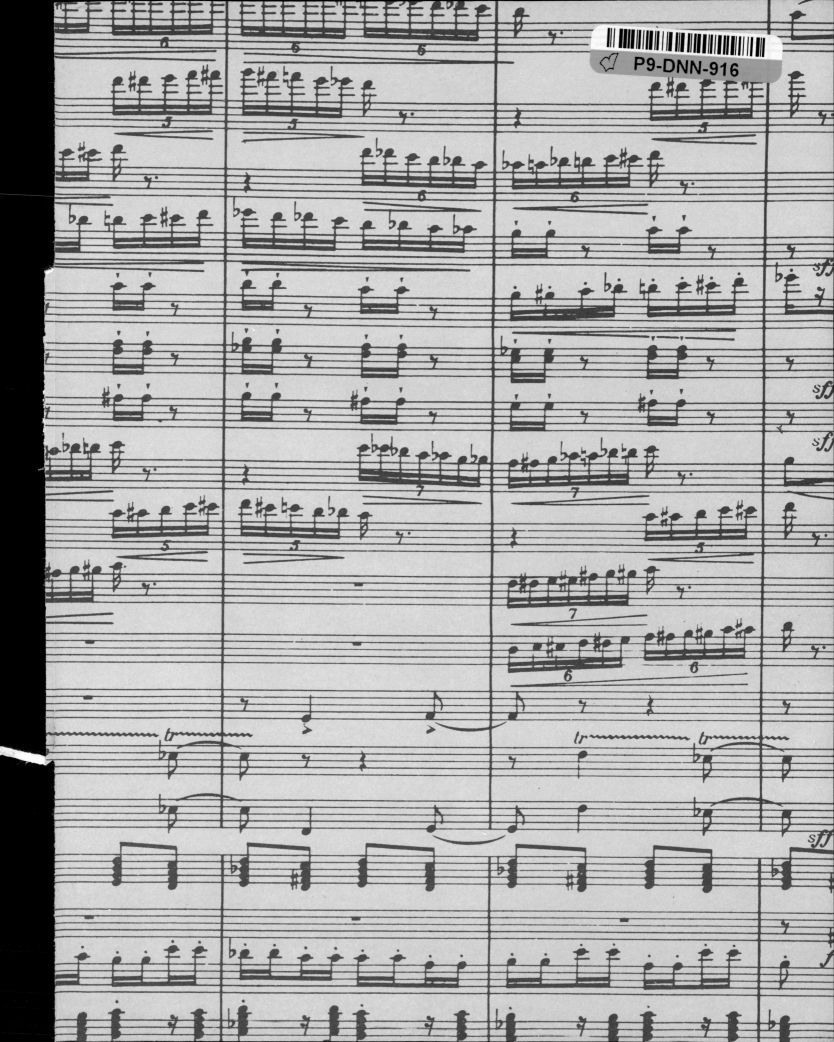

Music

An Illustrated Encyclopedia
Neil Ardley

Music

An Illustrated Encyclopedia

Neil Ardley

HAMLYN

Published 1986 by Hamlyn Publishing,
Bridge House, London Road, Twickenham, Middlesex

ISBN 0 600 36410 0

Printed in Italy

Contents

Author's Preface

Music was a mystery to me as a child – I dreamed (and still do) of being able to play wonderful music with absolutely no effort at all, but had no idea of what music involved or what it was all about. Asked to say something about Stravinsky – now among my favourite composers – I undoubtedly would have replied, as did the pupil of a friend of mine, that Stravinsky is a very rare kind of violin.

Music in fact came to me late but when it did arrive, it took me by force. I found music irresistible. Not content with just playing music, I began to write it and became a composer. I wanted to hear this music performed, so I also became a band leader for a while. My first great love in music was jazz, and then an increasing desire to explore new sounds led me to write pieces involving classical musicians and also rock performers. This in turn took me into recording and broadcasting studios. I became fascinated by the technology of music, and eventually turned to electronic and computer music – where I strongly believe the future of music lies.

This practical experience, aided by much listening and reading, has given me a wide appreciation of music. I now really do thrill to the powerful beat of good jazz and rock, the soaring flight of a great opera singer, the intriguing sounds of the folk music of Asia and Africa, the intricate architecture of classical music, and the spine-chilling sounds of electronic music. The reason is that I find in all good music – however it is made – the quality of individuality. The people who create the music, whether they are long-dead composers or performers who are very much alive, give us a unique experience of music that is totally their own. Making and receiving their music is being with them – indeed, almost inside them – and in this sheer ability to communicate so directly I've found that music has tremendous power.

In writing this encyclopedia of music, I've tried to combine my enthusiasm for music with the desire to inform. I hope to have created the kind of music book that would have seized my burgeoning interest in music and told me all that I wanted and needed to know. It's my one desire that, having read this book, you will not only know that it was Stradivarius who made rare violins but, far more important, have an appreciation of the quality of music as a whole. Best of all, may it help you to bring something of your own to the world of music.

Left The production of Offenbach's *Orpheus In The Underworld* at the English National Opera features striking scenery and costumes designed by Gerald Scarfe.

Neil Ardley
Christmas 1985

7

Introduction

How to use this Book

This encyclopedia is divided into separate chapters that explain the various kinds of music and ways of making music. You can read through these to get a general view of music as a whole, or study one chapter to learn about a particular aspect of music. The chapter called *The History of Music* will guide you through the growth of music from its very beginnings to the present day, for example, while the chapter on *Popular Music* describes all the different kinds of music that make a hit with the public. The contents page lists the chapters in this book, and the introduction to each chapter will tell you about the music that it contains.

Throughout the book, illustrations show you things about music that you will find interesting. These include photographs of famous musicians in action and artwork of

instruments, as well as pictures and diagrams that explain technical aspects of music in a visual way.

The encyclopedia can also be used as a reference book to find out facts about music and to answer any questions you may have. Consult the contents page to find the right chapter. For example, if you want to know about a certain musical instrument, turn to *The Instruments of Music*. Technical terms are covered in *The Mechanics of Music*. To find out about a favourite performer or composer, look in *Music Makers*. If there is a particular fact you need to know – like details of an instrument or a musician – you can also use the index at the end of the book.

Throughout this encyclopedia, you will find panels and boxes. These are separate sections on particular aspects of music or items of interest. The panel called *Electric Instruments and Sound Systems* on page 46, for example, explains with the aid of a large and detailed diagram how electric instruments make sound and also how these instruments, and performers using microphones, are connected into a powerful sound system for live shows. The box entitled *A Musical Riddle* on page 72 tells a fascinating story about a famous piece of music and has pictures of the composer and a ballet based on the music.

These are also many tables of information. These are of two main kinds – tables that contain the titles of famous pieces of music and tables that give the names of famous musicians. Tables of music give the titles of pieces that are well known and are good examples of a particular kind of music. They are enjoyable to listen to and many contain familiar tunes that you will recognize. Furthermore, many of the pieces are good pieces to play or sing if you are a performer. The tables give the full musical title and also a popular name, if the piece has one, together with a date. This is the year in which the piece was composed. The table of *Famous Pieces of Chamber Music* on pages 76

Below This illustration depicts a variety of simple and ornate instruments played in the traditional music of China. It appears on page 53.

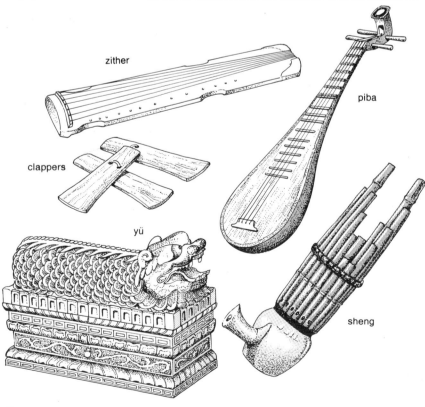

zither

clappers

piba

yü

sheng

8

and 77, for example, contains a variety of chamber works by famous classical composers and modern composers and also gives the instruments that play the music. In this table, you will discover the great string quartet and also find pieces that employ unusual combinations of instruments, such as Mozart's cheerful *Serenade* for 13 wind instruments and double bass and Milhaud's lively *Scaramouche* for two pianos.

The tables of famous musicians give the best performers, singers and groups. These are people who you can see on television or hear on radio and whose records and tapes you can find in shops and libraries. The table of *Ragtime and Boogie-Woogie Pianists* on page 108, for example, gives the names of the great pianists, such as Meade Lux Lewis and Jelly Roll Morton, who developed this form of popular music. There is also Joshua Rifkin, who revived ragtime and performs it in a new way. If you want to hear the best ragtime and boogie-woogie music, listen to the records and tapes of these pianists.

Famous records or tapes also appear in tables and in *Music Makers*. The album titles given are those of the original album and the date is the year in which it was first released. The table of *Famous Rock Albums* on page 116, for example, covers an important period in rock music and gives 12 records or tapes essential to any collection of rock.

Tables of operas, musicals and ballets give the place and date of their first performance. In this book, operas and ballet are normally called by their English name and only by the original foreign name if this name is more usual. Mozart's last opera is called *The Magic Flute*, for example, while Verdi's best-loved opera is referred to as *La Traviata*.

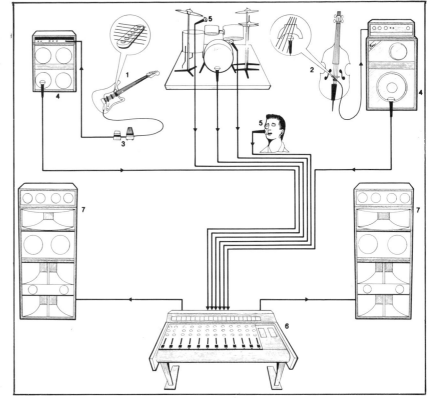

Above This panel on page 46 shows how electric instruments and sound systems work.

Right This diagram from page 35 explains the mechanism of a trumpet.

Below This table recommends 12 records or tapes covering a wide range of rock music. It appears on page 116.

Below This table from page 28 gives famous players of plucked stringed instruments. It includes jazz and folk performers as well as classical musicians.

Famous Musicians

Guitar
Julian Bream
Manitas de Plata
Django Reinhardt
Andrés Segovia
John Williams
Narciso Yepes

Harp
Osian Ellis
Sidonie Goossens
Marisa Robles

Sitar
Ravi Shankar

Twelve Famous Rock Albums

Title	Group or Artist	Date
Pet Sounds	The Beach Boys	1966
Sergeant Pepper's Lonely Hearts Club Band	The Beatles	1967
Electric Ladyland	Jimi Hendrix	1968
Beggars Banquet	The Rolling Stones	1968
Wheels Of Fire	Cream	1968
Tommy	The Who	1969
Hot Rats	Frank Zappa And The Mothers of Invention	1969
The Rise And Fall Of Ziggy Stardust	David Bowie	1972
Catch A Fire	Bob Marley And The Wailers	1972
Tubular Bells	Mike Oldfield	1973
Rumours	Fleetwood Mac	1977
The Clash	The Clash	1977

Making Music

Everywhere, people have ways of making and enjoying music. From a large orchestra or solo performer interpreting the music of great composers, through musicians or singers performing the traditional music of their people, to a band or group entertaining an audience or dancers with its own particular sounds – music is able in many different ways to give tremendous pleasure both to those creating it and to those listening. All with ears to hear will find endless delight in the immense variety that is the world of music.

Music is an art that people make together. Musicians may work with one another to produce music but even solo performers are not alone as they create music. There is always an audience listening intently to the music or maybe singing or dancing to it. As they perform, the musicians react to the way in which they each play and to the effect that their music has on the audience. A feeling often builds between all taking part that urges the music forward, making the musicians play with passion and creating a special performance unique to that occasion. This sharing in the creation of music gives it an appeal greater than other arts. Without understanding anything about it, music can move us physically and make us tap our feet or dance, and it can also move us emotionally, giving us feelings of joy or sadness. Furthermore the appeal of music is worldwide and its effects are still present if you listen to recordings of music, even those made long ago. The sheer power of music can cross time and space with ease.

Throughout the world, people make music in many kinds of ways and for different purposes. In this chapter, we look at the various forms of music making that people have devised and in which you may take part – either as a performer or a listener.

Symphony Orchestras

The largest collection of musicians you are likely to hear is a symphony orchestra. This kind of orchestra may contain more than a hundred players and it is usually named after the city in which it was founded. The orchestra normally plays there but may often visit other cities and countries on tour.

Symphony orchestras are mainly from Europe, Russia and North America, where there is a long tradition of playing composed music. You can see an orchestra in action at a concert hall, but a large part of an orchestra's time is spent in studios recording music for broadcasting and records.

This kind of orchestra is called a symphony orchestra because it plays the symphonies of Mozart, Beethoven and other composers. However, the musicians can play any type of music that is written for them and orchestras perform a wide range of classical music as well as playing for operas and ballets. Also, when you watch a film or a television play or listen to a pop singer, you will often hear a symphony orchestra in the background. But basically, symphony orchestras exist to give listening audiences performances of music written by the best composers.

These kinds of symphony orchestras employ professional musicians who make their living by playing music. There are also amateur symphony orchestras and youth orchestras in which the players perform just for enjoyment or to learn about orchestral music.

Far left Music has great power to move people. Performers like Mick Jagger of the Rolling Stones can thrill an audience, while events such as the Live Aid concerts in 1985 can raise huge sums for charity.

Below The Concertgebouw Orchestra, which is based at Amsterdam in The Netherlands, is among the world's finest symphony orchestras.

Left The various sections of the Concertgebouw Orchestra.

1 first violins
2 second violins
3 violas
4 cellos
5 double basses
6 woodwind
7 brass
8 percussion
9 harp
10 conductor

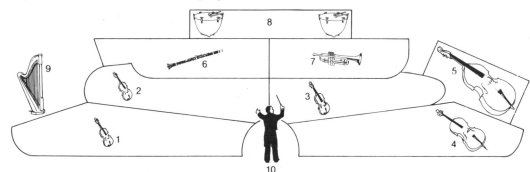

The Symphony Orchestra

A symphony orchestra contains four main sections of instruments: the strings, woodwind, brass and percussion sections. You can find out how these instruments work in the chapter on *The Instruments of Music*. Each section contains several different instruments, and good composers can write music which blends and contrasts the sections and their instruments, creating a wide variety of shifting sounds to enchant our ears.

The strings sit at the front of the orchestra because they are not as loud as the other instruments. To the left are the violins, which are divided into two groups, the first violins and second violins. The two groups usually play a different line of music. The violas are in the centre, to the right are the cellos and behind them the double basses. The total number of players in the string section may vary from one orchestra to another, but in each of the five groups the musicians normally all play the same notes.

The woodwind section is behind the strings and usually contains two flutes, two oboes, two clarinets and two bassoons. However, other instruments such as a piccolo, cor anglais, bass clarinet and contrabassoon may be added – either played

Below Karlheinz Stockhausen, the German composer, rehearses a symphony orchestra for a performance of his work *Inori*. Several composers like to conduct their own music so that an audience can hear the music exactly as the composer intends it to be performed.

by these or extra players. The brass section comes behind the woodwind and normally contains four French horns, two trumpets, three trombones and a tuba.

At the back is the percussion section, which contains two to four timpani, a side drum, bass drum, cymbals, gong, xylophone and other percussion instruments depending on the pieces that are played. Behind the violins there may be one or two harps and possibly a piano.

Any soloists, such as a pianist or violinist in a concerto, or singers are placed in front of the orchestra so that they can easily be heard.

Below Leonard Bernstein, the American composer, often conducts the music of other composers. He is renowned for his dramatic gestures and for the emotional and vivid interpretations that he demands of symphony orchestras.

The leader of the orchestra is the principal violin player, and this musician can direct the other players in the orchestra. However, the conductor is the person who is in charge of the performance of the music. Orchestras have their own resident conductor but also invite other conductors to perform with them.

As the orchestra plays, the conductor uses his or her hands, face and body to indicate to the players how they should play – how fast or how slow, and how loud or how soft. The music contains marks that show how it is to be played, but the conductor can interpret the music in his or her own way to give a special performance unlike that of other conductors. In fact, a lot of the conductor's work is done at rehearsals. There the conductor talks with the musicians and goes over the music with them to show them what is wanted. The conductor has to know every note that every musician in the orchestra is playing, and conducting requires a great amount of study as well as a strong personality that can dominate an orchestra.

Famous Symphony Orchestras

Berlin Philharmonic Orchestra
Chicago Symphony Orchestra
Concertgebouw Orchestra (Amsterdam)
London Symphony Orchestra
New York Philharmonic Orchestra
Paris Conservatoire Orchestra
Philadelphia Orchestra
Philharmonia Orchestra (London)
Vienna Philharmonic Orchestra

Famous Conductors

Claudio Abbado	Simon Rattle
Pierre Boulez	Georg Solti
Sergiu Celibidache	Leopold Stokowski
Colin Davis	Arturo Toscanini
Wilhelm Furtwängler	
Bernard Haitink	
Herbert von Karajan	
Otto Klemperer	
Lorin Maazel	
Riccardo Muti	
Seiji Ozawa	
André Previn	

Chamber Music

Much music written by classical composers is played by small groups of musicians. This kind of music is called chamber music because it is suitable for performance in a chamber or room. There may be from two up to a dozen or so musicians, and the composer treats them all equally. No particular performer features prominently, and in chamber music all the musicians play intently together. It is rather like a musical conversation in which everyone has something to say. An exception is music featuring a singer, but this is called vocal music rather than chamber music.

Orchestras known as chamber orchestras exist, but these are really small symphony orchestras. The most important kind of chamber group is the string quartet, which has two violins, a viola and a cello. Many professional quartets exist, made up of players who stay together a long time and often dedicate their lives to chamber music. This is important because the music has to be played with great sensitivity that only comes with people who know each other very well.

Most other professional chamber groups are made up of players who get together from time to time. Professional string quartets and other groups usually play in small concert halls to listening audiences. They tour a lot and also make broadcasts and recordings. Chamber music is ideal for small groups of amateur musicians. It is necessary to be able to read music well but the music can be very enjoyable to play because each part is important. There may not be an audience but great pleasure is to be had from making music together.

Above A string quartet performing at Covent Garden, London. The string quartet consists of two violins, a viola and a cello. It is the most important kind of chamber group and many musicians devote their musical lives to playing string quartets.

Famous String Quartets

Aeolian Quartet
Alban Berg Quartet
Amadeus Quartet
Arditti Quartet
Hungarian Quartet
Italian Quartet
Lindsay Quartet

Chamber Music Groups

Duos [two players]
2 pianos
Violin, piano
Cello, piano
Flute, piano

Trios [three players]
Piano trio Piano, violin, cello
String trio Violin, viola, cello

Quartets [four players]
String quartet 2 violins, viola, cello

Piano quartet Piano, violin, viola, cello
Flute quartet Flute, violin, viola, cello

Quintets [five players]
String quintet 2 violins, 2 violas, cello
Piano quintet Piano, 2 violins, viola, cello
Clarinet quintet Clarinet, 2 violins, viola, cello
Wind quintet Flute, oboe, clarinet, French horn, bassoon

Sextets [six players]
String sextet 2 violins, 2 violas, 2 cellos

Solo Music and Duets

Many people take up an instrument with the aim of joining a band, group or orchestra; however, as an alternative, there is plenty of music that can be played solo. Because just one person is performing, the music that results is very personal. The musician can play a piece exactly as he or she wants it to be heard, and both musician and listeners can get a great deal of pleasure from it. This is very true of musicians who are able to improvise on their own, such as church organists and jazz pianists. But it is also true of musicians who play written solo music, which allows a wide degree of interpretation by the performer.

Classical composers, especially those who were good performers themselves, wrote much solo music. Almost all of this music is for keyboard instruments, especially the piano, and solo piano works such as the sonatas of Mozart and Beethoven, and the ballades of Chopin, are great pieces of music. The organ and harpsichord are best played solo. J. S. Bach's magnificent keyboard music (which can also be played on the piano) is especially suitable for soloists. The guitar is another good solo instrument, and there is some excellent solo music for the violin and cello. Although much of this solo music is hard to play, most composers have written less difficult music and there are simplified arrangements of well-known music that are easier to play.

Duets are often played just for pleasure. They may be either special compositions or arrangements of well-known pieces normally for two instruments. However, one of the best instruments for duets is the piano. Four hands at one keyboard can produce rich and exciting music; there are excellent piano duets by Mozart, Schubert, Debussy and Ravel. (See page 80).

Left Keith Jarrett, the American pianist, specializes in solo performances in which he totally improvises the music that he plays. He performs with intense concentration, allowing the music to flow straight from his mind to his fingers as he creates it.

A Band Of Your Own

Some people like to play alone but are not content with just one instrument. They rig up an ingenious group of instruments that they can play at the same time – a guitar in both hands, a mouth organ, a drum on the back operated with a pedal, and a pair of cymbals between the knees, for example. Being a one-person band is fun, but it is perhaps easier to do with electronics. Modern electronic keyboards and organs can produce the sound of a whole band at the press of a few keys. And computer-driven instruments such as synthesizers can provide a complete electronic orchestra under the control of just one pair of hands. (See page 47).

Right A one-man band.

Light Orchestras and Big Bands

Performing or listening to the music of classical composers is only one way of enjoying music. Many musicians get both pleasure and employment from playing light music, which is tuneful, often rhythmic music to which millions of people listen or dance or have as a background sound at work or home.

This type of music is usually played by light orchestras and big bands. A light orchestra may be like a small symphony orchestra and contain similar string, woodwind, brass and percussion sections. A big band is different. It has a section of saxophone players, who may also play other woodwind instruments, a brass section of trumpets and trombones, and a rhythm section. The rhythm section contains a drummer who plays a set of drums called a drum kit, and possibly a percussionist, a double bass or bass guitar player, an electric guitar player, and a keyboard player who plays the piano and electric or electronic keyboards.

The rhythm section sets the beat of the music and keeps it moving along to make the music lively. Big bands often play for dancing and are also called dance bands. Light orchestras and dance bands may consist of a big band plus a string section. These bands and orchestras sometimes have a conductor, whose role is much less important than the conductor of a symphony orchestra.

Light orchestras, big bands and dance bands usually play well-known tunes that are arranged for them. An arranger takes the tune and writes a version of it for the orchestra or band to play. Often a singer and chorus is included.

An orchestra or band may be named after its leader, who directs the music in concerts, broadcasts and recordings and runs the whole outfit. But many orchestras and bands are employed by radio stations to play mostly for broadcasting.

Below The James Last Orchestra is one of the world's most popular light orchestras. The music is picked up by microphones and amplified, and the layout of the sections with the loudest instruments at the front enables the softer strings to be heard clearly.

1 keyboards
2 bass guitar
3 drums
4 guitar
5 percussion
6 brass
7 woodwinds/saxophones
8 violins
9 violas
10 double basses
11 cellos
12 conductor

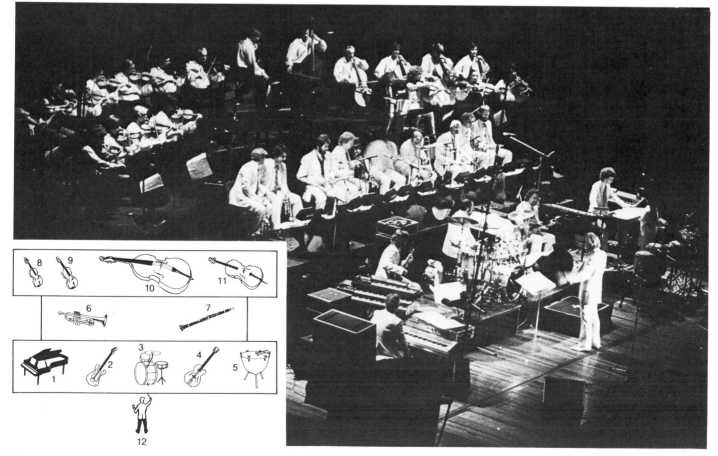

Brass Bands and Military Bands

Music played with a lively beat can get you up on your feet and moving in time to it. Music has therefore long been used for parades and other events in which people march. A band not only keeps everyone in step by playing marches but enhances the occasion with other exhilarating music. The musicians in the band have to march too so marching bands in which all the instruments can be played while walking have evolved. Because this is outdoor music, the instruments have to be both loud and rugged. These bands are of two types: brass bands and military bands.

Brass bands contain only brass instruments, apart from drums. The brass instruments used are cornets and a variety of horns as well as trombones. On the march, a big bass drum plays the beat and the band keeps in time with it. However, the sound of a brass band can be very expressive as well as stirring and brass bands also play to listening audiences at concerts, often in the open air. The bands play special music composed for

brass bands as well as arrangements of classical music and popular tunes.

Brass bands are usually made up of amateur musicians and a town or village band is a good place to learn a brass instrument. There are fierce competitions between rival bands that spur on the musicians to play their best.

Military bands are the bands attached to the armed forces and they too play for parades and ceremonial occasions as well as concerts. The military band is more elaborate than the brass band and in addition to brass contains woodwind instruments such as flutes, clarinets and saxophones as well as more drums and percussion instruments. Large kettledrums may be carried on horseback and the whole band is normally conducted by its director.

The musicians in military bands are professional musicians in that they are paid to perform. However, they are also regular soldiers and have military duties apart from their music.

Wind bands are civilian versions of military bands and many exist in schools. There are marching bands that play marches and other rhythmic music, and symphonic bands that play concerts.

Above A children's brass band parades through the centre of Warrington in England. Brass bands are very popular in northern England.

Jazz Groups

Playing jazz is a very different way of making music to performing in an orchestra or a brass or wind band. For a start, most or all of the music is improvised – that is, made up by the musicians as they play. In addition, the beat of the music is often more important than anything else. Most jazz musicians aim to make the music swing, which means keeping the beat springing effortlessly ahead as if it has a life of its own. You'll see the musicians' feet tapping and the audience moving or dancing with the beat. Jazz is a music which has a lot of joy and zest.

Jazz can be played by any number of musicians – and you can join in while the music is playing. Small groups of three, four or five musicians are common. There is always a rhythm section containing drums, bass and usually a keyboard or guitar to keep the beat moving. Over this often play brass or woodwind instruments, especially the trumpet, trombone, clarinet and saxophone. Singers can take part too. There are several styles of jazz, about which you can read in the chapter on *Popular Music*. Often a piece begins and ends with a tune that is either written or known by all the musicians taking part. In between, the players improvise, normally one at a time but sometimes together. Jazz is also played by big bands. In this case, much of the music is written and contains gaps for improvising players. It is performed with great rhythmic drive.

To play jazz, you need a good ear for music and a strong sense of rhythm – things that many people are born with but which you can develop with practice. The best performers can play jazz for a living and tour to perform in festivals, concert halls, night clubs, bars and pubs as well as making broadcasts and records. But for many musicians, it is more of a hobby and many amateur musicians get together to play jazz.

Some musicians completely improvise their music, either solo or in small improvising groups. All you need for this music is a good imagination to think up something worth playing. Any kinds of instruments or voice may take part, the aim being that every performance should develop well and be completely different.

Below The Count Basie Orchestra was one of the best big bands in jazz for nearly 50 years. Basie, whose real name was William Basie, led his band from the piano. His music was renowned for its fierce rhythmic drive.

Famous Jazz Musicians

Louis Armstrong	Duke Ellington
Count Basie	Gil Evans
Dave Brubeck	Benny Goodman
John Coltrane	Charlie Parker
Miles Davis	Oscar Peterson

These musicians appear on records with their own groups and as performers with other musicians.

Rock and Pop Groups

Rock and pop music is the most popular music in Europe and North America, though it is enjoyed by people all over the world. A performance by a good group can be a tremendous show, a riot of sound and colour that is as entertaining as it is musical. However, fans of a group may never get to see the group live at all, not least because many famous groups seldom perform in public and because groups may remain popular long after they break up. Instead, a diet of records and videos gives the public the music they want.

Rock and pop music covers a wide spectrum of styles, about which you can read in detail in *Popular Music*. However, they are basically fairly similar. The music usually has a powerful beat and consists of songs sung by members of a group. Sometimes a singer leads the group but often the musicians sing and play at the same time. The pieces may be played the same way every time, but some groups have musicians who can improvise and stretch the music out in live performances.

The smallest groups are duos – just two musicians, often playing an electric organ and drums. The music needs drums to produce a strong beat and a driving bass line

to push it along. The organist can play bass lines on the bass pedals of the organ, while playing tunes and accompaniments on the organ keyboards and singing – all at the same time! Such ability is pretty rare, so most rock groups have more players. A three-piece band usually has drums, bass guitar and an electric guitar or one or more keyboard instruments such as an organ, piano or synthesizer. Four-piece rock and pop bands are most common. The classic line-up is two electric guitars, bass guitar and drums. The lead guitar concentrates on the tunes while the rhythm guitar plays backing chords. In many bands, the rhythm guitar is replaced by an electric organ or a set of keyboards. To this line-up may be added other instruments, often a saxophone, trumpet or percussion.

Electronic bands may produce a similar kind of music but make many or even all of their sounds with synthesizers and computer-driven instruments. At the other end of the rock and pop spectrum are bands that incorporate folk music and they may have acoustic guitars, banjos or violins playing with electric guitars and a rhythm section of bass guitar and drums. Country music bands often feature the steel guitar, a kind of electric guitar with a singing tone which can slide from one note to another.

Rock and pop groups spring up as people get together to try out music that they know and like. They then usually develop to produce their own music. One or more members of the band may write the pieces of music, or just the tunes and words. The pieces themselves are developed in re-hearsals until the band is happy with the sound. It is not necessary to read music to be in a rock or pop band, but it helps. Many rock and pop performers work as session musicians, playing for other bands and singers in recording studios.

Below Police are one of the leading rock groups of the 1980s. The group contains three members – Sting (Gordon Sumner) on electric bass and vocals, Andy Summers on electric guitar and Stewart Copeland on drums.

Famous Rock and Pop Groups	
Beatles	Pink Floyd
Cream	Police
Fairport Convention	Rolling Stones
Fleetwood Mac	Status Quo
Genesis	Ultravox
Kraftwerk	Wham!
Led Zeppelin	Who

Folk Music

For many people throughout the world, music making is a custom or tradition that they learn from others around them. Music is played, often with singing and dancing, in time-honoured ways to entertain people and to accompany events, particularly religious ceremonies. This kind of traditional music is called folk music or ethnic music. It is seldom composed, or even written down, and continues as one generation hands the music and the methods of playing it down to the next.

Many different kinds of folk music exist throughout the world, most of them employing their own special instruments. You can read about folk music in *Music Around the World*.

Folk music is usually performed by musicians, both amateur and professional, for the people in their own or nearby communities. However, in some countries, professional musicians play traditional music more widely. They may bring the folk music of the country to people in cities and towns or they may recreate the folk music of the past for today's audiences.

Below These Indian folk dancers perform a traditional dance from Madras, in which they dress as horses and perch on stilts.

Singing

Just about everyone can make music if they want to. You don't have to learn an instrument: all you have to do is open your mouth and sing. Anyone can do it. Some people sound better than others of course, because singing requires an ear for music. But unless you are tone deaf and really cannot tell one note from another, you can develop a good ear even if you are not born with one.

Singing is a marvellous way of experiencing music. Because it is so natural and because it requires words, singing is one of the most expressive ways in which we can make music. It moves us deeply whether we sing ourselves or listen to song.

Solo Singing

Many people enjoy singing solo, usually with an accompaniment of some kind. This may vary from a guitar strummed by the singer or a piano played by an accompanist to a backing from a band or even music by a whole orchestra, as in opera. The tone of the voice and style of singing vary enormously. In classical music such as opera, singers are

Famous Vocal Groups

Abba
Beach Boys
King's Singers
Swingle Singers

For tables of singers, see Opera and Ballet *and* Popular Music.

trained to produce a strong voice with a wide range of notes. In popular music, singers use a more natural voice and rock and pop singers sound much more different from one another than classical singers. However, the range and power of their voices is not as great, so they often use microphones.

Choirs and Vocal Groups

The sound of people singing together – from the roar of a football crowd in full song to the hushed tones of a small church choir – can be as exciting or uplifting as any in music. But to have its greatest effect, vocal music for several singers must be sung in several parts. Instead of everyone singing the melody or tune together, most of the singers sing other musical lines or parts. The notes in all the parts must be in harmony with each other, which means that they must sound good when sung together. The harmony fills out the singing and gives it more character, just as playing the piano with two hands is better than using one finger. In the best vocal music, the different parts are like several tunes sung together; they can make the music move so that it may not need any accompaniment.

Most vocal music is in four parts. The highest, which is usually the melody, is the soprano part. Then come the alto, tenor and bass parts. Most people have a voice that fits one of these parts. ·

To sing in a choir or vocal group, you really need to be able to read music so that you can sing the notes you see on the page. You can learn to do this. If you can't read music, you can learn a part but you must be able to keep to it while all the other parts are singing at the same time. There is a vast range of music to sing. Symphony orchestras have a large choir or chorus for choral works, and churches and towns have choirs that sing at services and concerts. Many people join or form small vocal groups to sing for pleasure or possibly for profit. Choirs and vocal groups sing music that is composed for them, such as anthems and madrigals.

Above left This vocal group performs gospel songs at a religious meeting in Mississippi, USA. The members sing with great fervour to a lively backing by the musicians.

Above Ella Fitzgerald has been a leading solo singer in jazz since the 1940s. She performs popular songs in her own style, often changing the notes of a tune to give it a personal interpretation.

The Instruments of Music

Throughout the world, people make music with all kinds of instruments. Some are small and simple, like the tin whistle and the triangle. Others are mighty and complex, such as the enormous organs with their thousands of pipes that fill cathedrals with music, and carillons, the lofty tune-playing towers of bells that grace many towns and cities. As well as a host of conventional musical instruments, there are new electronic instruments that allow us to make all kinds of sounds with no physical effort whatsoever.

The belfry at Brugge, Belgium, contains one of the largest and most complex musical instruments – a carillon of bells that can play tunes. By contrast, this Indonesian man is playing one of the smallest and simplest instruments – a flute made from a hollow reed.

The urge to make music is ancient. We will never know when music began, for the first musical sounds must have been those of voices raised in primitive song. But eventually, people found that music can also be made with objects and the first musical instruments were born. They were simple constructions, the earliest known instruments being whistles made of hollow bones about 35,000 years ago.

Since then, people have invented all kinds of devices for making music. Yet all musical instruments played the world over, whether past or present and however primitive or complex, belong to seven main families of instruments. And these families are divided into acoustic and electric instruments

Acoustic Instruments

Acoustic instruments are instruments in which the sound comes from the body of the instrument itself. The quality of sound therefore depends on the way it is handled by the performer. The enormous variety of sound that the best musicians can get from acoustic instruments enables them to produce music of great power.

There are five families of acoustic instruments: strings, woodwind, brass, percussion and keyboard instruments.

All string instruments contain stretched strings. To get a sound, the performer either plucks the strings or slides a bow across them. These actions make the strings vibrate and they give out sound. The vibrating strings cause the body of the instrument to vibrate as well, making the sound louder. String instruments include the violin and guitar.

Woodwind instruments are pipes with holes along the side. They may be made of metal as well as wood. The player gets a sound by blowing into a mouthpiece at one end. This makes the air in the instrument vibrate and give out sound. Covering the holes with the fingers or by pressing keys makes the notes higher or lower. Woodwind instruments include the flute, clarinet and saxophone.

Brass instruments are basically coiled tubes of metal. The performer blows into a mouthpiece at one end to make music. This causes the air inside to vibrate and give out sound. A brass player gets different notes by blowing differently and by pressing keys or valves on the instrument. Brass instruments include the trumpet and horn.

To get a sound from a percussion instrument, you simply strike it with a stick or your hand, or shake it. The whole instrument then vibrates and gives out sound. Percussion instruments include drums and cymbals.

Keyboard instruments make their sounds in the same way as string, woodwind or percussion instruments. The player presses keys on the keyboard to operate a mechanism that produces the sound. In this way, each finger can produce a different note. On most other instruments only one note can be played at a time. Keyboard instruments include the piano and organ.

Electric Instruments

An electric instrument does not itself make the sound that you hear when it is played. The instrument is connected to an amplifier and loudspeaker like those in a record player but more powerful. The loudspeaker produces the sound. By operating controls on the instrument or the amplifier, the musician can make the sound louder or softer and change the quality of the sound. The kind of music made by electric instruments therefore depends on the equipment used and the way it is operated. Electric instruments are mostly used in popular music.

There are two types of electrically powered instruments: electronic instruments such as the synthesizer and electric instruments such as the electric guitar.

Good musicians can control their instruments and equipment to get very special sounds and make unusual music. This is particularly true of synthesizer players and computer musicians, who can produce a wider range of sounds and musical effects than any other instrumentalists.

Left Classical music is played on acoustic instruments. This is the famous Korean violinist Kyung-Wha Chung playing a violin concerto. Behind her is the violin section of a symphony orchestra.

Left Much popular music is performed on electric instruments. This group, Ultravox, is using several synthesizers and an electric guitar to get a wide range of sounds.

23

String Instruments

The instruments of the string family can be divided into two main groups. The first group contains instruments such as the violin and cello that are mainly played with a bow. The second group contains instruments such as the guitar and harp that are played by plucking the strings.

The Violin Family

This family of instruments is widely played and they make up the string orchestra and string section of every symphony orchestra. Individually, they have a rich, noble sound while a full string orchestra has a wonderful soaring quality. The violin is the smallest member of the family. The others, in order of increasing size, are the viola, cello or violoncello, and double bass or bass. The violin and viola are held under the chin, while the cello and double bass stand on the floor. All are normally played with a bow.

Each instrument has four strings except for the double bass, which may have five. The violin, viola and cello all give a bright, full sound when played well. When you see string players in action, you will notice that they shake their left hands as they press on the strings. This produces vibrato, a variation in the note that improves the sound of the instrument. They may also use mutes which fit on the bridge and make the sound soft and silvery. Other effects used by string players are tremolo, when they move the bow rapidly to and fro, and pizzicato, when they pluck the strings.

The double bass is more often plucked than the higher strings because it gives deep ringing notes that provide a strong foundation for the music. This is particularly true in acoustic jazz and popular music where, in combination with the drums, the bass sets the beat of the music and propels it forward.

Viols

The viols are bowed strings that were played before the violin family developed about 400 years ago. They are similar in shape and size, but have six strings and frets on the fingerboard. Frets are bars on the fingerboard that the player uses to find the right positions for the fingers. Viols are played upright, and they do not have as bright a sound as the violin family. You can hear them in concerts of early music. Viola da gamba is another name for a viol.

Above The violin family – the violin (1), viola (2), cello (3) and double bass (4).

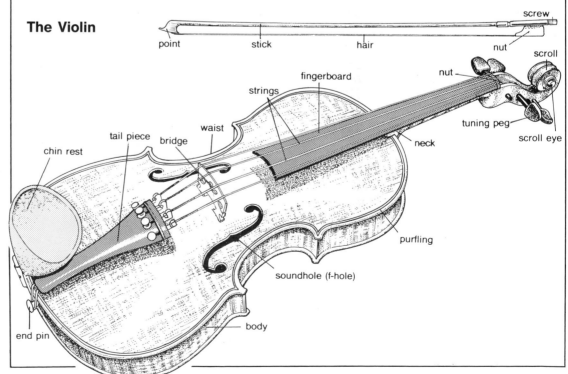

The Violin

screw, point, stick, hair, nut, scroll, nut, fingerboard, strings, tuning peg, scroll eye, neck, tail piece, bridge, waist, chin rest, purfling, soundhole (f-hole), end pin, body

Fiddles

The violin is also a popular instrument with folk musicians in Europe and North America, who can play it with great dexterity. It is often called a fiddle instead of a violin. However, there are many kinds of bowed folk instruments similar to the violin that are known as fiddles. They vary greatly in shape and may have one or several strings. They are often played upright, resting against the chest or supported on a long spike.

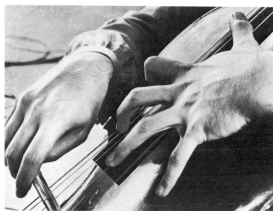

How String Instruments Make Music

Most string instruments have a set of strings that lie over a fingerboard at one end of the instrument. The strings are of different thickness so that they produce different notes: the heavier a string is, the lower the note that it sounds. The strings are stretched tightly between the bridge and the pegs at the end of the fingerboard. Stretching a string more tightly gives a higher note. The player tunes the instrument by adjusting the pegs until each string gives a particular note.

To play most string instruments, you use the fingers of one hand (usually the left hand) to press the strings down on the fingerboard. The notes that sound will depend on the length of string between your fingers and the bridge. The shorter the string, the higher the note. The other hand sounds the strings, either by using a bow or by plucking the strings. With string instruments, you can play one string at a time to give a tune or several strings at once to sound chords beneath a melody.

Above left Charlie Mingus, one of the best double bass players in jazz.

Above centre Mstislav Rostropovich, the famous cellist. His hands (top) show the power needed to play the strings.

Above right The trumpet marine is an old single-string instrument that produced trumpet-like sounds.

Famous String Music

Violin
J. S. Bach	*Violin Partita No 3 in E*	1720
Paganini	*24 Caprices*	1805
Beethoven	*Violin Concerto in D*	1806
Mendelssohn	*Violin Concerto in E minor*	1844
Bartók	*Sonata for Solo Violin*	1903

Viola
Berlioz	*Harold In Italy*	1834
Debussy	*Sonata for Flute, Viola and Harp*	1916
Walton	*Viola Concerto*	1927

Cello
J. S. Bach	*Suite No 3 for Cello*	1720
Tchaikovsky	*Variations on a Rococo Theme*	1876
Dvořák	*Cello Concerto in B minor*	1895
Richard Strauss	*Don Quixote*	1896
Britten	*Suite No 1 for Cello*	1964

String Quartet
Haydn	*Quartet No 81 in G major*	1799
Schubert	*Quartet No 14 in D minor* (*Death and the Maiden*)	1824
Borodin	*Quartet No 2 in D major*	1881

See also table of chamber music on page 76

String Orchestra
Mozart	*Eine Kleine Nachtmusik*	1787
Tchaikovsky	*Serenade for Strings*	1880
Mahler	*Adagietto* (from *Symphony No 5*)	1902
Vaughan Williams	*Fantasia on a Theme of Thomas Tallis*	1910
Stravinsky	*Apollo*	1928
Barber	*Adagio for Strings*	1936

Famous Musicians

Violin
Kyung-Wha Chung
Stéphane Grappelli
Arthur Grumiaux
Jascha Heifetz
Yehudi Menuhin
Itzhak Perlman
Isaac Stern
Pinchas Zuckerman

Cello
Pablo Casals
Pierre Fournier
Mstislav Rostropovich
Paul Tortelier

Bass
Ray Brown
Gary Karr
Scott LaFaro
Charlie Mingus
Niels-Henning Oersted Pedersen

Guitars and Lutes

This group of plucked string instruments is similar to the violin family in that they have a fingerboard with strings stretched between a bridge and tuning pegs. However, the fingerboard has frets on which the strings are pressed, and guitars and lutes are also played differently. They are held against the body, supported either on the legs if sitting or by a strap around the neck if standing. In addition, it is possible to play a melody and an accompaniment at the same time.

Guitar and lute players can get a wide range of sounds from their instruments by plucking the strings in different ways. They may also use a plectrum made from wood or metal to get a brighter sound from the strings. The principal difference between guitars and lutes is that guitars have flat backs and lutes are rounded.

The most popular guitar is the Spanish guitar or acoustic guitar. It has six strings and is capable of an enormous range of music, from concertos with orchestras through solo guitar pieces to simple accompaniments for singers. The twelve-string guitar is a type of acoustic guitar. It has six

Top right This painting, *The Concert* by Costa (about 1500), shows a man playing a lute. In the foreground is a kit, a small violin.

Right Andrés Segovia is the most famous classical guitarist in the world. Segovia, who comes from Spain, revived the use of the acoustic guitar as a classical instrument, developing ways of playing the instrument so that it could be heard clearly in concert halls. The foot stool raises the guitar to a comfortable position for playing.

pairs of strings, each pair normally being tuned to the same note, which can give it a bright strident sound. The acoustic guitar is not a loud instrument so it is often amplified using a microphone and loudspeaker. The electric guitar and bass guitar are described in the section on electric instruments.

The lute is an ancient instrument that was very popular in medieval times. It has recently been revived for the performance of early lute music. It has six or more strings.

Varieties of guitars and lutes are played in popular and folk music in many parts of the world. The balalaika is a triangular three-string guitar played in Russia, while the mandolin is a lute having four or five pairs of strings, often heard in Italy. There are also the bouzouki of Greece, a six-string long-necked mandolin, and the banjo of America, a strange instrument with a round drum-like body covered in parchment that originated in Africa. In India, several kinds of lutes are played, notably the sitar, vina and tambura. These may have sympathetic strings, which are extra strings that are not played but resonate as the other strings sound to give a shimmering effect.

The Acoustic Guitar

machine head

peg

fingerboard

frets

strings

body

bridge

fan struts

soundhole

Harps and Zithers

The harp stands upright and has a large set of open strings without a keyboard – 47 strings in the harp played in a symphony orchestra. Each string is tuned to a different note so that you get a scale if you run a finger over the strings, just like running a finger over the white notes on a piano keyboard. However, the harpist can make the notes sharp or flat by pressing pedals at the base of the harp. Though difficult to play, the harp can produce music of great beauty. Smaller harps without pedals are played in folk music to accompany singers.

Zithers are folk instruments which are part harp and part lute. They are played flat on a table and contain a set of open strings like a harp as well as some strings with a fingerboard like a lute. This arrangement enables the performer to play a tune on the fingerboard while strumming an accompaniment on the open strings.

The koto of Japan is a kind of zither that can produce the most delicate music. It has 13 open strings but each passes over a separate bridge that can be moved. In this way, the tuning of the strings can be changed to any notes required. Furthermore, by plucking a string on one side of the bridge and pressing it on the other, the note produced will rise and fall.

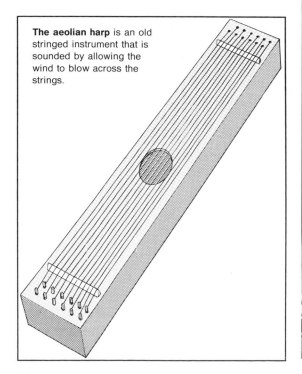

The aeolian harp is an old stringed instrument that is sounded by allowing the wind to blow across the strings.

Famous Music		
Guitar		
Vivaldi	*Guitar (Lute) Concertos in A major and D major*	*c* 1740
Tarrega	*Reminiscences of the Alhambra*	*c* 1900
Turina	*Fandanguillo*	1926
Villa-Lobos	*Preludes*	1940
Rodrigo	*Concierto de Aranjuez*	1939
Harp		
Mozart	*Flute And Harp Concerto in C major*	1778
Debussy	*Danse Sacrée et Danse Profane*	1903
Ravel	*Introduction and Allegro*	1906
Britten	*Suite for Harp*	1969

Left The strings of the harp are plucked with the fingers while the feet operate pedals to change the pitch of the strings. There are seven pedals, one for each of the notes A to G. The A pedal, for example, changes all the A strings to either A flat, A natural or A sharp.

Famous Musicians

Guitar
Julian Bream
Manitas de Plata
Django Reinhardt
Andrés Segovia
John Williams
Narciso Yepes

Harp
Osian Ellis
Sidonie Goossens
Marisa Robles

Sitar
Ravi Shankar

Woodwind Instruments

The instruments of the woodwind family can produce a wide variety of sounds, from the shrill piping of the piccolo to the deep gruff blurts of the bassoon. But woodwinds generally produce music of delicacy and grace. As they are able to sound only one note at a time, they mainly play melodies.

There are two main kinds of woodwinds: edge-blown instruments such as the recorder and flute, and reed instruments like the oboe, bassoon, clarinet and saxophone.

Edge-blown Instruments

In edge-blown instruments, the mouthpiece contains an edge over which the performer blows air. This action sets the air in the pipe vibrating to give a sound.

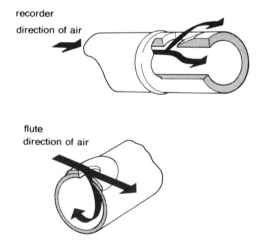

recorder
direction of air

flute
direction of air

Whistles A whistle is a simple woodwind instrument, often without any holes so that it can only sound one note. The mouthpiece has a square hole in which one side (the lip) has a sharp edge. It is this edge that sets the air vibrating as the whistle is blown. Tin whistles or penny whistles are long whistles with holes along the side. Whistles of this kind, which are sometimes called end-blown flutes, are played by folk musicians around the world with considerable dexterity.

Recorders The recorder has a mouthpiece like a whistle and eight holes. It has a light warm sound unlike the shrill tone of the tin whistle. The recorder is of ancient origin and

How Woodwind Instruments Make Music

All woodwind instruments are basically pipes, usually made of wood or metal, with holes along the side. The performer blows into a mouthpiece at one end, which makes the air inside the pipe vibrate and give out a note. However, only the air between the mouthpiece and the first open hole vibrates. To produce different notes, a woodwind player has to open or close some of the holes. The greater the length of vibrating air in the pipe, the deeper the note. If the performer closes all the holes, the whole pipe vibrates and sounds the lowest note obtainable.

In most woodwind instruments, some or all of the holes are covered with pads that are operated by keys. This allows the holes to be larger than the fingertips, giving a bigger sound. A system of keys also makes fingering easier so that the player can perform better. Without keys, complicated fingerings are needed. A range of high notes can be obtained either by blowing harder, by uncovering a hole or pressing a key at the back of the pipe, or by special fingerings. In this way, woodwind instruments can produce more than 40 notes even though the player has only eight fingers and two thumbs with which to get them.

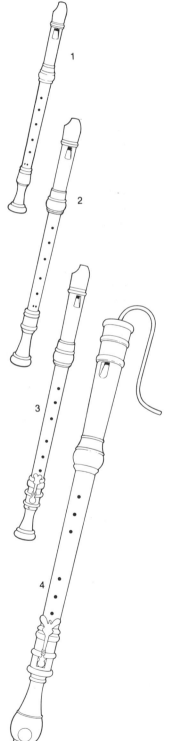

Left The saxophone section of the Glenn Miller Orchestra.

Below The recorder family – the descant or soprano recorder (1), treble recorder (2), tenor recorder (3) and bass recorder (4).

was very popular from about 1500 to about 1750. It was then replaced by the flute, which musicians preferred for its richer sound. However, interest in the recorder revived about 60 years ago and now it is often the first musical instrument that children learn to play.

Modern recorders are made of wood or plastic and come in six different sizes. The highest in pitch and smallest is the sopranino recorder. Then come the descant (or soprano) recorder, which is the most popular recorder, followed by the treble (or alto), tenor, bass and low bass recorders. Only the lower recorders have keys.

Flutes The flute has a lovely mellow breathy sound that brightens as it ascends in pitch, making it a valuable member of orchestras and bands as well as an attractive solo instrument. Flutes are side-blown woodwinds. The performer blows across a round hole in the mouthpiece, causing the edge of the hole to set the air in the flute vibrating. Most modern flutes are made of metal and all the holes are covered by key-operated pads.

The flute family has four principal members. The smallest and highest in pitch is the piccolo, whose piercing tones can often be heard in full flight high above the orchestra. Then comes the concert flute, the most popular flute. The alto flute and bass flute are larger, deeper-sounding flutes with a mysterious quality to their sound. The fife is a small flute without keys played in military and marching bands.

Above The flute family — the bass flute (1), alto flute (2), concert flute (3) and piccolo (4).
Below The flautist James Galway.

Reed Instruments

Reed instruments get their name because the mouthpiece contains one or two thin but stiff reeds. The player sets the reed or reeds vibrating by blowing into the mouthpiece, causing the air in the pipe to vibrate and sound.

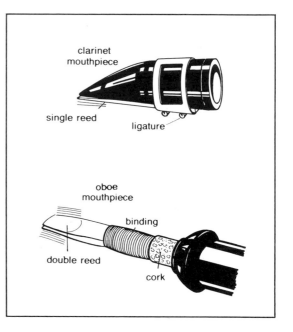

Oboes The oboe has a nasal, rather plaintive sound. The mouthpiece consists of a double reed made of two slices of cane bound together. The player inserts the double reed between the lips and blows through it. A larger and deeper oboe called the cor anglais or English horn is also played in orchestras.

Bassoons There are two kinds of bassoon: the bassoon and larger and deeper contrabassoon or double bassoon. They are big double-reed instruments similar to the oboe and have a deep rich sound. The pipe of the bassoon is folded in two (or into three parts in the contrabassoon) so that the fingers can reach the holes and keys.

Clarinets The clarinet has a mouthpiece containing a single reed, which is a slice of cane fixed over the opening of the mouthpiece with a metal band. The instrument has a beautiful liquid sound that becomes warm and dark when low but bright and piercing when high. The clarinet most often played is the soprano B flat clarinet, and it can be heard in all kinds of bands and orchestras.

Above The
clarinet family –
the bass clarinet
(1), basset horn
(2), soprano
clarinet (3) and
sopranino
clarinet (4).

Some players use the slightly larger A clarinet. The clarinet family also includes a small high-pitched sopranino clarinet, and the bigger and deeper basset horn and bass clarinet, which are curved and have an upturned bell (the end of the instrument) to direct the sound outwards.

Above Roland Kirk, the American jazz musician, was famous for playing several saxophones at once.

Below The soprano saxophone (1), alto saxophone (2), tenor saxophone (3) and baritone saxophone (4).

Saxophones Unlike the other woodwind instruments, which all have ancient or early origins and have developed to their present form over several centuries, the saxophone is an invention. It is named after its maker, Adolphe Sax, and it dates from about 1840. The saxophone or sax is a hybrid reed instrument, having a mouthpiece like the clarinet and a system of keys and conical pipe like the oboe. The pipe is wide and made of metal.

All these factors give the saxophone a very distinctive sound. In orchestras, military bands and dance bands, saxophones are played with a sweet, rather cloying tone. But in jazz, the tone of the saxophone has been developed into a wide range of very personal sounds by many musicians.

Unusual Woodwinds

The shawm is an early double-reed instrument similar to the oboe. It is still played as a folk instrument in many countries.

The mouth organ is a free-reed instrument. The sound comes directly from a set of metal reeds that vibrate at different rates when blown, each producing a different note. The mouth organ originated in China in ancient times.

The bagpipes are a set of pipes each containing a single or double reed that is blown by air from a bag. The bag is filled with air either by mouth or by a bellows tucked under one arm. At the same time, the bag is squeezed to send a constant flow of air into the pipes. One of these, the chanter, is fingered to play a melody while the others sound unchanging notes to produce a drone.

The ocarina is a round or egg-shaped kind of whistle. It may have a plunger to tune it to different notes.

The nose flute is a whistle or flute blown with the nose rather than the mouth. A finger may be used to block one nostril when playing.

The panpipes are a set of pipes played in folk music around the world. Each pipe sounds a particular note when blown across the top.

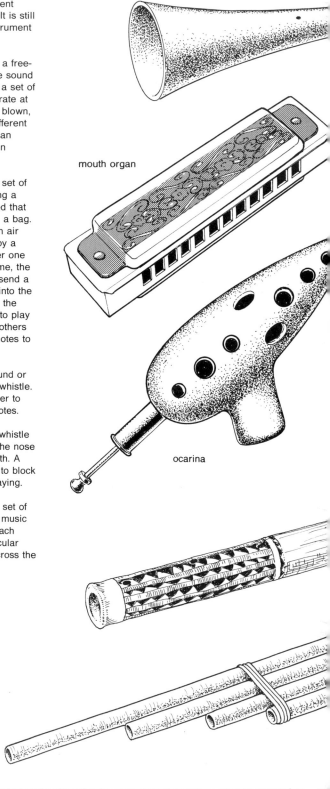

mouth organ

ocarina

Above Double-reed instruments – the contrabassoon (1), the bassoon (2), the cor anglais or English horn (3) and the oboe (4).

shawm

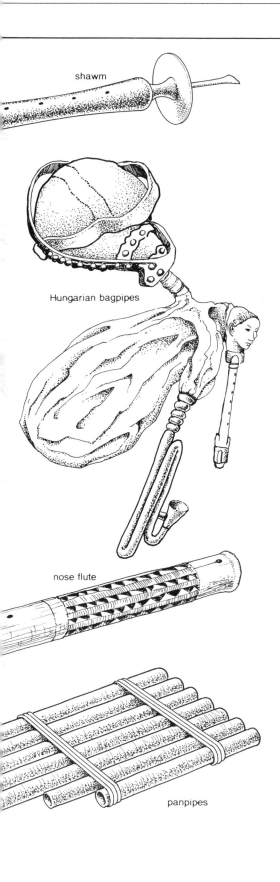

Hungarian bagpipes

nose flute

panpipes

Famous Woodwind Music

Flute

J. S. Bach	*Suite No 2 in B minor*	1730s
Mozart	*Flute Concertos No 1 in G major and No 2 in D major*	1778
Beethoven	*Serenade in D major for Flute, Violin and Viola*	1802
Debussy	*Syrinx*	1912

Oboe

Mozart	*Oboe Concerto in C major*	1778
Richard Strauss	*Oboe Concerto in D major*	1945

Bassoon

Mozart	*Bassoon Concerto in B flat major*	1774

Clarinet

Mozart	*Clarinet Quintet in A major*	1789
Mozart	*Clarinet Concerto in A major*	1791
Brahms	*Clarinet Quintet in B minor*	1891
Stravinsky	*Three Pieces for Clarinet*	1919

Famous Musicians

Recorder
Michala Petri

Flute
James Galway
Karlheinz Zöller

Oboe
Heinz Holliger
Thea King

Clarinet
Jack Brymer
Benny Goodman
Gervase de Peyer

Mouth Organ
Larry Adler

Panpipes
Gheorghe Zamfir

Soprano Saxophone
Sidney Bechet
John Coltrane

Alto Saxophone
Ornette Coleman
Paul Desmond
Johnny Hodges
Charlie Parker

Tenor Saxophone
John Coltrane
Stan Getz
Coleman Hawkins
Sonny Rollins
Ben Webster
Lester Young

Baritone Saxophone
Harry Carney
Gerry Mulligan
John Surman

Left Lester Young was one of the pioneers of the tenor saxophone in jazz.

Brass Instruments

Perhaps the most majestic and stirring sounds to be heard in music are those of brass instruments in full cry. The brilliance and richness of their sound never fails to thrill. Yet, played quietly or with mutes inserted to thin their tone, brass instruments can bring a haunting and mysterious air to music.

Brass instruments are basically long, coiled tubes made of brass or other metals. At one end, the bell, the tube flares out in order to project the sound forward. A mouthpiece shaped like a small cup or funnel is inserted in the other end. The player's lips, pressed into the mouthpiece, set the air throughout the instrument vibrating strongly, thereby producing the full, vibrant sound characteristic of brass.

There are two main types of brass instrument: cylindrical or conical, depending on the bore or shape of the tube.

Cylindrical Brass Instruments

In brass instruments with a cylindrical bore, most of the tube is the same diameter. The tube widens to form the bell near the end of the instrument. The main cylindrical brass instruments are trumpets and trombones, which can produce a very bright, often strident sound. This quality makes them the most widely played of brass instruments. Trumpets and trombones can be heard in orchestras, military bands, dance bands and in jazz, rock and pop music.

Trumpets The trumpet has three valves, which lower the pitch of the note being blown by one, two or three semitones. Pressing the valves in different combinations therefore lowers the note by up to six semitones, which is the greatest change needed to fill the gaps between the harmonics.

In addition to the standard trumpet, there is a smaller high-pitched clarino or Bach trumpet often used to perform the music of Bach and early composers, as well as a larger deep-sounding bass trumpet.

Trombones The trombone has no valves. Instead the player moves a slide to and fro to

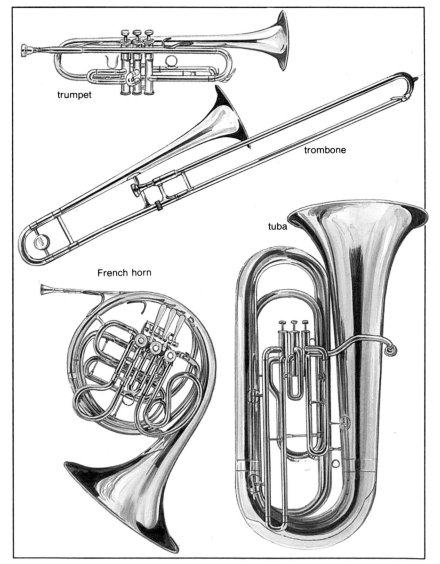

trumpet

trombone

tuba

French horn

Above Wynton Marsalis is a gifted American trumpet player who is adept at playing both jazz and classical music.

Above left A brass band in Germany mostly contains brass instruments with a conical bore.

produce the notes between the harmonics. Pushing the slide out lengthens the tube of the trombone and lowers the pitch of the note. It can be moved into six positions to lower the note by up to six semitones. However, a trombonist can also move the slide between positions to make one note slide into another, a marvellous trombone effect.

The trombone most often played is the tenor trombone. Bass trombones are also used to get deeper notes than the tenor trombone. They have an extra coil of tubing for this purpose.

Conical Brass Instruments

Most other brass instruments have a conical bore. The tubing widens after the valves and

How Brass Instruments Make Music

Just by varying the lip pressure, a brass player can produce a set of notes called harmonics. All bugle calls and many fanfares are made up of these harmonics, though the actual set of notes that sound may be different in different instruments. However, apart from buglers, brass players are not limited to just these notes but can play all the other notes between the harmonics as well.

Most brass instruments have valves to produce these other notes. The player uses a certain lip pressure to reach a particular harmonic that is higher than the note required. At the same time, one or more valves is pressed to lower the note to the required pitch. When a valve is pressed, it opens an extra section of tubing, making the length of vibrating air longer and thus lowering the pitch.

Getting the higher harmonics requires strong lip pressure and is difficult. This is why only good brass players can reach high notes and why performers sometimes 'crack' notes – they either get the wrong harmonic first or reach the right one but cannot sustain it.

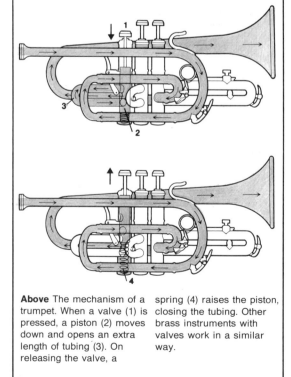

Above The mechanism of a trumpet. When a valve (1) is pressed, a piston (2) moves down and opens an extra length of tubing (3). On releasing the valve, a spring (4) raises the piston, closing the tubing. Other brass instruments with valves work in a similar way.

Famous Brass Music

Trumpet

Jeremiah Clarke	*Trumpet Voluntary*	1700
J. S. Bach	*Brandenburg Concerto No 2*	1721
Haydn	*Trumpet Concerto in E flat major*	1796

French Horn

Mozart	*Horn Concerto No 4 in E flat major*	1786
Richard Strauss	*Horn Concerto No 1 in E flat major*	1883
Britten	*Serenade for Tenor, Horn and Strings*	1943

Tuba

Vaughan Williams	*Tuba Concerto in F minor*	1954

Brass Section

Stravinsky	*Symphonies Of Wind Instruments*	1920
Janáček	*Sinfonietta*	1926

Unusual Brass Instruments

The alphorn or alpenhorn was originally used to send signals as its sound carried far among the Alps and other European mountains where it originated centuries ago. It is made of wood but blown like a brass instrument.

The sousaphone is a deep-sounding brass instrument made to fit over the player's shoulders so that it can be carried in marching bands. It was designed by and named after the famous American bandmaster John Philip Sousa.

The lur is an ancient bronze trumpet of Scandinavia. Lurs were made in pairs that twisted in opposite directions. The earliest that have been found are about 3,000 years old.

The didgeridoo is played by the Aborigines of Australia. It is made out of a tree trunk and played like a brass instrument.

The serpent is an old instrument named for its winding shape. It was blown like a brass instrument but had holes and keys like a woodwind instrument. The serpent was invented in 1590 and was played until about a century ago, when it was replaced by the tuba and bass horn.

The conch shell is one of several seashells that can be blown like a brass instrument. Shells have been used throughout the world since ancient times for signalling with sounds.

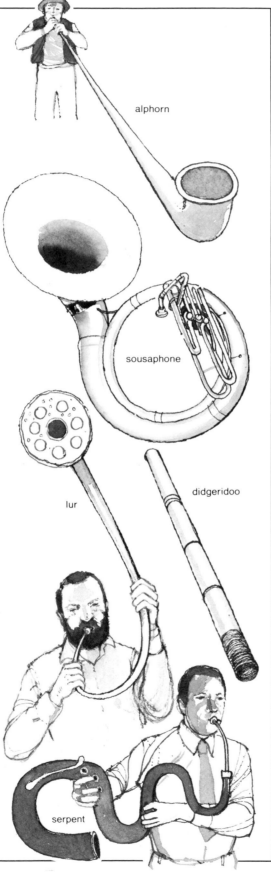

alphorn

sousaphone

lur

didgeridoo

conch shell

serpent

the bell may be very large. Many are called horns and they originated from hollow animal horns, which could be blown to sound signals or calls like hunting calls. These brass instruments include the French horn and tuba, which are mainly played in orchestras, and the horns played in brass bands. They have a warmer, less strident sound than trumpets and trombones.

French horn The French horn, which is often simply called the horn, has several coils of tubing. If unwound, it would be nearly six metres (20 feet) long – three times the size of a horn player! The French horn can therefore play notes as deep as a trombone but, in good hands, can also play high notes with a brilliant sound. You will often see horn players insert their hands into the bell. This changes the sound, giving it a thin but penetrating quality.

The kind of French horn most played is the double horn, which has two separate sets of coiled tubing. The player switches from one set to another to get certain notes.

Tuba The tuba is a massive, heavy instrument used to produce deep sonorous notes beneath the rest of the orchestra. Tubas come in several sizes and may have four valves, depending on the range of notes to be sounded.

Brass Band Instruments

Apart from trombones, brass bands contain conical brass instruments that are mostly different types of horns. The cornet is the highest-pitched along with the flugelhorn, both played in the same way as the trumpet. Lower in pitch are the alto, tenor and baritone horns, which are all like small tubas and have an upright bell. At the bottom end of the band are the euphonium and bass or bass horn, which are similar to the tuba.

Famous Musicians

Trumpet	Trombone
Maurice André	J. J. Johnson
Louis Armstrong	Jack Teagarden
Miles Davis	
Dizzy Gillespie	**French Horn**
Wynton Marsalis	Dennis Brain
	Barry Tuckwell

Percussion Instruments

Percussion instruments include instruments such as drums and cymbals that make noises rather than notes, as well as instruments like the xylophone that can produce musical notes. You strike or shake percussion instruments to play them, and the whole or part of the instrument vibrates to give a sound.

Watching and listening to percussion players in action, especially drummers, is exhilarating because of the energy they put into the music. Drums and other percussion instruments are essential to rock, jazz and pop music, marching bands and much folk music because they play the basic beat that gives the music life and makes it dance or move. The other musicians listen to the drums and percussion and emphasize the beat as they play.

In symphony orchestras, the percussion section sometimes plays in this way but the percussion instruments are more often used for effects. A roll on the drums followed by a crash of cymbals can bring the music to a climax, while quiet repeated drumbeats can make the music sound menacing.

Famous Percussion Music

Percussion

Varèse	*Ionisation*	1931
Bartók	*Music for Strings, Percussion and Celesta*	1936

Cimbalom

Stravinsky	*Les Noces (The Wedding)*	1923
Kodály	*Háry János Suite*	1926

Tubular Bells

Tchaikovsky	*1812 Overture*	1880

Famous Musicians

Drums	Vibraphone	Percussion
Ginger Baker	Gary Burton	James Blades
Billy Cobham	Lionel Hampton	
Gene Krupa		**Percussion Ensembles**
Elvin Jones		The Percussions Of Strasbourg (below)
Keith Moon (The Who)		
Buddy Rich		

The Drum Kit

In jazz, rock and popular music, the music is usually propelled by a drummer who sits at a drum kit containing a set of drums and cymbals. Playing with drumsticks, mallets or wire brushes in both hands and operating pedals with both feet, the drummer plays several of the instruments at the same time.

At the centre of the kit in front of the drummer is a snare drum, and beyond this are one or two bass drums played with mallets moved by pedals. Cymbals and tom-toms (drums of medium pitch) are fixed to the bass drum and mounted on stands placed around the drummer. To one side is the hi-hat, a pair of cymbals that the drummer can open or close with a pedal while playing on the upper cymbal.

Right Ginger Baker playing drums.

There are two main kinds of percussion instruments: untuned percussion instruments make noises and tuned percussion instrument produce musical notes.

Untuned Percussion

Drums are the principal untuned percussion instruments; they are of ancient origin and played in many forms in all kinds of music throughout the world. A drum is basically a cylinder with a skin stretched tightly over one or both ends. The skin is struck with the hands or fingers, or with a drumstick or soft mallet. The skin and air in the drum vibrate to produce the characteristic hollow thud of a drumbeat. The tighter or smaller the skin, the higher the sound.

The main kinds of drums used in orchestras and bands are: the side drum or snare drum, a medium-sized drum with a set of wires called a snare on the underside that add a crack to the sound; the tenor drum, a large drum with a full sound; and the bass drum, a big booming drum usually played on

Below An Indian drummer performs with a shehnai player.

Bottom Kettledrums are carried on horseback in this British military band.

Latin American Percussion

The popular and folk music of Central and South America features a group of unusual percussion instruments which are known as Latin American percussion. The players bang, shake and scrape the instruments in lively energetic rhythms that work together to make the music dance along.

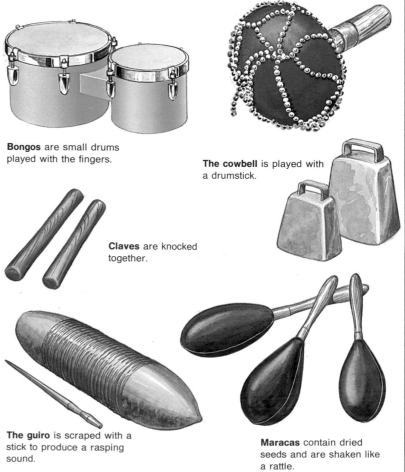

The cabaca may be shaken or rubbed to make the strings of beads rattle.

Bongos are small drums played with the fingers.

The cowbell is played with a drumstick.

Claves are knocked together.

The guiro is scraped with a stick to produce a rasping sound.

Maracas contain dried seeds and are shaken like a rattle.

its side. Kettledrums or timpani, which are tuned drums, are described below.

Cymbals and gongs are discs of metal that vibrate in complex ways to give crashing or ringing sounds. They are usually mounted on stands or suspended from frames, but pairs of cymbals may be clashed together. The gong is often called a tam-tam.

Other untuned percussion instruments commonly played in orchestras and bands include the tambourine, a small drum with jingles like tiny cymbals mounted in it that give a sparkling sound when it is struck or shaken. The wood block contains a slot and produces a bright hard sound when tapped. Castanets are a Spanish instrument consisting of a pair of hinged wooden shells clicked together between the fingers. The triangle is a triangular steel bar struck with a metal bar to give a high, penetrating, bell-like sound. The wind machine contains a large cylinder that is turned to imitate the howl of the wind.

Tuned Percussion

Timpani or kettledrums are the principal percussion instruments in the symphony orchestra. One percussionist plays two to four of them. Timpani are large round copper drums. The skin is stretched tight by screws around the drum, and the tightness can be changed to tune the drum to a definite musical note. You can see the percussionist doing this before and sometimes during a performance. However, many percussionists play pedal timpani, which have a pedal mechanism to change the pitch of the drum quickly.

The xylophone, vibraphone, marimba and glockenspiel all have sets of wooden or metal bars arranged like a piano keyboard. When struck with mallets, the bars ring and give out the same notes as piano keys. All except the glockenspiel have tubes beneath the bars which resonate when the bars above are struck. The bar causes the air in the tube to vibrate and produce the same note, making the sound louder.

Tubular bells consist of a set of steel tubes that ring like bells when struck with a hammer. The cimbalom or dulcimer looks rather like a grand piano without a lid or keyboard. It contains strings like the piano, which the performer strikes with mallets to make music.

Above Oscar Peterson, the virtuoso Canadian jazz pianist, with the Danish bass player Niels-Henning Oersted Pedersen.

Keyboard Instruments

On a keyboard, you can play a different note with each finger and thumb – and, with some keyboard instruments, you can also use your feet to control the sound or even play more notes. Keyboard players, such as pianists and organists, can therefore make great music on their own, and no other instruments can equal the keyboards for solo performances. Furthermore, the arrangement of keys is the same on all keyboard instruments. If you learn to play one keyboard instrument like the piano, you can easily take up another such as the organ or harpsichord or the electric and electronic keyboards described on pages 45 to 49.

Above This beautifully decorated harpsichord was made in France in the 1670s.

But keyboards are not only solo instruments; the piano is an excellent instrument for duets in which two people play the keyboard. Keyboard instruments are also often played in orchestras, both as a featured instrument in concertos and as part of the orchestra. And many jazz, rock and pop groups use keyboards.

Acoustic (non-electronic) keyboard instruments make their sounds in basically the same way as some string, woodwind and tuned percussion instruments. Instead of using the fingers and possibly the mouth to produce the music, pressing a key operates a mechanism that gives the sound.

Stringed Keyboard Instruments

All these instruments contain a set of stretched strings, one or more for each note. The three main types – clavichord, harpsichord and piano – use different methods for making the strings sound.

The clavichord is the oldest stringed keyboard, dating back to about 1400. It is not a common instrument today, mainly because its sound is very quiet. When a key is pressed, a metal blade fixed to the other end of the key rises and strikes a string which vibrates and makes a sound. One unusual feature of the clavichord is that you can get vibrato (make the note wobble in pitch) by moving the key up and down after striking it.

The harpsichord is also an old instrument, the earliest surviving harpsichord dating from 1490. Together with the spinet and virginals, which were small harpsichords played in the home, it was popular until about 1800. All were then ousted by the piano, but the harpsichord can be often heard today in performances of music of the 1700s.

When a key is pressed on a harpsichord, a mechanism called a jack moves and causes a plectrum to pluck a string. On releasing the key, a damper touches the string and stops it sounding. Harpsichords may also have buttons called stops, and two or even more keyboards, one above the other. Normally, the harpsichord has a bright, buzzy sound. By operating the stops or changing to another keyboard, the strings can produce different tones, making the instrument sound lighter or full and rich, for example. This is desirable because the volume of the harpsichord cannot be changed to make the music louder or softer.

The piano was invented by Bartolommeo Cristofori in Italy in about 1709 to overcome this problem. Its full name is pianoforte, which means 'soft-loud' in Italian. Inside the piano, felt-covered hammers hit the strings as the keys are played and then fall back to leave the strings sounding. Striking the keys of the piano harder makes the music louder.

Unusual Keyboards

The celesta or celeste gives soft bell-like chiming sounds. It is played in symphony orchestras. The keyboard operates hammers that strike metal bars suspended inside the celesta.

An accordion contains a set of free reeds blown by bellows that are pushed in and out while playing. Keyboards containing keys or buttons for each hand sound single notes or chords. The concertina is a similar instrument having button keyboards.

The hurdy-gurdy is a kind of keyboard violin. Instead of using the fingers to press the strings and produce notes, keys are operated to press the strings. At the same time, the player winds a handle which makes a drum rotate to rub the strings and cause them to sound. This folk instrument can be heard in Brittany, France.

The harmonium is a small organ containing free reeds. It often has pedals that are pushed to and fro while playing to work bellows that blow the reeds.

The prepared piano is an ordinary piano in which various objects are fixed to the string to change its sound. In this way, the piano can be made to produce unusual, often percussive, sounds.

harmonium

Left This is the keyboard of a carillon. The keys are wooden rods that are connected by wires to bells in a tower above. They are arranged like a piano keyboard, but the performer has to use his fists instead of his fingers.

Above The Japanese classical pianist Mitsuko Uchida.

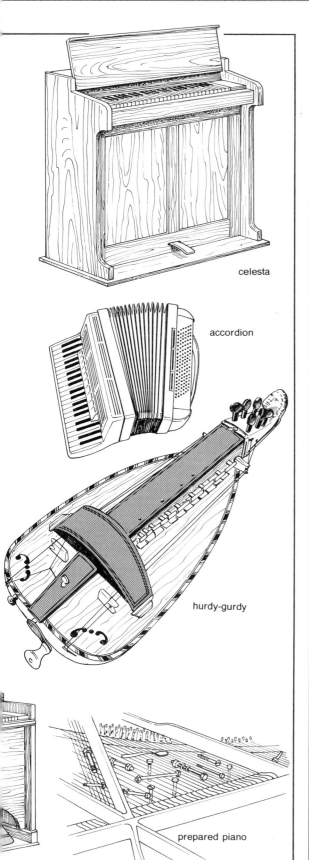

celesta

accordion

hurdy-gurdy

prepared piano

Famous Keyboard Music

Harpsichord

Scarlatti	*Keyboard Sonatas*	1722–57
Handel	*The Harmonious Blacksmith*	1720
J. S. Bach	*Goldberg Variations*	1742
Falla	*Harpsichord Concerto*	1926

Piano Solo

Chopin	*Waltzes*	1829–47
	Ballade No 4 in F minor	1842
Schumann	*Carnaval (Carnival)*	1835
Mendelssohn	*Songs Without Words*	1834–43
Liszt	*Hungarian Rhapsodies*	1847
Debussy	*Children's Corner*	1908
Ravel	*Gaspard de la Nuit*	1908

Piano Duets

Schubert	*Fantasia in F minor*	1828
Debussy	*Petite Suite*	1888

Piano Concertos

Mozart	*Piano Concerto No 21 in C major*	1785
Beethoven	*Piano Concerto No 5 in E flat major (Emperor)*	1809
Grieg	*Piano Concerto in A minor*	1868
Tchaikovsky	*Piano Concerto No 1 in B flat minor*	1875

Prepared Piano

Cage	*Sonatas and Interludes*	1948

Pipe Organ

Albinoni	*Adagio in G minor for Strings and Organ*	*
J. S. Bach	*Toccata and Fugue in D minor*	c1710
Widor	*Organ Symphony No 5 in F minor*	1880
Saint-Saëns	*Symphony No 3 in C minor*	1886
Messiaen	*L'Ascension*	1934

Celesta

Tchaikovsky	*Dance of the Sugar Plum Fairy* (from *The Nutcracker*)	1892
Bartók	*Music for Strings, Percussion and Celesta*	1936

* This work, often ascribed to Albinoni (1671–1750), was largely written by Remo Giazotto (1910–   ).

Famous Musicians

Harpsichord	Glenn Gould	Earl Hines
Ralph Kirkpatrick	Vladimir Horowitz	Keith Jarrett
George Malcolm	Arturo Benedetti Michelangeli	Thelonius Monk
Piano (classical)		Oscar Peterson
Martha Argerich	Murray Perahia	Art Tatum
Claudio Arrau	Artur Rubenstein	
Vladimir Ashkenazy	**Piano (jazz and rock)**	**Organ**
Daniel Barenboim	Keith Emerson	Carlo Curley
Alfred Brendel	Bill Evans	Peter Hurford
Paul Crossley	Errol Garner	Simon Preston
Clifford Curzon	Herbie Hancock	Karl Richter
		Lionel Rogg

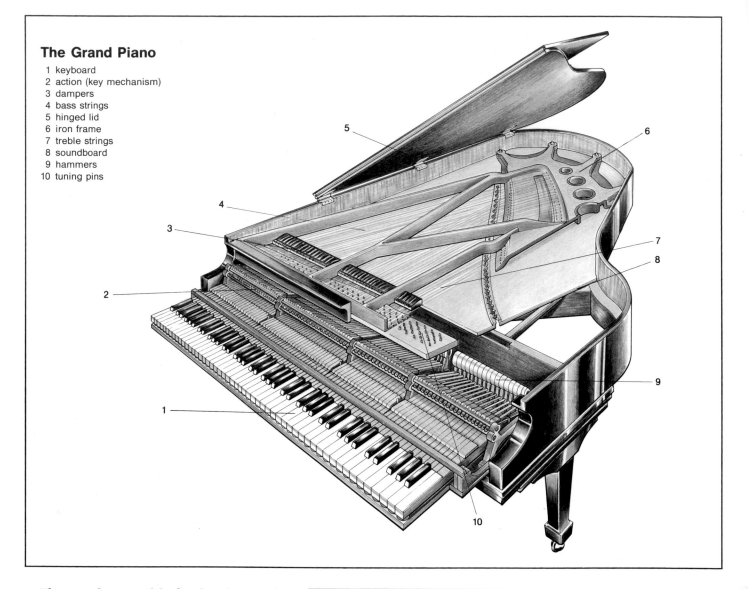

The Grand Piano

1 keyboard
2 action (key mechanism)
3 dampers
4 bass strings
5 hinged lid
6 iron frame
7 treble strings
8 soundboard
9 hammers
10 tuning pins

The grand piano of the kind we have today developed in the early 1800s. It has two strings for every note in the middle of the keyboard and three at the treble end. The keyboard normally has 85 keys but some pianos possess three extra keys at the treble end. There are usually two pedals. The soft pedal, operated by the left foot, quietens the sound. The right pedal stops the dampers from cutting off the notes so that they continue to sound when the keys are released. It is therefore known as the sustaining pedal, but is often wrongly called the loud pedal.

The upright piano is a smaller version of the grand piano with vertical strings. It has all the features of the grand piano but not such a rich sound.

Keyboard Mechanisms

Right The mechanism of an upright piano. Pressing a key (1) tilts the lever (2), pushing the jack (3) against the hammer (4). As the hammer strikes the string (5), the damper lever (6) pulls back the damper (7) from the string. The check (8) then holds the hammer near the string until the key is released. A grand piano works in a similar way.

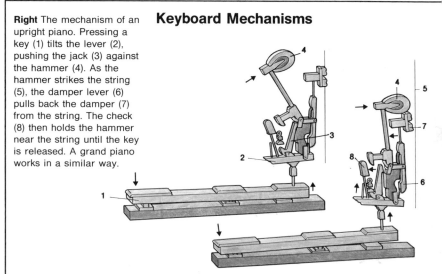

Pipe Organs

The pipe organ is the most versatile and most complex of all acoustic musical instruments. The biggest instruments have many thousands of pipes and can produce a vast array of sounds. The electric organ, which does not have pipes, is described on page 45.

When you play an organ, you have to decide on the sounds you want for the various sections of the music. You pull knobs called stops to get different sounds. Many organs also have two or more keyboards which are called manuals, each of which can be given its own particular sound. There may also be a pedalboard for the feet with another set of stops. Playing an organ is therefore not just a matter of fingering a keyboard. It also involves changing the stops and using different manuals as well as sounding deep bass notes with the feet. Furthermore, the notes cut off immediately the keys are released so great care is needed in fingering. Making the music louder and softer is done mainly by changing stops or manuals.

Good organists can produce tremendous music that is full of contrasting sounds. One moment the organ may whisper; the next, it may roar. Pipe organs are too big to move and are built permanently into halls and churches. They are usually played solo and organists may improvise the music. Choral music often has an organ accompaniment, and sometimes the organ is played with an orchestra.

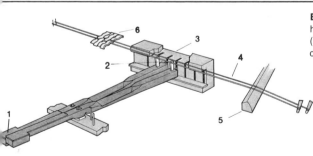

Above The mechanism of a clavichord. Pressing a key (1) causes a tangent (2) to rise in the rack (3) and strike a string (4). The part of the string between the tangent and the bridge (5) vibrates. The damping cloth (6) stops the other part of the string sounding.

Below The mechanism of a harpsichord. Pressing a key (1) makes a jack (2) rise, causing the plectrum (3) to pluck a string (4). On releasing the key, the damper (5) stops the string sounding.

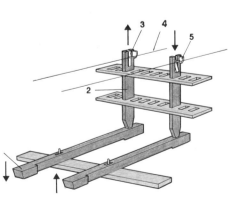

Above This beautiful pipe organ is at Salamanca in Spain. Magnificent organ music has been composed, especially by J. S. Bach, for such grand instruments.

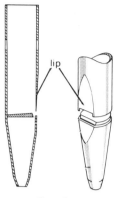

lip

flue pipes

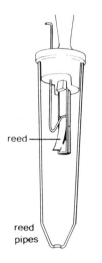

reed

reed
pipes

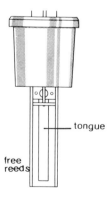

tongue

free
reeds

Above The three kinds of organ pipes.

How A Pipe Organ Works

A pipe organ is basically a large group of pipes that are blown mechanically. Fans powered by electricity blow air into a chamber inside the organ called the windchest. When the keys are pressed, valves in the windchest open and direct the air to certain pipes. The pipes make sounds in the same way as woodwind instruments, though they do not have fingerholes and the whole length of the pipe sounds. To get different notes, an organ has pipes of different sizes – from 2 centimetres (1 inch) up to as much as 19 metres (64 feet) in length.

The pipes are of three kinds. Flue pipes are like whistles and recorders. The air blows against a lip in a hole at the base of the pipe. Reed pipes contain a reed like that in a clarinet mouthpiece, and the air makes the reed vibrate to sound the pipe. There are also free reed pipes, which contain a metal tongue that makes a sound in the same way as the metal reeds in a mouth organ.

Pulling out a stop or changing manuals causes the airstream to flow to different sets of pipes when a key is pressed. Several pipes may sound the note required, or notes an octave or another interval below or above the note may be added. All the possible combinations give an enormous variety of tone colour to organ music.

The largest organs have five manuals, each of which can be thought of as operating a different smaller organ within the organ. The bottom manual sounds the choir organ, which has a light tone. Then comes the great organ, which produces the full, powerful sound characteristic of pipe organs. The third manual operates the swell organ, which has shutters that open and close on pressing a pedal to make the sound louder or softer. Then comes the solo organ, normally used to play melodies, and finally the echo organ, which gives soft echoing sounds.

Below The mechanism of a pipe organ. Pressing a key (1) causes a pallet (2) to open, allowing air to flow from the reservoir (3) through the wind chest (4) to a set of pipes (5) that sound a note. Operating a stop causes a slider (6) to mqve in or out, sending the air to sound different pipes in the set.

Electric Instruments

Electric musical instruments make sounds in a different way from acoustic instruments such as guitars and pianos, even though they may look similar. These instruments must be connected by a wire called a lead to an amplifier and loudspeaker to produce a sound. Instead of making the sound themselves, electric instruments produce a weak electric signal. The amplifier makes the signal stronger so that it is powerful enough to drive a loudspeaker, which produces the actual sound that you hear.

There are two main kinds of electric instruments. The electric guitar and some electric keyboards contain moving parts which generate the electric signal that goes to the amplifier. In electronic instruments like the synthesizer, the action of playing the instrument switches on electronic components such as microchips that produce the signal.

Electric Guitars

The standard electric guitar contains six strings like the acoustic guitar. Because its own sound is not heard, an electric guitar has a solid body that can be any shape required. The strings are made of metal and beneath each one is a pick-up containing a magnet and coil of wire. When a string is plucked, it vibrates and causes the magnetic field around the coil to vibrate. This action generates an electric signal in the coil, and this signal goes to the amplifier and loudspeaker to produce the sound of the guitar. Most electric guitars have volume and tone controls fixed to the body so that the player can easily control the sound.

The electric guitar is an important instrument in jazz, rock, blues, country and pop music. As a lead guitar, it can play tunes and solo lines with tremendous expression and power. As a rhythm guitar, the electric guitar is used to play chords in a rhythmic accompaniment. Many singers accompany themselves on the electric guitar.

The bass guitar has four strings tuned to the same notes as a double bass. It works in the same way as the electric guitar and is used to play lively, rhythmic bass lines in rock, jazz and pop (especially disco) music.

Electric Keyboards

The electric piano has a keyboard that operates hammers in the same way as an acoustic piano. The hammers strike stretched strings or metal rods or reeds that vibrate and generate signals in pick-ups. The clavinet is an electric clavichord that works in a similar way. These electric keyboards produce a variety of sounds, ranging from the bright percussive notes of the clavinet to the cloudy bell-like sounds of the Rhodes electric piano.

The electric organ was invented by the American engineer Laurens Hammond in 1939 as a small organ with the sound of a big pipe organ. In fact, the Hammond organ and other electric organs also produce special 'electric' sounds as well as the sounds of pipe organs. When the keys are pressed, electric signals go to an amplifier and loudspeaker inside the organ to produce a sound. The signals may be generated by tone wheels, which are metal discs that rotate to generate signals in pick-ups. Pressing the keys and operating the tone controls sends mixtures of these signals to the loudspeaker.

Modern electric organs produce an enormous range of sounds complete with automatic drum and percussion rhythms as well as automatic bass lines and accompaniments.

Famous Musicians

Electric Guitar
Eric Clapton
Charlie Christian
Jimi Hendrix
B. B. King
Wes Montgomery
Les Paul

Bass Guitar
Jack Bruce
Stanley Clarke
Jaco Pastorius

Electric Organ
Ray Charles
Billy Preston
Jimmy Smith

Left Jimmy Page, of the rock band Led Zeppelin, pioneered the use of the electric guitar to create a wall of sound.

Electric Instruments and Sound Systems

1. Electric instruments make only a very soft sound so they contain pick-ups that change the sound waves into a weak electric signal.

2. Some electric instruments are ordinary acoustic ones adaped for amplification. They contain a tiny microphone which changes the sound of the instrument into a weak electric signal.

3. The signal from the pick-up or microphone may go to one or more processing devices. These are often worked by pedals. They affect the signal so that the sound you hear is changed, for example, they give it an echoing quality.

4. The signal may then go to the performer's amplifier and loudspeaker unit. This controls the volume and tone of the music.

5. Singers and acoustic instruments have their own microphones.

6. The engineer operates the mixer to combine the signals from the instruments and microphones into one signal (or two signals for stereo sound).

7. The signal goes to a powerful amplifier that drives loudspeakers to produce the final sound.

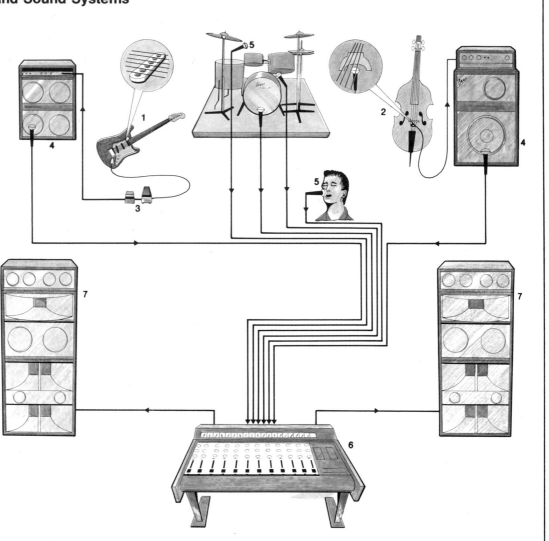

Electronic Instruments

Electronic instruments have given music a totally new realm of sound in the last twenty years. The main reason is that these instruments produce sounds in ways that are completely different from acoustic instruments. But another reason is that electronics makes possible new ways of putting sounds together to create music that has tremendous impact and power. Good electronic music produces vivid sounds of immense clarity that can surround you and draw you into the music in a way unrivalled by acoustic instruments.

Two scientific advances have brought about this electronic revolution in music. The first was the invention of the multitrack tape recorder, which can record many different sounds separately. The second was the development of electronic components such as integrated circuits and microchips, which led to the synthesizer and microcomputer. These inventions took place in the 1960s and 1970s. They have made electronic instruments available at no greater cost than acoustic instruments.

Electronic music making Inside electronic instruments such as synthesizers, electronic components produce electric signals that go to an amplifier and loudspeaker to make a sound. Portable electronic keyboards may contain their own speakers. Most synthesizers have keyboards, and pressing a key causes the components to generate a signal and produce a sound. Some synthesizers are monophonic and sound only one note at a time. Polyphonic synthesizers can produce chords. However, the kind of sound that you get depends on how you operate the controls on the synthesizer. You can press buttons to get pre-set sounds, or you can use the controls to get your own sounds and change them while you play. With programmable instruments, you can keep these sounds in the machine's memory or store them for later use. In this way, the synthesizer will immediately produce your own sounds whenever required without your having to operate the controls again. Musicians in a group play electronic instruments in this way.

You do not have to finger a keyboard to produce electronic music: some synthesizers can be played like a guitar or blown like a woodwind instrument. Percussion synthesizers have pads that you strike with sticks to produce a variety of drum-like sounds or unusual electronic noises.

Bands made up of all or some electronic instruments are only one form of electronic music making. The signal from a synthesizer can go directly to a tape recorder to be recorded. And with multitrack tape recorders, different sounds can be recorded separately on the same tape. When the tape is played back, the sounds are mixed together to produce the impression of a whole orchestra of electronic instruments — all played by one person! With some synthesizers, this technique of creating and mixing different sounds can be done by storing the music in the machine's memory and a multitrack recorder is not needed.

To make electronic music in this way, you need to know how to put music together, although you do not need to be able to play each part yourself. A special music computer or machine called a sequencer can be connected to the synthesizer or may be part of it, or the computer may contain its own sound generating microchips. Instead of playing the keyboard to make the music, you program the computer or sequencer with the notes that you want to hear. The machine will then produce the music automatically, enabling you to get effects that you could not obtain yourself.

Bottom left This electronic keyboard can produce the sounds of several acoustic instruments and automatic percussion rhythms, either by playing the keyboard and pressing the control buttons, or by programming the instrument's internal computer to play the music. It is made in Japan.

Below Vangelis, the Greek synthesizer musician, is a modern one-man band. He composes and performs all his music himself, building layer upon layer of sounds in his recording studio.

The First Electronic Instruments

Electronic music is in fact nearly a century old. The first electronic instrument was the telharmonium, which was invented by Thaddeus Cahill in New York in 1906. It had a large keyboard and banks of rotating electric generators which produced signals that travelled along telephone wires to those who wished to hear the instrument. The telharmonium weighed about 200 tons. Unfortunately, it interfered with telephone calls and was never used.

The first successful electronic instrument was the theremin, which was invented by Leon Theremin in Russia in 1920. It was played by waving a hand over a metal rod projecting from the instrument and gave an eerie sound.

The ondes marinot is an electronic instrument invented by Maurice Martenot in France in 1928. This has a keyboard and other controls to produce a voicelike sound. It is still sometimes played in symphony orchestras and may be seen and heard in the *Turangalîla Symphony* by Messiaen.

The first synthesizers were large and complex machines developed by RCA in the United States in the 1950s. However, the first synthesizer that was simple to use was invented by Robert Moog in the United States in 1963.

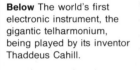

Below The world's first electronic instrument, the gigantic telharmonium, being played by its inventor Thaddeus Cahill.

How Synthesizers Work

To synthesize means to build up, and a synthesizer makes music by building up sounds. All sounds are mixtures of a main note that you hear and other higher but weaker notes called harmonics (see page 149). The strengths of the various harmonics give a sound its own particular quality. A bright sound like a violin has strong harmonics whereas the mellow tone of a flute has weak harmonics.

The synthesizer can produce so many different sounds because it creates the harmonics in the sound. With the controls, you can change the harmonics and alter the sound that the instrument produces. To do this, the electronic components in the synthesizer generate and then alter an electric signal as the keys and controls are operated. The final signal that emerges goes to an amplifier and loudspeaker to produce the actual sound that you hear.

Many synthesizers have components called oscillators that produce a signal, giving a sound with strong harmonics. There is also a noise generator, which produces a hissing noise. This sound or noise signal is then treated with a filter to remove some harmonics and strengthen others so as to give different kinds of sounds. The synthesizer also has a control

Computers in Music

Computers are making an increasing impact on music. Some microcomputers have sound generators that produce musical notes. You can program a computer to play a tune or a piece in several musical lines. Or you can write programs that make the sound generators work in unusual ways. You normally have to tell the computer the pitch, duration and volume of the sounds you want and possibly also the tone of the sound and ways in which the sound may change during a note. Special music programs are available to do this. These often display the music that you write on the screen of the computer or print it out for you. You may also be able to connect the computer via a standard connection to a synthesizer to increase the range of sounds that you can produce.

called an envelope generator that turns the sound signal on and off in various ways so that the notes start and stop quickly or slowly. This gives different kinds of notes, making sounds that ping or whoosh, for example.

Other synthesizers work differently. They use computer components to build up the sounds by combining together electric signals that give the harmonics. A microprocessor is required that must work very fast because the signals have to change rapidly as the sounds form.

In some kinds of synthesizers and computers it is possible to sample sounds. A real sound – either live from a microphone or recorded – is fed into the machine as an electric signal. The electronic components detect the harmonics in the sound and the way in which they change as the sound dies away. The machine then stores this information in its memory. The sound can then be heard at any pitch by playing the keyboard or programming the notes required. You can then change the sound, or possibly even 'design' entirely new sounds to be stored in the memory.

The vocoder is a kind of synthesizer used with the voice. It gives a spoken sound a pitch as if it were sung.

Famous Electronic Music

Stockhausen	*Gesang der Jünglinge*	1956
Stockhausen	*Kontakte*	1960
Walter Carlos	*Switched-on Bach*	1967
Kraftwerk	*Autobahn*	1974
Jean-Michel Jarre	*Oxygène*	1976
Boulez	*Répons*	1983

Famous Musicians

Chick Corea	Isao Tomita
Thomas Dolby	Vangelis
Brian Eno	Joe Zawinul

Below An electronic musician uses a light pen to operate a music computer.

Above Simon Stockhausen combines the acoustic sound of his soprano saxophone with electronic sounds in a concert of electronic works by his father, Karlheinz Stockhausen.

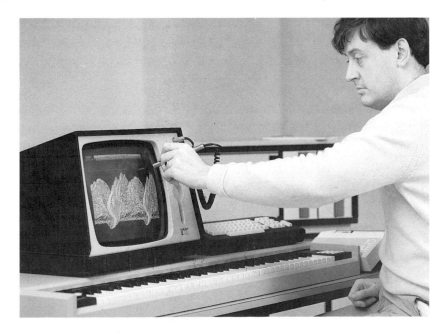

In addition to creating musical sounds, computers can handle electric signals at enormous speeds and can therefore process musical signals in all kinds of ways. The signals may come from microphones that pick up the sounds of live instruments or they may come from electronic instruments or tape recorders. The computer can take the signals and change them – adding new tones and altering the quality of the sounds, for example. It can then direct the signals to banks of loudspeakers so that the resulting sounds come from all directions and move around the listener – an extraordinary musical experience only possible in electronic music. In this way, electronic instruments and computers are opening up new and exciting directions in making and listening to music.

Music Around the World

Music is something that people everywhere seem to need to enhance their lives. Music has tremendous power to affect human feelings, especially when used to accompany words and movement in singing and dancing. It can raise or lower the spirits, help people work or relax, intensify religious experience and confer importance on ceremonies and occasions. Throughout the world, people have developed many distinctive ways of making music.

Each continent has developed a different kind of music, mainly because the continents are separated. In Asia, Africa, Australia and Europe, people did not hear the music of other continents and so developed their own ways of making music. In North and South America, different kinds of music arose as people from Europe and Africa came together.

Some kinds of music have since spread from their origins. Classical music arose in Europe and popular music in North America, and each kind of music has now permeated both these continents and is extending its influence further. For example, Korea has produced superb classical musicians and Japan excellent popular groups. However, all regions still possess their own particular ways of making music, producing different kinds of songs, dances and instrumental music played on an enormous variety of fascinating instruments. This traditional music, which is often called ethnic music or folk music, goes back centuries but remains steadfastly alive everywhere. Sometimes modern influences make their mark on it; elsewhere pure traditional forms are maintained or revived.

The Music of India

India is one of four main regions of Asia that possess their own kind of music. The other regions are China, Japan and Indonesia. All Asian or Eastern music has one basic similarity – a strong reliance on melody – but this does not mean that all Asian music is tuneful. The music is played or sung so that single lines of notes follow one another to create melodies. Asian music is noted for the way in which its melodies swoop and soar, often in a florid, decorated style.

Each region has its own type of melody and each sounds very different from the others, even to Western ears unused to Asian music. The reason is that each kind of music uses different scales of notes to create melody. These scales are unlike the major and minor scales that give classical and popular music their sound (see page 152),

Left Folk music was first recorded on wax cylinders. Nowadays, television teams like this crew at work in West Africa capture it in both sound and vision.

50

and they are most highly developed in the music of India.

Traditional Indian music is performed by small groups of musicians. There is a singer or a principal player who leads the music, often on a lute such as a sitar, and he or she is supported by accompanying musicians, often just a drummer and a player who sounds a drone. The reason that so few people are involved is that the music is mostly improvised. The players make up most of the music as they perform, and too many people would create chaos. The purpose of the music is to create and sustain a particular emotion or mood, such as joy, sorrow or peace. To do this, the performers choose a particular scale of notes for their piece, and both the scale and the piece of music are called a raga. There are many different ragas and each has its own quality of mood. It may be played only at a certain time of day or season of the year in order to produce the right effect. For example, a morning raga gives a different feeling to an evening raga.

The notes of a raga scale are chosen from the twelve notes of the chromatic scale,

Above This folk dance of Himachal Pradesh in northern India is performed to the music of ceremonial horns and drums.

which are the same as the notes of the black and white keys on a piano. However, a raga is not like a scale that people practise on the piano. Each raga has its own particular set of notes. The performers create music by choosing notes from the scale as they play, and they may sharpen or flatten the notes for special effect. The raga contains one main note called the vadi that is like a home note.

Indian Instruments

The tambura is a long-necked lute whose strings are plucked to sound the drone in a raga.

The vina is a lute with large gourds that resonate when the strings are plucked. It has a bright, buzzy sound.

The sitar, like the vina, is a lute. The strings can be pulled with one hand as they are plucked with the other to make the notes slide in pitch. It has several extra sympathetic strings that are not plucked but resonate to give a shimmering tone.

The sarangi is held upright and played with a bow. The strings are stopped with the fingernails, which can move along the strings to make the notes slide.

The tabla is a pair of drums played by both hands. Different strokes are given with the fingers or hands to get a wide variety of sounds.

The shehnai is a woodwind instrument blown with a double reed. It is traditionally played at weddings.

tabla

shehnai

tambura

sitar

vina

sarangi

This note is sounded by the drone, and the way in which the other notes sound against it gives the raga its particular feeling.

A whole raga has two or three set sections, but it lasts as long as the performers feel they are sustaining the right mood. It opens with the alap, which is meditative without any rhythm or pulse. The singer or lead player explores the scale of the raga, producing notes that may slide, tremble, zig-zag, or rush up or down to produce all kinds of melodic phrases and effects that wring as much emotion from the scale as possible.

The players may next proceed to the jor, an interlude that introduces a steady pulse to take the raga into its final rhythmic section. The drums then enter, playing in a rhythm called a tala. The tala has a set number of beats to the bar, varying from 3 to more than 100. The rhythm may be unusual to Western ears, often containing 5, 7, 11 or 14 beats. Furthermore, these are subdivided into irregular groups – 14 beats may be made up of four groups of 5, 2, 3 and 4 beats. The final section may begin with a short composed melody in the raga scale called the gat, and the performers then continue to improvise, often using this melody in various ways. The beat of the drums raises the excitement, and the raga becomes more and more rhythmic and possibly faster. The music gets wilder and wilder until it suddenly ends, the raga

explored to the full. It may last for hours.

None of this music is written down. The performers learn the ragas and gats and develop ways of performing them over many years. The singers have to be able to interpret the words used in a raga in many different ways. The players may strive to imitate the voice as they play, giving their melody tremendous expression.

Left A singer from northern India accompanies himself on a two-string lute.

Left In India, ragas are often played by a small group of musicians, especially this combination of tabla (left), tambura (centre) and sitar (right). The tabla provides an exciting rhythm and the tambura a drone over which the sitar, here played by Ravi Shankar, improvises melodic phrases. This kind of traditional music is known as Indian classical music.

Right The sheng, a kind of a Chinese mouth organ.

Chinese Music

Unlike Indian music, the traditional music of China is composed and not improvised. It may be written or handed down from teacher to pupil and memorized, but it does not change from one performance to another. One reason for this is that Chinese music aims to describe things, particularly scenes and situations, and so has to be very precise in its effect on listeners. Because the music is composed, a wide range of instruments can be played together in orchestras to get a great variety of sounds.

One of the principal forms of Chinese music is opera. The productions are highly stylized; some of the actors have their faces painted in different colours to represent their roles. An opera consists of several acts and each has a descriptive title, rather like a newspaper headline. In each act, a character first enters to explain the situation and then the actors sing songs, accompanied by an orchestra containing instruments like flutes and mouth organs, strings such as lutes and fiddles, and percussion instruments such as drums and clappers. The orchestra also plays interludes between scenes, and the music may contain special tunes that depict

Chinese Instruments

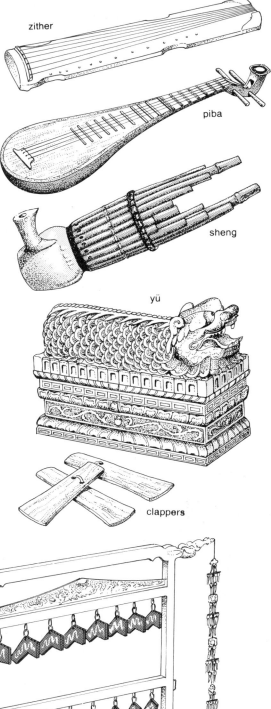

zither

piba

sheng

yü

clappers

sonorous stones

The zither has a set of strings that can be plucked in different ways to give a variety of sounds. Harmonics, which have an ethereal other-worldly sound, are used to bring zither pieces to a climax.

The piba is a lute that is played as a solo instrument as well as in small ensembles and orchestras.

The sheng is a type of mouth organ. The player blows into the wind-chest and covers holes on the pipes to produce notes. Inside the pipes, metal strips vibrate to give the sounds.

The yü is a wooden instrument carved in the form of a tiger. It is played by scraping a rod along its back.

Clappers are two pieces of wood that are banged together to give a sharp crack.

Sonorous stones are sets of suspended stones of ancient origin that are struck with a hammer to produce notes.

particular actions or emotions, for example joy, drunkenness, anger or quarrels.

The music that is written for musicians and singers to perform is also very descriptive. Famous pieces exist for the zither and lute with titles such as *Mist And Rain On The Lake* and *Cold Crows Playing With Water*. The songs are comparatively simple but the instrumental pieces may be complex, often with a slow prelude and then several variations of a tune.

Much Chinese music, however varied the instruments and its descriptive powers, uses a simple five-note scale, known as the Chinese pentatonic scale, to create melody. This scale can be produced with the notes C D E G A, or with the black notes on the piano. Playing pairs of notes in this scale a fourth apart – such as G C, E A, and D G – gives a very Chinese sound.

Japanese Music

The music of Japan resembles that of China in several ways. Japanese music consists mainly of composed melody that is either written or handed down. It is often descriptive and music is used in stylized theatre productions like opera in China. However, Japanese music sounds quite different from Chinese music, mainly because it uses different scales to build its melodies. Much of the music features two pentatonic (five-note) scales that contain different notes from the Chinese pentatonic scale. On the white notes of the piano, the Japanese pentatonic scales are A B C E F and E F A B D. Unlike Chinese melody, both these scales give a semitone (E F) which creates a characteristic haunting sound.

The traditional Japanese theatre is called the noh theatre. A typical production contains two acts; in the first, the principal character has been reincarnated as another person, and the second act then shows the character's former life. The actors wear masks and there is a chorus that comments on and describes the action. Words are chanted, and the music accompanies the chants and dances as well as providing musical introductions and interludes. The music consists of sinuous melody played on a

Japanese Instruments

The shakuhachi is a simple bamboo flute that is blown across the end of the tube and not across a hole in the side. The fingers can be slid over the holes and the flute tilted to produce sliding sounds.

The shamisen is a three-stringed lute. The strings are plucked with the right hand using a plectrum, and stopped on the unfretted neck with three fingers of the left hand.

The koto is a zither with 13 strings usually tuned to notes of the Japanese five-note scales. The bridges are moved to change the notes. As the right hand plucks the strings, the left can press the strings on the other side of the bridges to vary the pitch and give the music more expression.

The wooden fish is a wooden slit drum used in Buddhist ceremonies in Japan and also throughout Asia. It is struck with a padded stick.

shakuhachi

shamisen

koto

wooden fish

Left The traditional kind of Chinese opera is performed with elaborate costumes and highly stylized gestures and movements. The false beard is worn to signify authority.

Right In Japan, kabuki performances are acted in front of a traditional backdrop of a pine tree and on-stage musicians playing shamisens, flutes and drums.

flute against complex rhythmic patterns performed on three drums.

Music is also used in the two other kinds of Japanese theatre: the bunraku theatre and kabuki theatre. The bunraku theatre is a puppet theatre, with the characters portrayed by large puppets that are often handled by puppeteers dressed in black on the stage. A person sings and narrates the story, often a bloodthirsty or romantic legend, accompanied by the shamisen, the Japanese lute. There are also musical interludes. The kabuki theatre often presents the same type of plays as the puppet theatre but with human actors. There are two groups of musicians, both playing shamisens, flutes and percussion. One ensemble is on the stage and accompanies the narrative and dance, while the other, off-stage group provides music for the songs.

There is also much music for soloists and instrumental groups. The shakuhachi, the Japanese end-blown flute, the shamisen and the koto, the 13-string zither, are the principal traditional instruments, and they often accompany singers. These instruments produce solo music of great sensitivity. The shakuhachi, for example, is blown using the tongue and with breathing effects to create a wide range of sounds. One famous shakuhachi piece called *Tenderness Of Cranes* features trilling birdlike sounds that depict the affection of parent birds for their young.

The traditional togaku music features orchestras playing instruments such as flutes, double-reed pipes, mouth organ, zither, lute, drums and gongs. The orchestra performs traditional tunes and dances, but slows the melodies down so that they can be performed in a very florid style with much embellishment. The mouth organ sounds clusters of high notes, a very unusual effect, and different parts of the orchestra may play in different scales that clash to give strange sounds.

Above A traditional Korean orchestra contains the Japanese koto (centre) and a drum and flute.

The Music of Indonesia

Indonesia consists of a long chain of islands in south-east Asia, among them Java and Bali. The music of these islands is very unusual, both because of its instruments and its scale systems. As in China and Japan, the music is principally composed melody that is written or handed down. But unlike other Asian music, Indonesian music is mostly played by large orchestras. These are called gamelans and may contain 30 to 40 players.

Most orchestras in the world consist of musicians who bring standard instruments to the orchestra. A gamelan is totally different. Each town or village may have its own gamelan and the instruments of the gamelan are made by one instrument maker. They are tuned to the notes of the Indonesian scales but the pitch of the notes is not standard. Each instrument maker produces slightly different instruments so that one gamelan sounds slightly different from another. Also, the instruments may be made of different materials; a rich village will have bronze instruments whereas a poor one may only be able to afford iron or bamboo instruments.

Gamelans play on all kinds of occasions for all kinds of purposes – for weddings, social gatherings, concerts, dances, entertainment on radio and television and so on. They may feature singers and dancers as well as performing instrumental music. The music itself has a unique and beautiful sound because the performers mostly strike their instruments, playing xylophones or metallophones (xylophones made of metal), chimes, gongs and drums. Zithers, flutes and fiddles may also be played in the gamelan, but the music is mainly gong and bell sounds.

Gamelan music consists of composed melodies that the various musicians interpret in different ways at the same time. Usually, the higher instruments play more notes, producing decorative versions of the melody, while the lower instruments keep to the melody. The music falls into sections, each finishing with a stroke of a large gong. There may be abrupt changes of speed, and

Gamelan Instruments

The saron is a large deep-sounding metallophone with thick bronze bars suspended over a wooden trough that resonates as the bars are struck with a mallet.

The gong ageng is a large gong that produces a deep ringing sound.

The bonang is a set of small gong-chimes that are tuned to different notes of the scale and mounted horizontally on a frame.

The gender is a smaller high-sounding metallophone with resonating tubes beneath each bar.

The gambang is a wooden xylophone played with two sticks. It covers two to four octaves.

saron

gender

gambang

gong ageng

bonang

Left A gamelan orchestra on the island of Bali in Indonesia. A gamelan may contain many musicians who play highly involved pieces from memory with amazing precision.

great contrasts of tone colour, rhythm and volume as various instruments combine in different patterns. The musicians may play together with great virtuosity and astonishing precision, producing music that is very exciting.

As in China and Japan, the music of Indonesia is built on pentatonic scales. There are two scales. The five notes of the slendro scale divide the octave into five equal steps, producing a scale that sounds like the Chinese pentatonic scale. The pelog scale is yet another Asian five-note scale with an individual sound. On the white keys of the piano, it is E F G B C. The two scales are used separately and are not mixed together.

Music in Australia

The music of the Aborigines – the original black inhabitants of Australia – is the most unusual of any kind of traditional music in the world. Cut off from the rest of the globe until Europeans began to settle there two centuries ago, the Aborigines developed their music in total isolation over several thousand years. It is probably the oldest music that is still being performed, and it is totally different from any other music.

The Aborigines make music to accompany rituals and dances, and the style, which can be complex, is handed down and not written. The music is vocal, with singers and chanters producing all kinds of vocal sounds as well as words. These do not adhere to any particular system of notes, for the Aborigines never developed instruments that play the notes of a scale. The vocal music is accompanied by the beating of simple percussion instruments such as sticks and rattles, and hand-clapping. In addition, there may be the extraordinary sound of the Aborigine's single main instrument – the didgeridoo.

The didgeridoo is made from a long hollow branch. It is blown like a horn at one end to give one deep note, but the player uses the tongue and mouth and makes vocal noises at the same time to create a rich, buzzy sound rather like a loud jew's harp. The player breathes in through the nose while still playing, so that the didgeridoo sounds a continuous drone beneath the voice, and varies the tone to produce elaborate rhythms.

The European settlers brought their folk music with them and produced new songs in this tradition. The best-known of these Australian songs is *Waltzing Matilda*.

Right An Australian Aborigine plays a didgeridoo (foreground).

African Music

Musically, Africa consists of two parts. In North Africa, the music belongs to the Asian melodic tradition and basically consists of a florid musical line. This is because North Africa is mainly Arab and thus linked to the Middle East. But south of the Sahara desert, a completely different kind of music is to be heard: this is the music of black Africa.

The many tribes of Africa take part in music making to a greater degree than people in any other part of the world, and music plays a central role in everyone's life. This does not mean that all Africans are musicians; much of the music is performed by professional musicians or people who specialize in music. But most people are or learn to be musical and readily join in a song or a dance.

Music in Africa is something that brings people together. There are all kinds of social songs to mark occasions, such as a successful hunt or the birth of a child, and songs that accompany activities like drinking songs and work songs make life more enjoyable. Music is important in ceremonies, especially religious rituals, and it is often performed to entertain people, for example at markets. People also make music to communicate with others — protests are often made in song, and people pass on knowledge such as

Below A pair of African drummers beat out driving rhythms.

African Instruments

To make music, Africans have a wealth of musical instruments. Almost everywhere, people play xylophones of various sizes. Large xylophones may rest over pits in the ground and may be played by several musicians at once, while smaller instruments hang round the player's neck. This instrument may have originally come from Indonesia and, as there, it is played with great virtuosity. The thumb piano is another very popular instrument that is African in origin. It has metal tongues that are plucked by the thumbs to produce a twanging sound. Rattles are also found all over Africa, usually made of natural objects, and drums of all kinds are played everywhere. Hourglass drums can be squeezed while playing to change the pitch of the note.

Wind instruments include wooden flutes and panpipes and also horns actually made of animal horn or ivory as well as wood. These horns may be blown at the side instead of the end, and some have holes along them to produce extra notes. There are also several types of string instruments, including zithers, harps and fiddles. The musical bow is a one-string instrument that may be held in the mouth to make the notes resonate.

history and news by singing to one another. Some African tribes can even send signals or messages by playing hollowed logs known as 'talking' drums. The messages are simple and readily understood, such as a warning that an enemy is approaching.

African Rhythm

African music has one special feature and that is its use of rhythm and beat, which is more highly developed than in any other traditional music in the world. The music proceeds at a regular speed with a constant beat, often emphasized with vigorous playing and hand-clapping to thrust it along — especially in the 'hot' music of West Africa.

Everyone plays percussively, not just the drummers, percussionists and xylophone players. Wind players spit out short, hard notes and string players pluck or hit the

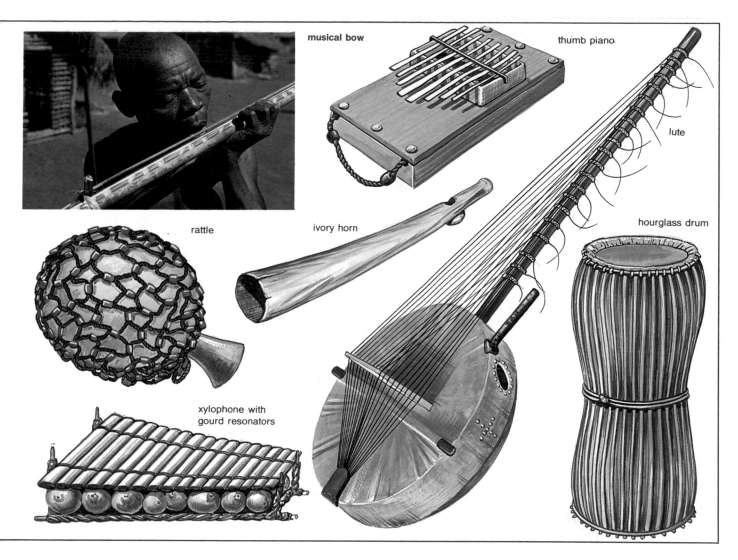

musical bow

thumb piano

lute

rattle

ivory horn

hourglass drum

xylophone with
gourd resonators

strings with great verve. Singers give full-blooded voice to a song and dancers may explode with energy. The fierce rhythmic drive that can result unites the people taking part in the creation of their music.

To make the music as energetic as possible, small groups of people play together with or without singers and dancers. Melodic instruments such as xylophones or singers may repeat simple, tuneful and rhythmic phrases over and over again, often using call-and-response patterns in which one person is answered by others. They may vary the phrases, possibly making up variations on them, and playing different phrases together. There is no scale system to give an exotic sound as in Asian or Eastern music. The phrases may have a Western flavour and can even sound together to give Western harmony.

Beneath the melodic phrases, the regular beat acts as an anchor on which rhythmic patterns are repeated over and over by percussive instruments such as drums, rattles and bells. But these rhythms are not the same as each other. The players may use different rhythmic patterns of various lengths, or play the same patterns but start them at different times. Overall, the patterns overlap with each other to give a springing, rhythmic interplay that is tremendously exciting.

Western influences have made their mark on African music in recent years, for example in the use of harmony and of instruments such as the electric guitar. These elements have been absorbed to produce popular urban forms of African music, such as highlife music in West Africa and kwela in South Africa.

Music in Europe

Europe, including Russia, has given the world the wealth of composed music that we call classical music. This music, which has developed over the last thousand years, is put together in much more complicated ways than most ethnic or folk music and it has to be written down and played or learnt from written music. The various kinds and developments of classical music are described in *Classical Music* and *Opera and Ballet*.

However, as well as classical music, Europe has a long tradition of music made by ordinary people for their own pleasure. This music consists of folk songs and dances whose tunes, usually composed long ago, are handed down from generation to generation. These songs and dances are many and varied. Epic songs and ballads tell stories, some recounting true events of the past, others legends. There are love songs, work songs like sailors' shanties, and children's songs and nursery rhymes. How-

European Folk Instruments

The Scottish bagpipe has several drone pipes. The chanter produces a scale in which some notes are slightly sharp, giving the instrument its special sound.

The gusle is a one-string fiddle of Yugoslavia. Folk singers accompanying themselves on the gusle sing epic songs that may last for hours.

The double recorder is from Eastern Europe. The player may play the same tune on both pipes, or use one of them to sound a drone beneath a tune played on the other pipe.

The dulcimer is laid on a table and the strings plucked to produce a melody and accompaniment. This is a Swedish dulcimer.

The tiple is a Spanish shawn, which is a kind of oboe. It has a strident reedy sound and is often played outdoors.

gusle

Scottish bagpipe

Left Greek musicians playing a three-string fiddle (left) and a lute (right). These instruments are heard in the traditional music of Crete.

Above The Irish folk band Clannad. The musicians play and sing folk songs using traditional instruments such as the Irish harp and a tin whistle as well as guitars and a double bass.

double recorder

dulcimer

tiple

ever, the original meanings and purposes of folk songs and dances may now be long forgotten. Dances are usually danced by groups of people with set patterns of movements in chains, lines and circles. They often mark occasions such as festivals and weddings, but may go back many centuries to pagan times when dances were magic rituals thought to bring good fortune.

In many parts of Europe, traditional music is no longer common but is kept alive by enthusiasts. However, its effects are widespread. Popular music, especially folk-rock and country music, owes much to European folk song and much classical music is based on folk tunes and dance rhythms.

Right Four European folk dances – Morris dancing in England (1); the Highland Fling, a sword dance from Scotland (2); the trepak, an energetic Russian dance (3); and Greek dancing (4), in which a line of people follows a leader.

Below centre South American Indians playing conch shells. The shells have a round hole at one end and can be blown with the lips in the same way as a brass instrument to give a booming sound.

Below A flamenco dancer in Spain.

Although Europe contains many different languages and cultures, its folk music has several features in common. This is probably because it developed under the influence of classical music and church music during the Middle Ages. Like this music, it usually contains melodies that are based on major and minor scales or the ancient Greek modal scales (see page 152 and 124), and it has harmonies that may be produced by people singing different notes or by accompanying instruments such as the guitar or harp.

Much European folk music also consists of a tune played over a lively rhythm without any harmony or of a melody played over a drone, as in bagpipe music, which exists throughout Europe.

European Folk Tunes

Folk songs and dances are usually performed to tunes made up of set patterns of melodic phrases and the tunes are often repeated, as in the verses of a song. This regular structure is characteristic of European folk music, and it comes from the way that folk poetry is organized into schemes of lines that rhyme in various patterns. Similarities can be shown by using the letters A B C etc to indicate the different kinds of melodic phrases used. Four-line patterns using just two identical or similar melodic phrases (A and B) are very common, especially the patterns AABA (*Drink To Me Only*) and ABAB (*Auld Lang Syne*).

Unlike Asian music, most European folk tunes are played and sung in a straightforward way without much ornamentation. And unlike African music, the rhythm is generally very simple, being made up of bars with two, three or four basic beats, though it may be played in a lively style.

Eastern Europe and Spain

The music of Eastern Europe – Hungary, Rumania, Bulgaria, Greece and Yugoslavia – is rather different from that of Western Europe. The forms of the folk songs and tunes have much more variety. In addition, the melody may be highly embellished with the voices or instruments wandering around a note, and the rhythms are often irregular, frequently using five-beat and seven-beat bars, for example. In some cases, the number of beats in the bar may change from one bar to another. This is due to the influence of Asian music, and the melodies may also have an Eastern sound produced by using notes in the scale C D E flat F sharp G A flat B C, which is known as the gypsy scale. This scale also gives Spanish music much of its flavour, especially the exciting flamenco music of the Spanish gypsies.

The Asian and Eastern influences in the music of Spain and Eastern Europe is due to invasions of these regions by Asian peoples such as Turks and Arabs in past centuries.

The Music of America

The continent of America – North, Central and South America – has a fascinating range of music. This is because it is large and is home to many different peoples whose ancestors came from other parts of the world. Many of their original styles of music are preserved, but new and exciting kinds of music have come about and developed as people mixed.

Above The harp plays an important part in the music of this Peruvian band.

Left Brazilian Indians blow pairs of long pipes in a religious ceremony.

Right The haunting sound of the panpipes is often heard in South American folk music.

American Indian Music

The first inhabitants of America were the American Indians, who crossed from Asia many thousands of years ago. In North America, their music has changed little and their songs and dances help the Indian tribes to preserve their identity. The music features simple melodies, often repeated many times to any words the singer cares to use, and can be very rhythmic. The main instruments played are flutes and whistles, and rattles and drums.

Several Indian tribes have interesting views on the origins of their music. Some maintain that no new songs are ever composed and that all their music has always existed. Others believe that new songs come only in dreams or visions.

Latin America

In Latin America (Central and South America), the folk music brought by Spanish invaders and settlers greatly affected the indigenous music, and there is little left of the original Indian tradition. Most of the folk songs and dances have tunes that are of Spanish origin. The way in which pairs of singers or instruments often perform a melody, with one always singing a third (three notes) below the tune, is a very characteristic feature that comes from Spanish music. However, the music may also be given an Indian sound by using the panpipes of the Indians. These instruments are made of wood or pottery and may be as large as the person playing them. The guitar and harp, which are of European origin, are also common.

Another feature of much Central and South American music is its lively and driving rhythm, and this is due to the influence of African music first brought by African slaves. Percussion instruments (shown on page 38) play rhythms that

Above The carnival in Rio de Janeiro, Brazil, throbs with music as bands dressed in extravagant costumes roam the streets. Brazilian music is renowned for its dancing rhythms.

Right A steel band rehearses in the West Indies. The instruments, which are made from oil drums, produce a lovely mellow ringing tone.

overlap to drive the beat along, a strong feature of African music. In this way, several well-known Latin American dances such as the samba, rumba and conga were born.

Caribbean Music

The African heritage is particularly strong in the music of the Caribbean islands, such as Jamaica, Trinidad and Haiti. The songs and dances of religous ceremonies contain the call-and-response patterns of Africa as well as fierce drumming. Jamaica and Trinidad have produced two famous song styles: reggae and calypso. They feature a strong but relaxed beat and place great importance on words, reflecting the use of song for protest and comment in Africa. Trinidad gave the world a completely new musical sound in the 1940s with the invention of the steel band, which contains instruments called pans that were originally made from oil drums. The pans have panels of metal that produce notes with a ringing sound when beaten with mallets. The steel band contains sections of pans of various sizes that play the melody, accompaniment and bass line of a tune, together with a rhythm section of drums and percussion that drives the beat along.

North America

The music of North America has had a great impact on the world. There the music of the American Indians had no effect on the white pioneers and settlers and the black people transported from Africa to work as slaves and their descendants; it was completely disregarded. The rhythmic drive of Africa combined with the melody and harmony of Europe to create the various styles of popular music, such as jazz, rock, soul and country music, that are described in *Popular Music*. In this century these have swept across North America and Europe and have also made their mark elsewhere.

However, folk music enthusiasts still preserve the traditional forms of black music and white music that developed in the United States during the 1800s and early 1900s. These include the rhythmic work songs of the black people and also their field hollers. These were simple, repeated calls that became the blues with the addition of harmony provided by the guitar, which

probably came from Mexico. The interaction of black and white religious music produced spirituals, such as *Swing Low Sweet Chariot*. These derive from European hymns, but may be given a rhythmic treatment quite unlike anything sung in a European church.

The tradition of European folk music

continues in the various communities made up of descendants of white settlers. However, the music has sometimes gained an American style all its own, often with a rhythmic drive provided by the example of black music. The lively square dance, for example, is the American version of the more refined European quadrille. In the southern states, particularly the Appalachian mountains, the dances, such as jigs and reels, and songs, such as ballads, that came from Britain and Ireland, developed into the hillbilly and bluegrass music that are the basis of country music. The main instruments of this music are the guitar, banjo, mandolin, dulcimer, violin and mouth organ and here there is a worldwide array of origins. The banjo is originally African, the mouth organ Chinese and the guitar Arab, while the other instruments are from different parts of Europe.

Above Dr Humphrey Bate and the Possum Hunters pioneered country music, an American traditional music that developed mainly from European folk music. In 1925, it became the first hillbilly band to appear on the Grand Ole Opry radio show, which has made country music famous throughout America.

Classical Music

Unlike popular and folk music, classical music is seldom played with a strong beat that will make you want to get up and dance to it. It is music more for listening to than moving to, and is sometimes called 'serious' music. But as well as appealing to the intellect, classical music is music that is capable of producing a great range of feelings in both performers and listeners. It can be stirring one moment and sad the next, or harsh and ugly then beautiful and tender.

Classical music is the name usually given to music written by composers in Europe, North America and Russia over the past 400 years or so. It includes music by such famous names as Bach, Beethoven and Tchaikovsky. Classical music is always written down and the performers, who range from symphony orchestras to solo musicians and singers, always play the notes that the composer has written. However, they may interpret the music in their own style so that the way in which a piece is played or sung will vary from one performance to another, keeping it fresh.

Because it does not change from one performance to the next, a piece of classical music reveals more and more of itself as you get to know it. You can revel in a favourite work again and again because a good composer designs the music so that all the various parts of it fit well together. He or she makes the notes follow each other in such a way as to pull you into the music, always eager to hear what is coming next yet thrilled with what has just gone. With each hearing, you will discover more and more in the music as you begin to recognize the different parts and realize how they fit together to make classical music work for you.

There are four main types of classical music depending on how it is performed: orchestral music, chamber music, solos and duets, and vocal music. Classical composers also write music for opera and ballet, which are described in the next chapter.

Orchestral Music

Orchestral music requires a large group of players, normally a symphony orchestra. In the music of composers such as Bach, Haydn, Mozart and Beethoven, the orchestra contains a big string section but only small

Left The conductor André Previn and violinist Kyung-Wha Chung recording a violin concerto. They and the leader of the orchestra are intently discussing how they should play the concerto, aiming to give a performance in which they can fully express their feelings about the music. Most classical musicians like to interpret the written music that they play in this way so that they can give individual performances.

woodwind, brass and percussion sections. Later composers wrote music for more instruments to get a wider range of sounds from the orchestra and there may be well over 100 players.

The main kinds of classical music played by orchestras are symphonies, concertos, variations, overtures and suites. These names indicate a particular way of composing the music and not the instruments that take part. Orchestras also play a wide range of descriptive pieces usually with evocative titles. This music aims to portray whatever is depicted in the title, for example a landscape or a story.

Below The composer Igor Stravinsky conducting a concert of his own music. Stravinsky, often considered the greatest classical composer of this century, wrote his music very carefully so that it would be clear to performers exactly how it should be played. He did not like musicians to interpret his music in their own way, fearing that they would lessen the individuality that he had brought to it.

Symphonies

The symphony is the greatest kind of music achieved by the classical composers of the past. In composing a symphony, a composer aimed to stretch his or her abilities to the utmost. The result is a long work and one that is made up of contrasts. A symphony is in separate sections called movements – normally three or four at contrasting speeds, though sometimes two movements may be played without a break between them. And each movement is itself made up of contrasting musical ideas, containing different themes or tunes and different combinations of instruments, all woven skilfully together to form an ever-evolving tapestry of sound.

The first symphonies, those of Haydn and Mozart, set a pattern for later composers. The first movement is usually quick and is composed in sonata form which has several sections. First there may be an introduction, perhaps slow and mysterious to contrast with what follows or maybe just a couple of loud chords to announce the start of the symphony. Then come two themes, one after the other; this is called the exposition section. After this, the composer takes the themes, breaking them up and weaving them together in the development section, often to build up to a climax. Then the complete themes come back again in the recapitulation section, and finally a section called the coda concludes the movement.

The second movement is normally slow and stately after the bustle of the first movement, consisting mostly of a tranquil tune. Next there often comes a minuet and trio, which are dance tunes played at a moderate pace. The fourth and last movement is usually a fast finale. It is often similar to the first movement in form or it may be in rondo form, having a main tune that is repeated several times with musical interludes. The symphony may then end with a climax and loud concluding chords.

However, this is only an overall scheme that acts as a basic contrasting design for the symphony. Composers have developed it in many ways, as you can hear by listening to the four great symphonies described on the next page. In the hands of such gifted composers, the symphony becomes music of immense power.

Four Great Symphonies

One of the best symphonies ever composed is the *Symphony No 40 in G minor* by Mozart. G minor is the key of the music. Many composers wrote several symphonies, and it is usual to give both the number and key of a symphony so that it is not confused with any other symphony. This symphony by Mozart has lovely tunes and you can easily hear how he uses them to build the symphony, fitting them together both elegantly and effortlessly to create music of great beauty. It was composed in July 1788, when Mozart was at the height of his powers.

Another very famous symphony is the *Symphony No 5 in C minor* by Beethoven, completed in 1808. Beethoven uses the contrasts of the symphony for intense dramatic effect. It has the same four-movement scheme as the early symphonies but Beethoven uses it in a very different and much more powerful way. The symphony opens with the famous four-note 'fate' theme, which has been likened to fate knocking at the door. Beethoven twists and turns this in all kinds of ways to do battle with an appealing second theme. The second movement is peaceful with a lovely, slow melody repeated several times in various guises, sometimes with simplicity, sometimes with grandeur. The third movement is a scherzo – a lively piece of music. Beethoven brings back the fate theme, this

Above Tchaikovsky is renowned for the warmth and emotion of his music, which abounds with tuneful melodies and dramatic effects. Both these qualities are to be found in the *Pathétique Symphony*, his last and greatest work.

time to contrast with an elegant tune and a section of scurrying music. Then mysterious drumbeats link this movement to the last movement, in which two grand and triumphant themes bring the symphony to an exultant ending.

Tchaikovsky's *Symphony No 6 in B minor* is known as the *Pathétique Symphony*. Composed in 1893, it was Tchaikovsky's last work and is highly emotional while being very tuneful. There are four movements but they are very different from the earlier symphonies. The first is active and passionate with great contrasts of sound. Then comes a lilting dance with five beats to the bar, a very unusual rhythm. The third movement develops into a brisk, grand march while the finale, in utter contrast, is one of the saddest pieces of music ever written.

Few composers in this century have attempted symphonies. An exception is Stravinsky, who often took the forms of the past and used them in his own way to create music of tremendous vitality. The *Symphony In Three Movements* was written during World War II and the events excited Stravinsky's musical imagination as he composed. Like all symphonies, it uses contrasting elements to build the music, especially insistent rhythms with sudden harsh stabbing chords that recall marching soldiers and the clamour of battle and episodes of uneasy calm.

The Sound of the Orchestra

A good composer is an expert at orchestration, which is the art of blending and contrasting the sounds of the instruments of the orchestra. The aim is to make the overall sound as attractive as possible and the best kind of sound for the music. The composer will also try to produce an individual orchestral sound unlike those of other composers.

Two excellent pieces to hear that demonstrate how composers can use instruments are *Variations And Fugue On A Theme of Purcell* (also known as *The Young*

Person's Guide To The Orchestra) by Britten, and *Concerto For Orchestra* by Bartók. Both these works, which were composed in the 1940s, contain sections in which the different instruments are heard by themselves and in which they are mixed together to produce all kinds of orchestral sounds.

Other composers who exploit the sound range of the orchestra in their music include Berlioz, Wagner, Mahler, Richard Strauss, Tchaikovsky, Rimsky-Korsakov, Stravinsky, Prokofiev, Debussy and Ravel.

Right Beethoven's third symphony is known as the *Eroica Symphony*, meaning heroic symphony. Beethoven originally intended this great work to be a tribute to Napoleon. However, when Napoleon crowned himself emperor – as portrayed in this painting by David – Beethoven angrily crossed out Napoleon's name on the title page of the symphony (inset).

Famous Symphonies

Leopold Mozart and Michael Haydn	*Toy Symphony*	1780
Mozart	*Symphony No 41 in C major (The Jupiter Symphony)*	1788
Haydn	*Symphony No 104 in D major (The London Symphony)*	1795
Beethoven	*Symphony No 3 in E flat major (The Eroica Symphony)*	1803
Schubert	*Symphony No 8 in B minor (The Unfinished Symphony)*	1822
Berlioz	*Symphonie Fantastique*	1830
Mendelssohn	*Symphony No 4 in A major (The Italian Symphony)*	1833
Brahms	*Symphony No 4 in E minor*	1885
Tchaikovsky	*Symphony No 5 in E minor*	1888
Dvořák	*Symphony No 9 in E minor (The New World Symphony)*	1893
Mahler	*Symphony No 5 in C sharp minor*	1902
Prokofiev	*Symphony No 1 in D major (The Classical Symphony)*	1917
Shostakovich	*Symphony No 5 in D minor*	1937
Messiaen	*Turangalîla Symphony*	1948

Above Dvořák's *New World Symphony* was composed on his arrival in America, when he was greeted by the Statue of Liberty in New York harbour.

Concertos

A concerto is a long piece of music to be played by a solo performer with a symphony orchestra. The soloist has a leading role and a concerto is intended to show how brilliantly he or she can play. It is rather like a discussion – or sometimes a duel or even a battle – between the soloist and orchestra in which neither intends to be outdone.

Most well-known concertos have three movements. The first is usually fairly fast and often in sonata form like a symphony (see page 67). However, there is usually one important difference. Towards the end of the movement, the soloist may play a cadenza. This is a section in which the soloist performs alone, using the themes of the concerto to produce a dazzling exhibition of virtuoso playing. In early concertos the composer did not write the cadenza but left it to the soloist to improvise or work one out. In the violin concerto by Beethoven, for example, the cadenza normally played is by the great violinist Fritz Kreisler and not by Beethoven at all. However, in later concertos, the composer wrote the cadenza.

The second movement of a concerto is usually slow and it often leads directly into the third movement, which is normally brisk and often in the form of a rondo.

Many composers also wrote concertos in which two or even three soloists perform together against the orchestra. These are known as double and triple concertos, referring to the number of soloists. The concerto grosso, which means great concerto, is another type of concerto in which the music features a group of instruments playing on their own against the orchestra. The concerto grosso was a popular form with J. S. Bach (especially in the famous six *Brandenburg Concertos*), Vivaldi and Handel, as well as Stravinsky in this century.

Some other pieces of music are known as concertos but are not really concertos at all. Bartók's *Concerto For Orchestra*, for example, has no soloists but features individual and virtuoso playing within the orchestra. At the opposite extreme is the *Italian Concerto* by J. S. Bach, which is a solo work for the harpsichord without an orchestra. It contrasts the sounds of different keyboards in a way similar to the interplay between the soloist and orchestra in a concerto.

Famous Concertos

Piano

Mozart	*Piano Concerto No 21 in C major*	1785
Beethoven	*Piano Concerto No 5 in E flat major*	1809
	(The Emperor Concerto)	
Chopin	*Piano Concerto No 1 in E minor*	1830
Schumann	*Piano Concerto in A minor*	1841
Liszt	*Piano Concerto No 1 in E flat major*	1849
Grieg	*Piano Concerto in A minor*	1868
Saint-Saëns	*Piano Concerto No 3 in B minor*	1869
Tchaikovsky	*Piano Concerto No 1 in B flat minor*	1875
Brahms	*Piano Concerto No 2 in B flat major*	1881
Rachmaninov	*Piano Concerto No 2 in C minor*	1901
Prokofiev	*Piano Concerto No 3 in C major*	1921
Gershwin	*Piano Concerto in F major*	1925
Bartók	*Piano Concerto No 1 in A major*	1926
Ravel	*Piano Concerto No 2 in G major*	1931

Violin

Beethoven	*Violin Concerto in D*	1806
Paganini	*Violin Concerto No 1 in D major*	1817
Mendelssohn	*Violin Concerto in E minor*	1844
Bruch	*Violin Concerto No 1 in G minor*	1868
Brahms	*Violin Concerto in D major*	1878
Tchaikovsky	*Violin Concerto in D major*	1878
Sibelius	*Violin Concerto in D minor*	1903
Berg	*Violin Concerto*	1935
Prokofiev	*Violin Concerto No 2 in G minor*	1935
Bartók	*Violin Concerto No 2 in B minor*	1938
Hindemith	*Violin Concerto*	1939
Walton	*Violin Concerto*	1939

Cello

Schumann	*Cello Concerto in A minor*	1850
Saint-Saëns	*Cello Concerto No 1 in A minor*	1875
Dvořák	*Cello Concerto in B minor*	1895
Elgar	*Cello Concerto in E minor*	1919
Delius	*Cello Concerto*	1925
Walton	*Cello Concerto*	1956
Shostakovich	*Cello Concerto No 1 in E flat major*	1959

Other Instruments

Vivaldi	*Flute Concerto No 2 in G minor* *(La Notte)*	1730
Mozart	*Horn Concerto No 4 in E flat major*	1786
Mozart	*Clarinet Concerto in A major*	1791
Haydn	*Trumpet Concerto in E flat major*	1796
Walton	*Viola Concerto*	1927
Rodrigo	*Concierto de Aranjuez* (for guitar)	1939
Richard Strauss	*Oboe Concerto in D major*	1945

Double and Triple Concertos

J. S. Bach	*Double Violin Concerto in D minor*	1723
Mozart	*Flute and Harp Concerto in C major*	1778
Beethoven	*Triple Concerto for Violin, Cello and Piano in C major*	1804
Brahms	*Double Concerto for Violin and Cello in A minor*	1887

Overtures

An overture is a short orchestral piece originally designed to precede the performance of an opera or a play and put the audience in the right mood. The famous overtures of Mozart and Rossini are of this kind. It later became a short piece of descriptive music in its own right, especially in the overtures of Mendelssohn and Tchaikovsky. In the *Hebrides Overture*, which was composed in 1830 and is often called *Fingal's Cave*, Mendelssohn portrays the Hebrides islands, while Tchaikovsky's *1812*

Above right The Italian pianist Maurizio Pollini plays a piano concerto with the Austrian conductor Karl Böhm and the Vienna Philharmonic Orchestra.

Right A visit to Fingal's Cave, on the island of Staffa in the Hebrides, Scotland, inspired Mendelssohn to compose his famous *Hebrides Overture*.

Left The British clarinettist Jack Brymer records a clarinet concerto.

Overture (1880) commemorates the victory of Russia over Napoleon in that year.

Overtures are tuneful pieces of music that are very enjoyable. An overture is often played at the beginning of a concert before the main works on the programme, and it helps to settle both orchestra and listeners.

Right Nicoló Paganini, the Italian violinist, is best known for the famous theme from his *Caprices* for the violin on which Brahms, Rachmaninov and several other composers have composed sets of variations.

Famous Overtures		
Mozart	*Overture to The Marriage Of Figaro*	1786
Mozart	*Overture to The Magic Flute*	1791
Beethoven	*Leonora Overture No 3*	1806
Beethoven	*Egmont Overture*	1810
Rossini	*Overture to The Barber Of Seville*	1816
Schubert	*Rosamunde Overture*	1823
Mendelssohn	*Overture to A Midsummer Night's Dream*	1826
Rossini	*William Tell Overture*	1829
Berlioz	*Le Carnaval Romain (Roman Carnival)*	1844
Tchaikovsky	*Romeo and Juliet Fantasy Overture*	1869
Brahms	*Academic Festival Overture*	1880

Variations

A piece of music that has the word variations in its title, like Dohnányi's *Variations On A Nursery Theme*, composed in 1916, or Ives' *Variations On America* (1891), is one of the easiest kinds of classical music to appreciate. It is often called a theme and variations because it begins with a theme or tune. In the variations mentioned above, the theme is *Twinkle, Twinkle, Little Star* and *God Save America* (which is the same tune as *God Save The Queen* and *My Country, 'Tis Of Thee*). The theme is played at the beginning and then it is played over and over again for the rest of the piece. However, each time it is repeated, the composer creates a variation on the theme by changing it in some way.

Composers often write variations on themes by other composers. Famous orchestral pieces of this kind include Brahms' *Variations On A Theme Of Haydn (St Anthony Chorale)*, composed in 1873, and Rachmaninov's *Rhapsody On A Theme Of Paganini* (1934), which is a set of variations even though it is called a rhapsody. The theme and variations is not limited to orchestral music, and is used by composers in all kinds of music. Other well-known variations include J. S. Bach's *Goldberg Variations* (1742) for harpsichord, and *Piano Sonata No 11 in A major* (1778) by Mozart.

A Musical Riddle

One of the most interesting set of variations is Elgar's *Enigma Variations*, composed in 1899. Elgar portrayed his closest friends in these variations which are as lovely as they are loving, especially the slow and moving *Nimrod* variation. However, Elgar deliberately left out the theme on which he composed the variations and refused to identify it, hinting only that it is a well-known tune. Some people believe that the unheard theme is *Auld Lang Syne*, but no one has yet been able to name it.

The *Enigma Variations* by Elgar (above) is also danced as a ballet (below) in which Elgar's friends appear.

Suites

A suite is a group of short pieces that are either played separately one after the other or as one continuous piece of music with linking passages between them. Suites were originally sets of dances, as in the orchestral suites of J. S. Bach. Later composers wrote suites that are collections of pieces taken from long works such as ballets and operas. They contain the main tunes of the work but the music is performed on its own without any dancing or singing. Listening to a suite of this kind is a good way of enjoying the music in a ballet or opera without having to sit through the whole work.

Descriptive Music

This kind of music aims to portray something in music. The flow of notes should give the listener the impression of whatever the composer intends to depict, such as turbulent music for a battle or storm, fast rhythmic music for a race, quiet slow music for sadness and so on. Descriptive music is often called programme music, the programme being the subject that is described in the music. This is often a story, like *Scheherezade* by Rimsky-Korsakov, and another favourite subject is landscape or nature, as in Debussy's *La Mer (The Sea)*.

Descriptive music suits the orchestra because of the wide range of sounds that are available to a composer. The pieces generally have titles giving the subjects they are intended to depict. Many orchestral descriptive pieces are called symphonic poems or tone poems. In addition, many suites and overtures are descriptive music and so too is much music in opera and ballet as well as some music for small groups or solo instruments. Music that is not descriptive, such as most symphonies and concertos, is called abstract music or absolute music.

Top right Handel composed his famous suite known as the *Royal Fireworks Music* for this grand firework display in London in 1749. It celebrated the Peace of Aix-La-Chapelle.

Right Many early suites are sets of dances such as this allemande.

Famous Suites

Handel	*Water Music*	1717
J. S. Bach	*Orchestral Suite No 3*	c 1730
	(contains *Air On The G String*)	
Handel	*Royal Fireworks Music*	1749
Bizet	*Jeux d'Enfants (Children's Games)*	1871
Bizet	*L'Arlésienne (The Girl From Arles)*	1872
Bizet	*Carmen*	1875
Stravinsky	*The Firebird*	1910
Ravel	*Daphnis And Chloe*	1912
Stravinsky	*Pulcinella*	1920
Walton	*Façade*	1922
Prokofiev	*Lieutenant Kijé*	1934

Listening to descriptive music allows you to give full rein to your imagination. Using the title and perhaps notes on a record sleeve or in a concert programme, you can picture the scenes portrayed in the music in your mind. However, this is not essential and you can listen to a descriptive piece just as music if you prefer. Although the subject may have inspired the composer to write the music in a particular way, a good composer will still make the music worth hearing as music on its own without considering its subject.

Below Debussy's orchestral work, *La Mer*, is similar to this painting *The Slave Ship* by Turner. In their different ways, both composer and painter seek to convey an impression of the movement of the sea.

Right Gershwin's *An American In Paris* is a musical portrait of Paris in the 1920s, when this photograph was taken.

Famous Pieces of Descriptive Music

An American In Paris (1928) Gershwin depicts an American visitor reacting to the atmosphere of Paris, complete with taxi horns.

Carnival Of The Animals (1886) Saint-Saëns calls this piece a 'grand zoological fantasy' and it is a parade of animals (including pianists), portrayed with affectionate humour.

Finlandia (1899) This is a tribute to Finland by Sibelius, its most famous composer.

Four Seasons (c 1725) A set of concertos by Vivaldi in which scenes and events of the seasons, such as falling on the ice in winter, are represented.

La Mer (*The Sea* – 1905) This marvellous evocation of the sea was written by Debussy while visiting the resort of Eastbourne on the south coast of England.

L'Après-Midi D'Un Faune (*The Afternoon Of A Faun* – 1894) This piece by Debussy illustrates a poem. It portrays a faun lazing in the afternoon sunshine and has a remarkable sense of atmosphere.

Pastoral Symphony (1808) Beethoven wrote this symphony, whose proper title is the *Symphony No 6 in F major*, to express his fondness of life in the countryside. It includes the sounds of a brook, peasants' merrymaking, a storm and bird calls amid much delightful music.

Peter And The Wolf (1936) Prokofiev wrote this musical tale for children. Instruments portray animals and characters in the story, and a performance often contains a narrator telling the story.

Pictures At An Exhibition (1874) Mussorgsky wrote these musical descriptions of ten paintings by a friend for the piano. However, it is often played in an orchestral version written by Ravel in 1922.

Scheherezade (1888) Rimsky-Korsakov composed this musical version of *The Arabian Nights* in which Scheherazade, represented by a violin, recounts tales to the sultan in order to save her life.

The Little Train Of The Caipira (1930) This charming piece by Villa-Lobos depicts a train journey that he made in Brazil. It is the second of a set of pieces called *Bachianas Braşileiras*.

The Planets (1916) These are vivid portrayals by Holst of the gods after whom the planets are named.

The Sorcerer's Apprentice (1897) Dukas illustrates the story of a wizard's apprentice who finds he can cast a spell but then cannot stop it working.

Till Eulenspiegel (1895) The lively music of this symphonic poem by Richard Strauss depicts the merry pranks of Till Eulenspiegel, a hero of German legend.

Vltava (1880) This is one of a set of six symphonic poems by Smetana called *Ma Vlast (My Country)*. The country is Czechoslovakia and *Vltava* portrays the River Vltava.

Chamber Music

Chamber music is a type of classical music that is played by small groups of musicians without any singing. There are usually two to five performers but chamber music can be played by up to about a dozen people. It is music on a small and friendly scale with all the players contributing more or less equally to a piece. Unlike much orchestral music, players do not have to spend ages waiting to make an entry; all the musicians play most of the time.

The kinds of pieces played in chamber music are mostly abstract music. There is little descriptive music, mainly because there are not enough players to produce the wide variety of sounds that composers need to portray a subject. Chamber music therefore often sounds much the same; there is not a lot of variation in sound within a piece or from one piece to another. The way to enjoy chamber music is to listen to each player separately and hear how all the parts fit together to create the music. You will then recognize how the players answer one another and how they play with or against each other. Listening to chamber music is different from orchestral music, but just as satisfying. The pieces can be equally tuneful and also lively — they are by no means dull.

Left The stage and film musical *Kismet* contains several well-known songs, including *And This Is My Beloved* and *Baubles, Bangles And Beads*. The music is in fact by the Russian composer Borodin, and these tunes come from his second string quartet, a famous chamber work.

Kinds of Chamber Music

Before orchestras existed, composers only wrote for small groups of musicians called consorts. The early forms of chamber music, written before about 1750, were often sequences of dances each containing set sections of music. Another form called the fantasia or fantasy was also popular. This was a freer form in which the music could vary and develop in different ways.

Early chamber music is often performed by a few instruments, usually strings, with a continuo. The continuo is a section of one or more instruments – often a keyboard such as a harpsichord or organ plus a deep string instrument – that plays a bass line and accompanying chords under the other instruments. Important composers of early chamber music include Corelli and Purcell.

Many early chamber pieces were called sonatas; the music was played on instruments as opposed to cantatas, which were pieces that were sung. However, from about 1750, a sonata came to mean a work in three or four movements. One or more of these was usually in sonata form and others could be a theme and variations or a rondo, as in a symphony (see page 67). In fact, a sonata can be thought of as a symphony on a small scale. In chamber music, the term sonata came to be restricted to a piece for two players, usually a violin or cello plus a piano and called a violin sonata or cello sonata respectively. Pieces for larger groups are given names that indicate the size of the group: a trio for three players, a quartet for four and so on. A table of these chamber groups is given on page 14. The most important is the string quartet, which consists of two violins, a viola and a cello.

As these chamber groups developed, so too did the music. The continuo disappeared and all instruments took on equal roles – especially in forms such as canons (see page 130) and fugues (see page 133), in which the players imitate each other's music. The instruments used in chamber music are mainly string instruments, often with the addition of a piano and sometimes a horn or clarinet, though some composers also wrote chamber music for groups of wind instruments. Later composers chose unusual combinations of instruments to give a much wider tonal range to their chamber music.

Famous Pieces of Chamber Music

J. S. Bach
The Musical Offering (1747)	flute, 2 violins, continuo

Bartók
String Quartet No 2 in A minor (1915)	2 violins, viola, cello
Sonata for Two Pianos and Percussion (1938)	2 pianos, percussion

Beethoven
Septet in E flat major (1800)	violin, viola, cello, double bass, clarinet, bassoon, French horn
Violin Sonata No 5 in F major (Spring Sonata – 1801)	violin, piano
Violin Sonata No 9 in A major (Kreutzer Sonata – 1802)	violin, piano
Piano Trio No 6 in B flat major (Archduke Trio – 1811)	violin, cello, piano
String Quartet No 12 in E flat major (1824)	2 violins, viola, cello

Borodin
String Quartet No 2 in D major (1881)	2 violins, viola, cello

Brahms
Horn Trio in E flat major (1865)	French horn, violin, piano
Violin Sonata No 1 in G minor (1879)	violin, piano
Clarinet Quintet in B minor (1891)	clarinet, 2 violins, viola, cello

Debussy
String Quartet in G minor (1893)	2 violins, viola, cello
Sonata for Flute, Viola and Harp (1916)	flute, viola, harp

Dvořák
Piano Quintet in A major (1887)	piano, 2 violins, viola, cello
String Quartet No 12 in F major (American Quartet – 1893)	2 violins, viola, cello

Franck
Violin Sonata in A major (1886)	violin, piano

Haydn
String Quartet No 38 in E flat major (Joke Quartet – 1781)	2 violins, viola, cello
String Quartet No 77 in C major Emperor Quartet – 1797)	2 violins, viola, cello

Mendelssohn
Octet in E flat major (1825)	4 violins, 2 violas, 2 celli
Cello Sonata No 2 in D major (1843)	cello, piano

Messiaen
Quatuor Pour La Fin Du Temps (Quartet For The End Of Time – 1941)	clarinet, violin, cello, piano

Milhaud
Scaramouche (1937)	2 pianos

Mozart
Serenade No 10 in B flat major (1781)	13 wind instruments, double bass

String Quartet No 17 in B flat major (Hunt Quartet – 1784)	2 violins, viola, cello
Clarinet Quintet in A major (1789)	clarinet, 2 violins, viola, cello
Nielsen	
Wind Quintet (1922)	flute, oboe, clarinet, bassoon, French horn
Ravel	
String Quartet in F major (1903)	2 violins, viola, cello
Introduction And Allegro (1906)	harp, flute, clarinet, 2 violins, viola, cello
Saint-Saëns	
Septet for trumpet, piano and strings (1881)	trumpet, piano, 2 violins, viola, cello, double bass
Schoenberg	
Verklärte Nacht (Transfigured Night – 1899)	2 violins, 2 violas, 2 celli
Schubert	
Piano Quintet in A major (Trout Quintet – 1819)	piano, violin, viola, cello, double bass
String Quartet No 14 in D major (Death And The Maiden – 1824)	2 violins, viola, cello
Octet in F major (1824)	clarinet, bassoon, French horn, 2 violins, viola, cello, double bass
Cello Sonata in A minor (1824)	cello, piano
String Quintet in C major (1828)	2 violins, viola, 2 celli
Schumann	
Piano Quintet (1842)	piano, 2 violins, viola, cello
Shostakovich	
String Quartet No 8 in C minor (1960)	2 violins, viola cello
Sibelius	
Voces Intimae (1909)	2 violins, viola, cello
Stravinsky	
*L'Histoire Du Soldat (The Soldier's Tale – 1917)	violin, double bass, flute, clarinet, trumpet, trombone, percussion
Octet for Wind Instruments (1923)	flute, clarinet, 2 bassoons, 2 trumpets, 2 trombones
Tchaikovsky	
String Quartet No 1 in D major (1871)	2 violins, viola, cello
Webern	
Five Movements for String Quartet (1909)	2 violins, viola, cello

*This was originally composed as a stage work complete with narrator and dancers. However, the music is often performed alone as a chamber work.

Music for One Instrument

Classical music contains a wealth of music that can be played on one instrument. Almost all of this music is for keyboard instruments, particularly the piano. This is because the keyboard allows all the fingers and thumbs of both hands to produce notes. Furthermore, the notes played can range greatly in pitch and the volume or tone of each note can be controlled by the performer. One keyboard can therefore produce all kinds of music – from cascades of notes to simple rhythms and from great crashing chords to quiet lilting tunes. There are also piano duets in which two pianists play one keyboard between them, producing an even wider variety of sounds from the instrument.

String instruments, mainly the guitar, violin and cello, can also produce solo music that is just as complete as solo keyboard music. By sounding two or more strings at once, the solo musician can play chords, a melody with accompaniment or even separate musical lines. There is also a little solo music for wind instruments, principally the flute, that play only one note at a time. However, modern musicians are developing methods of sounding more than one note, sometimes by humming one note while playing another! New ways of performing are exploited in Berio's set of *Sequenzas* (1958–75) for various unaccompanied instruments.

Solo Forms
Early classical music contains many suites of dances and free-flowing fantasias for solo instruments that are similar to these forms in chamber music. There are several other solo forms, some of which are also found in other kinds of classical music. A chaconne or passacaglia has a theme that is repeated over and over again under or behind the rest of the music. A partita is another name for a suite, or an air (theme) and variations like those in chamber and orchestral music. A fugue consists of separate musical lines that imitate one another and intertwine – rather like several people singing a round, except that the musician has to play all the separate

parts at the same time. A prelude is an opening piece, often in a suite or before a fugue, but may also be a short piece on its own. A toccata is a fast and dazzling piece designed to show off the virtuosity of the performer. These forms are normally one-movement pieces and two of them may be combined to give longer compositions, as in a toccata and fugue.

The sonata is a larger piece of solo music, normally in several movements and composed in the same form as a sonata for a chamber group or a symphony for an orchestra (see page 67). From the early 1800s, other solo one-movement forms emerged. Some are derived from dances, such as the waltz, polonaise and mazurka. The nocturne (night piece) is a short, dreamy piece and the ballade (ballad) a longer poetic one. The étude or study is designed to test the player's ability, while the impromptu is intended to suggest improvisation (although the music is written out in full).

Descriptive Music

Some solo music is descriptive and may bear evocative titles. Debussy's *The Snow Is Dancing* from *Children's Corner* (1908) is a lovely impression of swirling snowflakes, for example. To portray its subject, descriptive music may contain various sound effects that the instrument can produce, such as pedal effects on the piano. Some pieces that have formal names such as sonatas or preludes sometimes have a descriptive title as well. Beethoven's *Moonlight Sonata* and Chopin's *Raindrop Prelude* are examples, but in some cases these descriptive titles were given to the music after it was written and they do not necessarily reflect the composer's intentions.

Right The German organist Karl Richter in action. The pipe organ is a superb instrument for solo music as it can produce such a wide range of sounds. The organist can play on different keyboards and pull out various stops to vary the sounds made by the organ.

Left The Australian guitarist John Williams plays a solo concert of classical guitar pieces. Although the instrument has only six strings, a good guitarist can use his or her fingers to obtain many different kinds of sound from the strings, giving light and shade and great expression to solo music.

Left The famous solo guitar piece *Reminiscences Of The Alhambra* portrays the stately beauty of the Alhambra, the Moorish palace at Granada in Spain.

Famous Pieces For Solo Piano

Bartók
For Children (1909)

Beethoven
Sonata No 8 in C minor (*Pathétique Sonata* – 1798)
Sonata No 14 in C sharp minor (*Moonlight Sonata* – 1801)
Für Elise (1808)
Diabelli Variations (1823)

Brahms
Waltz No 15 in A flat major from *Waltzes* (*Opus 39* – 1865)
Rhapsody in G minor (1879)

Chopin
Revolutionary Study (*Étude No 12 in C minor* – 1829)
Grande Valse Brilliante (*Waltz No 1 in E flat major* – 1831)
Nocturne in E flat major (*Opus 9 No 2* – 1831)
Fantasie-Impromptu (1834)
Raindrop Prelude (*Prelude No 15 in D flat major* – 1839)
Ballade No 4 in F minor (1842)
Heroic Polonaise (*Polonaise No 6 in A flat major* – 1842)

Debussy
Clair De Lune from *Suite Bergamesque* (1890)
La Soirée Dans Grenade from *Pour Le Piano* (1901)
Golliwogg's Cakewalk from *Children's Corner* (1908)
La Fille Aux Cheveux De Lin (*The Girl With The Flaxen Hair*) from *Préludes* (*Book 1* – 1910)

Granados
The Maiden And The Nightingale from *Goyescas* (1911)

Liszt
Hungarian Rhapsody No 2 in C sharp minor (1847)
Liebestraum No 3 (1850)

Mendelssohn
Spring Song from *Songs Without Words* (*No 30* – 1842)

Messiaen
Vingt Regards Sur L'Enfant Jésus (*Twenty Gazes Upon The Child Jesus* – 1944)

Mozart
Turkish Rondo from *Sonata No 11 in A major* (1778)

Fantasia and Sonata (*No 14*) *in C minor* (1784)

Mussorgsky
Pictures At An Exhibition (1874)

Rachmaninov
Prelude No 1 in C sharp minor (1892)

Ravel
Pavane Pour Une Infante Défunte (*Pavane For A Dead Infanta* – 1899)
Sonatine (1905)
Gaspard De La Nuit (1908)

Satie
Trois Gymnopédies (1888)

Schubert
Sonata No 13 in A major (1819)
Fantasia in C major (*Wanderer Fantasy* – 1822)
Impromptu in G flat major (*Opus 90 No 3* – 1827)
Moment Musical in F minor (*Opus 94 No 3* – 1828)

Schumann
Carnaval (*Carnival* – 1835)
Kinderscenen (*Scenes From Childhood* – 1838)

Below The serenity of moonlight – seen here at a lake in Finland – has inspired several pieces of classical music, notably Debussy's *Clair De Lune*, originally a piece for solo piano. Beethoven's equally famous *Moonlight Sonata*, also for solo piano, gained its title because the first movement has a mysterious air. However, Beethoven composed the music without a thought of moonlight; the title was given to it by someone else later.

Famous Piano Duets

Brahms
Hungarian Dances (1869)

Debussy
Petite Suite (1888)
En Blanc Et Noir (1915)

Fauré
Dolly Suite (1897)

Mozart
Sonatas For Piano Duet (1765–87)

Ravel
Ma Mère L'Oye (Mother Goose – 1910)

Schubert
Marches Militaires (1818)
Grand Duo (1824)
Fantasia in F minor (1828)

Stravinsky
Easy Pieces (1914–17)

Above Mozart composed several excellent piano duets, which he here performs with his sister. In places, the two pianists have to cross hands. Listening to the music is their father, Leopold Mozart.

Famous Music For Other Solo Instruments

Cello

J. S. Bach	*Cello Suites 1–6*	1720
Britten	*Suites 1–3 For Unaccompanied Cello*	1964–71

Flute

C. P. E. Bach	*Flute Sonata in A minor*	1747
Debussy	*Syrinx*	1912

Guitar

Sor	*Fantasias*	1826
Granados	*Danzas Españolas*	1900
Tarrega	*Recuerdos De La Alhambra (Reminiscences Of The Alhambra)*	c1900
Turina	*Fandanguillo*	1926

Harpsichord

Couperin	*Harpsichord Suites*	1713–30
Handel	*Harpsichord Suites 1–8*	1720–33
J. S. Bach	*The Well-Tempered Clavier (48 Preludes And Fugues)*	1722 & 1744
Scarlatti	*Keyboard Sonatas*	1722–57

Note: Many performances of harpsichord works are played on the piano.

Organ

J. S. Bach	*Toccata and Fugue in D minor*	c1710
Liszt	*Prelude and Fugue on Bach*	1885
Franck	*Chorales*	1890
Messiaen	*L'Ascension*	1934

Violin

J. S. Bach	*Violin Partitas 1–3*	1720
Telemann	*Fantasias For Unaccompanied Violin*	1735
Paganini	*Caprices 1–24*	1805

Vocal and Choral Music

Vocal and choral music is music that people sing either with or without accompanying instruments. Vocal music is performed by one singer or a small group of singers whereas choral music is sung by a choir or chorus of many singers, sometimes together with solo singers.

The sound of the human voice can bring great power and feeling to music. This is not only because the words that are sung have particular meanings to which we may respond strongly; the actual tone of the voice greatly affects the music too. A large choir in full voice creates a sound that is tremendously stirring and thrilling, while the ghostly sound of a melody sung without words is one of the most mysterious in all music.

In classical music, composers usually take words to set to music and rarely write their own words. Classical vocal and choral music grew out of plainsong, which was a simple chant sung in church, and folksong. The words are therefore often religious in character or they may express people's feelings or tell stories. The composer then fashions the music to enhance or reflect the meaning of the words. A sacred (religious) work may become an act of worship for composer, performer and listener, while a secular (non-religious) piece may entertain. Yet although vocal and choral music is so different from instrumental music in purpose, a good composer will write the music so that it can still be enjoyed without finding meaning in the words or even without understanding them. You can thrill to the *Hallelujah Chorus* by Handel without experiencing any religious fervour, or find a Schubert song moving without being able to speak German.

Below At performances of Handel's *Messiah*, one of the best-known choral works, it is traditional to stand for the *Hallelujah Chorus*. The reason is that King George II was so impressed by the music that he rose to his feet and everyone else followed suit, a custom that has continued ever since.

Singing Voices

CHILDREN
High soprano The highest child's voice, of great clarity and purity.

Treble The lowest child's voice, fuller than the high soprano.

WOMEN
Soprano The highest woman's voice, clear and penetrating in quality.

Mezzo-Soprano The mid-range woman's voice, having qualities of both soprano and contralto.

Contralto The lowest woman's voice, full and rich in quality.

MEN
Counter-tenor An unusually high man's voice, clear but not shrill. Also called alto, it employs the high falsetto register.

Tenor The highest man's voice that does not use falsetto. It can have tremendous power.

Baritone The mid-range man's voice, rich and full in sound.

Bass The lowest man's voice, deep and strong in quality.

Solo Singing

In classical music, many singers give concerts of songs accompanied by a pianist. Many songs are poems that are set to music, and arrangements of folk songs are also common.

A particular kind of solo singing with the piano is known as lieder, which is the German word for songs. The songs are often poems put to music, normally in German. Composers of lieder include Brahms, Mahler, Mendelssohn, Schubert, Schumann, Richard Strauss and Wolf. Their works include song cycles, which are groups of songs that tell a story or are similar in mood.

Classical concerts may contain songs or song cycles in which a singer is accompanied by a group of musicians or a full orchestra, sometimes with a choir as well. Unlike opera, these songs are not intended to be performed with any action, scenery or special costumes, though they may still be sung in a very dramatic way.

Below The British singer Janet Baker performs a concert of lieder. These are poetic solo songs, normally in German, accompanied by the piano.

Famous Vocal Works

Lieder (solo song cycles with piano)

Schubert	*Die Schöne Müllerin*	1823
	(The Fair Maid Of The Mill)	
Schubert	*Die Winterreise (Winter Journey)*	1827
Schumann	*Dichterliebe (Poet's Love)*	1840
Wolf	*Mörike Lieder*	1888
Brahms	*Four Serious Songs*	1896
Mahler	*Kindertotenlieder (Songs On The Death Of Children)*	1904

Songs with Orchestra or Ensemble

Berlioz	*Les Nuits D'Été (Summer Nights)*	1834
Brahms	*Alto Rhapsody*	1870
Grieg	*Peer Gynt*	1875
Delius	*Sea Drift*	1903
Mahler	*Das Lied Von Der Erde (The Song Of The Earth)*	1908
Berg	*Five Orchestral Songs*	1912
Butterworth	*A Shropshire Lad*	1912
Schoenberg	*Pierrot Lunaire*	1912
Lambert	*The Rio Grande*	1929
Canteloube	*Songs Of The Auvergne*	1930
Britten	*Les Illuminations*	1939
Britten	*Serenade For Tenor, Horn And Strings*	1943
Villa-Lobos	*Bachianas Brasileiras No 5*	1945
Richard Strauss	*Four Last Songs*	1948
Boulez	*Le Marteau Sans Maître (Mallet Without Master)*	1954

Part Singing

When a group of people sing together informally, they often all sing the same tune. This is called singing in unison. However, people with musical ability or vocal training can sing other melodies at the same time that harmonize with the tune. This is called part singing and each musical line, including the tune, is called a part. You can hear the difference between unison and part singing in a church. The congregation normally sings a hymn in unison whereas the choir will sing it in parts.

Part singing fills out the music and makes it more expressive. It also enables songs to be sung without any accompaniment, and many vocal groups and choirs sing unaccompanied. In vocal groups, one or two people may sing each part, whereas in a choir each part is sung by a larger number of people.

There are normally four parts. The top one, which often sings the tune, is the soprano part. Then come the alto, tenor and bass parts. A fifth part, the descant, may be added above the tune. Composers of vocal and choral music limit the range of each part so people can sing their part comfortably.

Part singing developed in medieval times. One of the first part songs was the round, in which all the parts have the tune but begin one after the other. Children still sing rounds, such as *Row Row Your Boat*, *London's Burning*, *Frère Jacques* and *Three Blind Mice*. Composers then began to write vocal pieces in which the parts were separate melodies, often with different words. The parts became independent as two types of vocal works developed: motets and madrigals. In these the voices imitate or answer one another or intertwine in complicated musical patterns.

A motet is usually a religious piece in several parts to be sung by a choir or vocal group, often in the Catholic church. Composers of motets include J. S. Bach, Brahms, Byrd, Lassus, Machaut, Palestrina, Tallis and Victoria. In the Anglican church a motet is called an anthem.

A madrigal is normally a secular piece and may be serious or light-hearted. Madrigals are intended for small vocal groups but may be sung by choirs. The singing is usually, but not always, unaccompanied. Composers of madrigals include Byrd, Gesualdo, Gibbons, Monteverdi, Morley, Palestrina, Tomkins and Wilbye.

Below The choir at King's College Chapel in Cambridge, England, is renowned for its singing. Boy choristers sometimes sing the soprano part in church choirs, giving the music an ethereal quality appropriate to its surroundings. Men sing the lower parts.

Choral Music

Choral music is often singing on a grand scale complete with massive choirs and orchestras, though sometimes an organ has to substitute for an orchestra. The music may also feature solo singers who take leading roles in the music. The works may be sacred or secular. The mass is a sacred choral work in which the words are settings of five parts of the Catholic liturgy – the *Kyrie, Gloria, Credo, Sanctus and Benedictus*, and *Agnus Dei*. There is also a requiem mass, which contains the *Introit* and *Dies Irae* instead of the *Gloria* and *Credo*. These sacred works may be performed in church.

A grand choral work such as an oratorio or cantata usually tells a story, often one from the Bible. It is performed without action, costumes or scenery. Solo singers often portray characters or a narrator, often in an aria, which is a song with a melody, or a recitative, in which the words are sung in a kind of recitation. The choir or chorus sings in parts behind or with the solo singers and in choral sections. These may include chorales, which are like hymns, and fugues, in which the parts imitate one another.

Famous Choral Works

Oratorios

J. S. Bach	*St John Passion*	1723
J. S. Bach	*St Matthew Passion*	1729
J. S. Bach	*Christmas Oratorio*	1734
Handel	*Messiah* (contains *Hallelujah Chorus*)	1741
Haydn	*The Creation*	1798
Mendelssohn	*Elijah*	1846
Stainer	*The Crucifixion*	1887
Elgar	*The Dream of Gerontius*	1900
Honegger	*Le Roi David (King David)*	1921
Walton	*Belshazzar's Feast*	1931
Tippett	*A Child Of Our Time*	1941
Penderecki	*St Luke Passion*	1965

Cantatas

J. S. Bach	*Cantata No 4 (Easter Cantata)*	1707–8
J. S. Bach	*Cantata No 208* (contains *Sheep May Safely Graze*)	1713
J. S. Bach	*Cantata No 147* (contains *Jesu, Joy Of Man's Desiring*)	1723
Mozart	*Exsultate Jubilate*	1773
Berlioz	*The Damnation Of Faust*	1846
Coleridge-Taylor	*Hiawatha*	1898
Orff	*Carmina Burana*	1935
Prokofiev	*Alexander Nevsky*	1939
Britten	*St Nicolas*	1948

Far left A performance of the *Mass in B minor* by J. S. Bach, one of the greatest choral works. Although this mass and other such pieces of choral music are religious works, they are often performed by choirs and symphony orchestras in concert halls.

Left Many choirs, like this Welsh male voice choir performing at an Eisteddfod (a music festival), sing unaccompanied pieces in their concerts.

Church and Religious Music

Monteverdi	*Vespers*	1610
Vivaldi	*Gloria*	1708
J. S. Bach	*Mass in B Minor*	1738
Mozart	*Coronation Mass*	1779
Mozart	*Requiem Mass*	1791
Beethoven	*Missa Solemnis*	1823
Berlioz	*Requiem Mass*	1837
Brahms	*German Requiem*	1868
Verdi	*Requiem Mass*	1874
Fauré	*Requiem*	1887
Britten	*War Requiem*	1961
Stravinsky	*Requiem Canticles*	1966

Choral Symphonies and Other Choral Works

Tallis	*Lamentations*	c1550
Purcell	*Ode For St Cecilia's Day*	1683
Beethoven	*Symphony No 9 in D minor (Choral Symphony)*	1824
Borodin	*Polovtsian Dances (from Prince Igor)*	1890
Debussy	*Sirènes (from Nocturnes)*	1900
Vaughan Williams	*Sea Symphony*	1909
Ravel	*Daphnis And Chloe*	1912
Stravinsky	*Symphony Of Psalms*	1930
Britten	*Spring Symphony*	1949

An oratorio generally demands a large choir or chorus or even two choirs, several soloists and an orchestra. A cantata is a choral work on a smaller scale with perhaps only a few singers and instruments and possibly without any soloists. A passion is a kind of oratorio that portrays in music the suffering, death and resurrection of Jesus Christ. It is therefore often performed at Easter.

Other kinds of choral music include symphonies in which a choir sings with the orchestra, descriptive music in which a choir is added to the orchestra for effect, and choral settings of songs either with or without an orchestra.

Choirs, especially male voice choirs, also perform music that is written to be sung without any accompaniment. Often this music consists of arrangements of songs and pieces that exploit vocal effects, and it requires accurate part singing. So that everyone in the choir begins in the same key, a piano often sounds the key note of the piece of music before the choir starts. All the singers then pitch their opening note in relation to the key note.

Opera and Ballet

Opera and ballet take music out of the concert hall and into the world of the theatre, creating arts that are a feast for the eyes as well as the ears. Both fuse music with the drama or comedy of the stage, opera using voices raised in song and ballet the movements of dancers. At their best, performances of opera and ballet are intensely moving experiences, capable of producing feelings such as joy and anger, triumph and despair, even more strongly than music alone.

Opera and ballet are powerful arts that draw devoted audiences around the world. In the East, they are performed in traditional musical styles (see pages 53 and 54), while Western opera and ballet use classical music. But powerful though they may be, opera and ballet do not thrill everyone. People who are unfamiliar with them often think that they are boring and silly. However, the spectacle of the performers singing or dancing a story is not meant to look real. Both opera and ballet have their own ways of putting across action and thoughts which are unlike those in other performing arts like the theatre or cinema. To condemn opera and ballet as absurd is to close one's ears and eyes to their magic. If in doubt, there is one way you can find out whether the magic works for you and that is to go and see an opera or ballet. There is no substitute for a live performance.

Opera

An opera, like a play, usually tells a story. But it is more than a play with songs, which is called a musical or musical comedy (see page 104). In an opera, the music continues

for all or most of the time and it strengthens and enhances the mood and action of the story. The power of the music draws you into the story, whether it be tragic, funny, heroic or mysterious.

Opera needs great singers who are also good actors, eye-stunning sets and costumes, and a good orchestra and conductor. But even with all these, you may still find an opera difficult to understand and enjoy. The words are not always very clear and they may be sung in a foreign language. Reading about the opera first helps in understanding the action, and some opera houses project a translation of the words above the stage. Seeing an opera on television or video, or in the cinema, with sub-titles avoids these problems. Furthermore, the opera may be filmed on location in real places, which makes it very exciting to watch.

What Happens in an Opera?

The story of an opera is called its libretto. The composer of the music may write the libretto too, as Wagner did, but usually another person called the librettist provides the story. This may be a new story or a version of an existing book or poem – Shakespeare has proved very popular, there being several

operas based on *Macbeth* and *Othello*, for example. Usually the stories are fiction, normally either comic, dramatic or romantic, but some are based on historical events and others on legends.

Like plays, most operas are divided into parts called acts, often with an interval between each one, usually to change the scenery. One-act operas are short operas without an interval. An opera may begin with an overture, which is a piece of music played by the orchestra before the curtain rises. The overture sets the right mood for the opening scene and often contains music from the opera. Shorter orchestral pieces called preludes may then come before each act. Alternatively, the opera may begin with a prelude or start immediately without any introductory music at all.

Each act of the opera then develops the story. The leading singers portray the main characters in the story. There are also minor figures and there may be a chorus, often as a crowd. The leading singers are given tuneful arias which they sing alone with the orchestra, often to express their thoughts and emotions. The singers also sing together in duets, trios, quartets and larger groups, each with his or her own vocal line. The

Far left The ornate interior of La Scala, the opera house at Milan, contrasts with the shell-like exterior of the Sydney Opera House. Both convey the prestige of opera.

Left A rehearsal at the English National Opera of Stravinsky's opera *Le Rossignol (The Nightingale)*. The conductor is rehearsing the singers in their costumes and with the scenery. However, the orchestra is not yet required so a pianist provides the music.

arias, duets and songs for several singers are the most famous pieces in operas, and the action may stop as the audience applauds the singers.

However, these special pieces cannot carry the story along all the time. In between, the characters need to converse to keep things moving and their words need to be heard clearly. In some operas, these words are spoken but in many operas, they are sung. In early operas, these parts of the opera are sung as a recitative without any particular tune and with a simple accompaniment. But later operas are not split up into separate sections like this. The music and singing are more continuous with the orchestra surrounding the singers in arias and then retreating into the background when the action has to be advanced. The music can help to describe what is happening on stage. For example, in Wagner's operas, which he preferred to call music dramas, special themes are used to identify the characters and objects and these themes are woven into the music in different ways as the story unfolds.

Creating an Opera

An opera begins as an idea in the head of a composer or a librettist, who may be a famous author or poet. The composer and librettist meet and outline the story if it is a new one, or they work out an operatic treatment if they are using an existing story. They may be invited by an opera company to write the opera. If not, they will probably persuade a company to stage the opera when it is finished. Years of work may lie ahead and neither would want their efforts to go unheard.

Below Jonathan Miller (left) directs the opera singer Philip Langridge in his production of Britten's opera *The Turn Of The Screw*.

Right Opera singers and ballet dancers may have to wear unusual costumes in special productions, yet they must still be able to sing and dance with ease. This dancer is testing his movements as he is dressed for a role as a peanut in Tchaikovsky's ballet *The Nutcracker*.

The libretto of the opera is usually written first. The composer then sets the words to music and writes music to go with the action on stage. The composer will probably ask the librettist to change some of the words or action to fit the music as it is composed, and their collaboration is likely to continue until the last note is written. As the opera nears completion, the opera company prepares to stage it. A producer is appointed, the leading singers and a conductor are engaged and a designer is chosen.

The producer, who may also be a well-known producer or director in the theatre or cinema, is in charge of the whole production and decides how the opera will be performed on stage. He or she chooses the movements of the singers and directs their acting in countless rehearsals – at first in rehearsal rooms and then on stage as the first night approaches. The designer, who may be a famous artist, sketches the scenery and costumes, making models if necessary. He or she then directs the construction and painting of the scenery, oversees the making of costumes and choice of props, and plans the stage lighting. Meanwhile, the conductor and composer are rehearsing the singers. The conductor may specialize in opera but many conductors who conduct opera also conduct symphony concerts. At first, the singers work with the répétiteur, who plays the music on the piano and also coaches the singers. Later, the conductor rehearses the singers with the orchestra.

Eventually, after months of work, the opera is ready. The final rehearsals take place on stage with the orchestra. The first performance is given and the opera is then repeated several times. If it is successful, it will be revived. This means that the opera will be staged again with the same production, and possibly the same singers, a year or more later.

Most of the operas that you can see in an opera house are not new operas or even revivals of new operas. They are usually new productions of old operas in which the producer and designer stage their own particular version of an opera. The music is the same, of course, though some scenes may be cut or added. A new production of an opera will be revived several times if it is successful.

Kinds of Opera

Chamber opera An opera for a few singers and a small orchestra, such as *The Turn Of The Screw* by Britten.

Grand opera Generally, an opera in which all the words are sung and none are spoken. Also an opera with a serious story, particularly a spectacular production of an epic historical drama, such as *William Tell* by Rossini and *Aida* by Verdi.

Light opera or **operetta** A short opera with spoken dialogue and an amusing story, such as *Orpheus In The Underworld* by Offenbach and *The Pirates Of Penzance* and other works by Gilbert and Sullivan.

Opera buffa An early comic opera, such as *The Marriage Of Figaro* by Mozart and *The Barber Of Seville* by Rossini.

Opéra comique Not comic opera but an opera originally having spoken dialogue, such as *Carmen* by Bizet and *Faust* by Gounod.

Opera seria An early opera on a serious subject, often based on legend or history, such as *Idomeneo* by Mozart.

Left A scene from the light opera *The Pirates Of Penzance* by Gilbert and Sullivan.

Five Famous Operas

These five operas are frequently performed at opera houses all over the world. They represent the main kinds of stories that are told in opera and each is highly enjoyable in its own way.

The Barber Of Seville by Rossini is a comedy based on a play by Beaumarchais. It is set in Seville in Spain in the 1600s and tells of the efforts of Count Almaviva to marry Rosina against the wishes of her guardian Dr Bartolo, who wishes to marry her himself. With the aid of Figaro the barber, the count adopts a variety of disguises to trick Dr Bartolo and win Rosina. Things inevitably go haywire and confusion reigns, but the wily Figaro eventually sorts everything out and all ends happily.

The music is witty and good-humoured, and it contains the famous aria *Largo al factotum* in which Figaro sings of his life. Other comedies in opera include *The Marriage Of Figaro* by Mozart, in which Figaro, the count and Rosina appear again, and *Der Rosenkavalier* by Richard Strauss. Many operettas are also comedies, among them *The Merry Widow* by Lehár and *Die Fledermaus* by Johann Strauss.

Carmen by Bizet is a drama based on a novel by Merimée. It is set in and around Seville in 1820. Don José, a soldier, falls in love with Carmen, a wild gypsy girl. Carmen taunts Don José and forces him to desert from the army and join a band of smugglers with her. However, Carmen is also courted by Escamillo, a bull fighter, who wins her heart. At the bull fight, Don José begs Carmen to return to him but she proudly refuses, whereupon he kills her.

Carmen has the most exciting and tuneful music in all opera. It includes many famous songs, the best known being the Toreador's song. Other famous operatic dramas include *Tosca* by Puccini, *Rigoletto* by Verdi, *Peter Grimes* by Britten and *Faust* by Gounod.

Above A production of Verdi's spectacular opera *Aida*, which is set in ancient Egypt.

Above right A scene from the dramatic film of Bizet's opera *Carmen*, made in 1984 and starring Julia Migenes-Johnson as Carmen and Placido Domingo as Don José. Here Carmen taunts Don José when he has to arrest her.

Right A comical incident in Rossini's opera *The Barber Of Seville* in which Figaro, the barber, shaves a customer.

La Bohème by Puccini is a romantic love story based on a novel by Murger. It is set in Paris in 1830. Rudolfo and his friends are poor writers and artists. Mimi, who lives nearby, has lost her key and seeks Rudolfo's help. They fall in love and begin to enjoy life together despite their poverty. However, Rudolfo discovers that Mimi is very ill and becomes distraught because he has no money for medicine. His friends try to help but Mimi dies.

The music of *La Bohème* is extremely moving. It contains the beautiful aria *Your Tiny Hand Is Frozen*. Other famous love stories in opera include *La Traviata* by Verdi, *The Bartered Bride* by Smetana and *Eugene Onegin* by Tchaikovsky.

The Flying Dutchman with music and libretto by Wagner is based on legend. The action takes place on the coast of Norway in the 1700s. The opera is a ghost story about the Flying Dutchman, who is condemned to sail the seas for ever, setting foot on land only once every seven years. Once ashore, the Dutchman offers Daland,

a sea captain, all his treasure to marry Daland's daughter Senta. Senta agrees, but the Dutchman finds out that she is loved by Erik, a hunter. He reveals the truth about himself and sets sail yet again, abandoning her. Senta throws herself into the sea to be united with the Flying Dutchman in death.

Wagner's music evokes the sea and the mystery surrounding the Dutchman with great power. Other operas based on legends include Wagner's cycle of four operas known as *The Ring Of The Nibelung* and also *Tristan And Isolde, Orpheus And Eurydice* by Gluck, *Dido And Aeneas* by Purcell and *The Trojans* by Berlioz.

Aida by Verdi is a historical opera based on a story by Mariette. It is set in ancient Egypt and recounts the love of Aida and Radames, a general. Aida, the daughter of the King of Ethopia, is a slave to Amneris, who is the daughter of the King of Egypt. Radames wages war against Ethiopia and is awarded the hand of Amneris by her father. Radames prefers Aida and plots to escape. However he is condemned for treachery and dies with Aida.

Aida has scenes of tremendous spectacle matched by stirring music. Among other historical epics in opera are *War And Peace* by Prokofiev, *Boris Godunov* by Mussorgsky and *Prince Igor* by Borodin.

Famous Opera Singers

Soprano	Contralto	Baritone
Maria Callas	Kathleen Ferrier	Geraint Evans
Kirsten Flagstad	Helen Watts	Dietrich Fischer-Dieskau
Mirella Freni		Tito Gobbi
Victoria de Los Angeles	**Tenor**	Benjamin Luxon
Birgit Nilsson	Carlo Bergonzi	Sherill Milnes
Leontyne Price	Jussi Björling	Hermann Prey
Elisabeth Schwarzkopf	Enrico Caruso	John Shirley-Quirk
Beverly Sills	José Carreras	
Joan Sutherland	Placido Domingo	**Bass**
Kiri Te Kanawa	Luciano Pavarotti	Owen Brannigan
	Peter Pears	Boris Christoff
Mezzo-Soprano	Robert Tear	Tom Krause
Janet Baker	Jon Vickers	Ruggero Raimondi
Teresa Berganza		
Marilyn Horne	*Note: These singers may also perform*
Yvonne Minton	*other vocal music as well as opera.*

Famous Operas

English Name*	Original Name	Composer	First Performance
The Abduction from the Seraglio	Die Entführung aus dem Serail	Mozart	Vienna 1782
Aida	Aida	Verdi	Cairo 1871
Ariadne on Naxos	Ariadne auf Naxos	Richard Strauss	Stuttgart 1912
The Barber of Seville	Il Barbiere di Siviglia	Rossini	Rome 1816
The Bartered Bride	Prodaná Nevěsta	Smetana	Prague 1866
The Beggar's Opera	The Beggar's Opera	Gay	London 1728
Billy Budd	Billy Budd	Britten	London 1951
La Bohème	La Bohème	Puccini	Turin 1896
Boris Godunov	Boris Godunov	Mussorgsky	St Petersburg 1874
Carmen	Carmen	Bizet	Paris 1875
Cavalleria Rusticana	Cavalleria Rusticana	Mascagni	Rome 1890
The Coronation of Poppaea	L'Incoronazione di Poppea	Monteverdi	Venice 1642
Cosi Fan Tutte	Cosi Fan Tutte	Mozart	Vienna 1790
Dido and Aeneas	Dido and Aeneas	Purcell	London 1689
Don Giovanni	Don Giovanni	Mozart	Prague 1787
The Elixir of Love	L'Elisir d'Amore	Donizetti	Milan 1832
Eugene Onegin	Evgeny Onegin	Tchaikovsky	Moscow 1879
Falstaff	Falstaff	Verdi	Milan 1893
Faust	Faust	Gounod	Paris 1859
Fidelio	Fidelio	Beethoven	Vienna 1805
Die Fledermaus	Die Fledermaus	Johann Strauss	Vienna 1874
The Flying Dutchman	Der Fliegende Holländer	Wagner	Dresden 1843
The Force of Destiny	La Forza del Destino	Verdi	St Petersburg 1862
Der Freischütz	Der Freischütz	Weber	Berlin 1821
Hansel and Gretel	Hänsel und Gretel	Humperdinck	Weimar 1893
Idomeneo	Idomeneo	Mozart	Munich 1781
Jenůfa	Jenůfa	Janáček	Brno 1904
Lohengrin	Lohengrin	Wagner	Weimar 1850
The Love of Three Oranges	L'Amour des Trois Oranges	Prokofiev	Chicago 1921
Lulu	Lulu	Berg	Zurich 1937
Macbeth	Macbeth	Verdi	Florence 1847
Madame Butterfly	Madama Butterfly	Puccini	Milan 1904
The Magic Flute	Die Zauberflöte	Mozart	Vienna 1791
Manon	Manon	Massenet	Paris 1884
Manon Lescaut	Manon Lescaut	Puccini	Turin 1893
The Marriage of Figaro	Le Nozze di Figaro	Mozart	Vienna 1786
A Masked Ball	Un Ballo in Maschera	Verdi	Rome 1859
The Mastersingers of Nuremberg	Die Meistersinger von Nürnberg	Wagner	Munich 1868
The Merry Widow	Die Lustige Witwe	Lehár	Vienna 1905
The Midsummer Marriage	The Midsummer Marriage	Tippett	London 1955
A Midsummer Night's Dream	A Midsummer Night's Dream	Britten	Aldeburgh 1960
Moses and Aaron	Moses und Aron	Schoenberg	Zurich 1957
Norma	Norma	Bellini	Milan 1831
Orfeo or Orpheus	La Favola d'Orfeo	Monteverdi	Mantua 1607
Orpheus and Eurydice	Orfeo ed Euridice	Gluck	Vienna 1762
Orpheus in the Underworld	Orphée aux Enfers	Offenbach	Paris 1858
Othello	Otello	Verdi	Milan 1887
I Pagliacci	I Pagliacci	Leoncavallo	Milan 1892
Parsifal	Parsifal	Wagner	Bayreuth 1882
The Pearl Fishers	Les Pêcheurs de Perles	Bizet	Paris 1863
Pelléas and Mélisande	Pélleas et Mélisande	Debussy	Paris 1902
Peter Grimes	Peter Grimes	Britten	London 1945
Porgy and Bess	Porgy and Bess	Gershwin	New York 1935
Prince Igor	Knyaz Igor	Borodin	St Petersburg 1890
The Rake's Progress	The Rake's Progress	Stravinsky	Venice 1951

English Name*	Original Name	Composer	First Performance
The Rhine Gold	*Das Rheingold*	Wagner	Munich 1869
Rigoletto	*Rigoletto*	Verdi	Venice 1851
The Ring of the Nibelung	*Der Ring des Nibelungen*	Wagner	Bayreuth 1876
(The Rhine Gold; The Valkyrie; Siegfried; Twilight of the Gods)			
Salome	*Salome*	Richard Strauss	Dresden 1905
Siegfried	*Siegfried*	Wagner	Bayreuth 1876
The Tales of Hoffmann	*Les Contes d'Hoffmann*	Offenbach	Paris 1881
Tosca	*Tosca*	Puccini	Rome 1900
La Traviata	*La Traviata*	Verdi	Venice 1853
Tristan and Isolde	*Tristan und Isolde*	Wagner	Munich 1865
The Trojans	*Les Troyens*	Berlioz	Karlsruhe 1890
Il Trovatore	*Il Trovatore*	Verdi	Rome 1853
Turandot	*Turandot*	Puccini	Milan 1926
The Turn of the Screw	*The Turn of the Screw*	Britten	Venice 1954
Twilight of the Gods	*Götterdämmerung*	Wagner	Bayreuth 1876
The Valkyrie	*Die Walküre*	Wagner	Munich 1870
War and Peace	*Voina i Mir*	Prokofiev	Leningrad 1946
William Tell	*Guillaume Tell*	Rossini	Paris 1829
Wozzeck	*Wozzeck*	Berg	Berlin 1925

*Some operas are so well known by their original name that they have no English name

Left A production by Jonathan Miller of Verdi's opera *Rigoletto* transposes the action to twentieth-century America and turns the principal characters into gangsters. Unusual productions like this can make opera more exciting than the traditional staging.

Left Even the most famous operas were not immediately successful. Bizet's *Carmen* shocked its audience when it was first staged in 1875, and sadly Bizet died before it became a hit. Puccini's *Madame Butterfly*, seen here at the English National Opera, was booed and jeered at its first performance in 1904, even though Puccini had already composed several very successful operas. He then revised the score and *Madame Butterfly* has been popular ever since.

Ballet and Dance

Few can resist the physical power that music has to make us move. Musicians throughout the world know that a strong beat can get people up on their feet and dancing in response to the music. In popular music, particularly in disco music, the beat is driven hard to make people dance with great energy. Dancing to music can make you feel ecstatic and abandoned; it liberates you so that you can express the feelings that you get from the music. In this way, people who cannot make music are able to perform and be musical in their own fashion.

This has been true for centuries, but in the past people danced in a more formal way than most do today. Until about 1800, people danced in groups, performing set movements to pieces like minuets and gavottes – rather like country dancing or square dancing today. Then people began to dance in couples, using a variety of steps rather than set movements. These kinds of dances included the polka and waltz and were often lively. People who go old-time dancing still do these kinds of dances. In this century, people continued to dance in couples, often in showy dances like the tango or charleston. These kinds of dances are performed nowadays in ballroom dancing.

However, the style of dancing became much looser and more abandoned with such crazes as the jitterbug, jive and twist from the 1940s to 1960s. Disco dancing, in which people may dance by themselves in a very free style, is a recent development. It is the culmination of some three centuries of progress in which the beat of dance music has become ever stronger and the style of dancing has generally become less rigid and more individual and energetic.

This kind of dancing is known as social dancing; people dance to enjoy themselves and as an excuse to get together. Ballet is quite different in style and purpose. If social dancing is the equivalent of popular music, then ballet is the equivalent of classical music. Each performance of a ballet is always staged with the same number of principal dancers performing the same movements, which are specially created for the ballet, to the same music. Ballet is normally performed

Left Ballroom dancing is a popular leisure activity. Here couples dance at a competition, which is why they each have a number. The dances have set movements that the couples must perform with grace and precision.

on a stage with full scenery and costumes. The dancers express a meaning as they dance; this may be the outline of a story or simply a beautiful pattern of movements.

Seeing a Ballet

Ballets are staged in theatres or opera houses by ballet companies. Several countries have their own national ballet companies, notably the Bolshoi Ballet in Russia, the Royal Ballet in Britain and the Royal Danish Ballet in Denmark. There are also companies founded in particular cities, such as the New York City Ballet in the United States, as well as other companies often named after their founders like the Ballet Rambert in Britain and the Joffrey Ballet in the United States.

These companies usually have a home in a particular city but may tour to appear in

Above Break dancing is a very free and highly energetic style of dancing that people perform on their own, often in the street.

other cities and countries. But if you cannot get to see live ballet, you can see ballets on television or video, and in the cinema. These productions are usually recordings or films of ballets being danced on a stage.

A ballet is often performed in one act without an interval, but many great story-telling ballets contain two or more acts and may take up a whole evening. The story is often well known, such as *Romeo and Juliet* by Shakespeare or *The Sleeping Beauty*, which is a fairy tale. Sometimes it may be an original story, as in *Swan Lake* and *Petrushka*. However, some ballets are abstract. The dancing interprets the music without using a story, or there may be a simple outline on which the dancing is based. Notable among these ballets are *Les Sylphides*, which is a set of dances in the romantic tradition, and *Apollo*, in which the dances portray arts such as poetry and mime.

The action of the ballet, whatever its meaning, is danced by several principal dancers and supporting dancers possibly with a corps de ballet, who dance as a group.

The individual dancers perform solo dances and also dance in small groups. These dances have French names, such as a *pas de deux* for two dancers. Overall, the way in which the dancers and corps dance to the music in order to express the action and meaning of a ballet is similar to the way in which the singers and chorus in an opera perform to act out the plot of the opera. But where singers use words, the dancers make movements and gestures that portray or mime their meanings. The dancing, when performed with great artistry and feeling, can be very moving.

Staging a Ballet

The creation of a new ballet usually begins with an idea for a ballet by a ballet company or a choreographer, who devises all the movements that the dancers will perform. The director of the ballet company may then ask a choreographer to create the ballet or the choreographer may ask a company to put on the ballet. Either way, the choreographer is going to need some music. In many

Below A ballet called *Tonsile Involvement* by the American choreographer Alwin Nikolais. In modern dance, the movements of the dancers and the production may convey an abstract theme or idea rather than portray a story as in romantic and classical ballet.

cases, he or she will take some existing music and create a story or an abstract ballet to go with the music. But sometimes, the choreographer asks a composer to write the music for the ballet that he or she has in mind.

When the music is ready, if it is new, the choreographer begins to create the ballet in his or her mind. The choreographer chooses the dancers, who will often be people who have worked with the choreographer before, and a designer is appointed to design the scenery and costumes. Rehearsals now begin in which the choreographer works out the movements of the ballet with the dancers, using a pianist or a tape to provide the music. As the dancers learn the movements, the designer watches and gets ideas for the scenery and costumes. As with opera, the designer may be a famous artist.

When the dancers are ready, stage rehearsals begin with the scenery and costumes. The orchestra rehearses the music with the conductor and then plays for the dancers. The first performance is given, followed by several more performances during the season. Like a new opera, the ballet will be revived if it is successful and may be danced again in several seasons. The music and design will be the same, but there may be new dancers. They can learn their

movements from the choreographer, assisted by dance notation in which the movements are written down in a kind of shorthand and possibly by video recordings of performances.

If a ballet is a classic, like *Swan Lake*, then ballet companies everywhere want to perform it year after year. Instead of repeating the original production, new choreographers often create fresh ways to dance the ballet complete with different sets and costumes.

Above Dancers at the Danish Ballet School practise exercises and positions.

Left The British choreographer Frederick Ashton teaches the movements of one of his ballets to the dancers who will perform it. Choreographers are themselves dancers or former dancers.

The History of Ballet

Ballet began in the late 1500s as dance entertainments at the royal courts in Italy and France. The ballets were danced to entertain the king and queen and their guests or to mark special occasions such as a coronation. They often told legends about gods and heroes. The dances became more and more spectacular, especially in the elaborate ballets danced at the court of the French king Louis XIV. The king was a good dancer himself and became known as the Sun King after he danced the part of Apollo, the sun god, in a ballet in 1653.

By 1700, the style of dancing had advanced so much that trained professional dancers were required. Opera-ballets containing an equal mixture of opera and ballet became popular, many being composed by Rameau and Lully. (A ballet may still form part of an opera today, but this is unusual.) Ballet then moved into the theatre and ballets that told a story began to be performed as works of art in their own right. The early 1800s was the era of romantic ballet with its moving stories like *Giselle* and graceful leaps and elegant steps in which the dancers began to dance on the points of their toes. In the late 1800s, this style reached a peak of expression with the classical era of ballet – above all in the ballets of Tchaikovsky.

The turn of the century saw a reaction against classical and romantic ballet, which had become too formal and fixed in style for progress. New ballets, especially those by Stravinsky, were more natural in action and much wider in their range of expression and meaning. This development began a whole new school of modern dance in which the dancers express themselves much more freely. Today, ballet companies throughout the world work in all the styles of the past and also produce new experimental ballets.

Top right The French king Louis XIV dressed for his role as Apollo.

Right The Swedish-Italian dancer Marie Taglioni (centre), seen here in 1845, was the most important ballerina of the romantic period.

Three Romantic Ballets

These three ballets are among the most famous ballets of the romantic era. They were all created in Paris in the mid-1800s and have been popular ever since.

La Sylphide (The Sylph) This ballet was originally created in 1832 by Filippo Taglioni to music by Schneitzhoeffer. However, a later version with music by Løvenskjold is now danced. The story is set in Scotland and tells of James, a young farmer, who is entranced by a sylph (a fairy). She entices James away from his wedding but then disappears. James is tricked by a witch into believing that a magic scarf will bind the sylph to him; instead, it brings her death.

Giselle was created in 1841 by Coralli and Perrot to music specially composed by Adam. It is based on a German legend. Giselle, a peasant girl, loves a villager who unbeknown to her is a count. But when the truth is revealed, another girl claims him and Giselle kills herself. The ghosts of maidens then appear to the count and urge him to dance to death. Giselle's ghost saves him as dawn arrives and the ghosts disappear.

Coppélia was created by Saint-Léon in 1870 to music specially composed by Delibes. The story is about Dr Coppélius, a toy maker, who builds a life-like doll called Coppélia. Franz believes the doll to be real, as does Swanilda who loves Franz. However, Franz prefers Coppélia and tries to visit her. Dr Coppélius captures Franz in order to bring Coppélia to life. But he is tricked by Swanilda, who dresses up as the doll and rescues Franz.

Below A performance of *Giselle*.

Three Revolutionary Ballets

These three ballets were created for the Ballets Russes, the ballet company directed by Sergei Diaghilev that revolutionized ballet in the early 1900s. They pioneered a style of ballet in which the music, choreography and design all fuse together to produce rich and dramatic works of art. The music for all three ballets, specially composed by Stravinsky, is so thrilling that it is often performed on its own.

The Firebird was created by Fokine in 1910. The Firebird, a magical bird, is captured by Ivan, a hunter. He releases the Firebird in exchange for one of her magic feathers. A princess appears and warns Ivan that he must leave, as the evil enchanter Kastchey has her in his power, but he stays. Kastchey imprisons Ivan, who summons the Firebird with the feather. She leads Kastchey and his followers in a dance that exhausts them. Ivan finds a large egg that contains Kastchey's soul and breaks it to free himself and the princess.

Petrushka was created by Fokine in 1911. The ballet is set in a fair at St Petersburg. A magician appears and displays three puppets – which he then brings to life. Petrushka suffers with a hopeless love for the pretty Ballerina, who prefers the brutish Moor. He tries to win her, but the Moor pursues Petrushka and kills him. The magician then shows the crowd that Petrushka is only a puppet after all. But the ghost of Petrushka then appears, terrifying the magician.

Three Classical Ballets

These three ballets were all created in Russia in the late 1800s to music specially composed by Tchaikovsky. With their spectacular dancing and exciting, tuneful music, they represent the height of classical ballet.

Swan Lake was first performed in 1877, but did not prove successful. The ballet that is now so popular was created by Petipa and Ivanov in 1895. It tells of Prince Siegfried who breaks the spell cast on a beautiful girl, Odette, that transforms her into a swan by day.

The Sleeping Beauty was created by Petipa in 1890. It recounts the tale of Princess Aurora, who as a baby is placed under a spell which will cause her to fall asleep if she ever pricks her finger. When Aurora has grown up, the wicked fairy Carabosse gives her a spindle. She pricks her finger and the curse comes true. After a century of sleep, Aurora is awakened by the kiss of Prince Florimund. They marry at a glittering wedding attended by fairy-tale characters.

The Nutcracker was created by Ivanov in 1892. It begins with a Christmas party at which Clara and Fritz are given some toys, including a nutcracker doll. That night, Clara creeps downstairs to play with the nutcracker. The toy soldiers come to life and, led by the nutcracker, do battle with the mice in the house. Clara kills the Mouse King, whereupon the nutcracker turns into a prince who takes her on a magical journey to the Kingdom Of Sweets. The Sugar Plum Fairy greets Clara, and a marvellous entertainment of dances is performed in her honour.

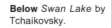
Below *Swan Lake* by Tchaikovsky.

The Rite Of Spring was created by Nijinsky in 1913. It is set in prehistoric times. A tribe of people dance in ritual frenzy as they prepare for the spring sacrifice. A maiden is chosen by the elders of the tribe, and she dances herself to death.

Stravinsky's music, with its stabbing rhythms and savage sounds, caused a riot at the first performance and Nijinksy's choreography was lost. However, the score was soon recognized to be a masterpiece and the ballet is now performed in many different versions.

Left In Stravinsky's ballet *The Rite Of Spring*, the chosen one is thrown into the air.

Ballet Movements

Arabesque The dancer stands on one leg and bends forward with the other leg pointing backward.

Attitude The dancer stands upright on one leg with the other pointing forward or backward.

Battement A kicking movement in which one foot is moved and then returned to its original position.

Brisé The dancer leaps and beats one leg against the other before landing on both feet.

Développé A movement in which a bent leg is slowly straightened.

Entrechat The dancer leaps into the air and crosses both legs several times.

Fouetté A rapid turn on one leg with a whipping motion of the other leg.

Jeté The dancer leaps into the air with one foot and lands on the other.

Pas de chat The dancer leaps and raises both feet so that the toes almost touch.

Pas de poisson The female dancer leaps and is caught by her partner.

Pirouette A turn executed on one foot.

Plié The legs are bent with the feet and knees turned outwards.

Relevé Rising on to the tips of the toes or ball of the foot.

Sur les pointes Dancing on the points of the feet or on tip-toe. The ballet shoes contain blocks that support the feet in this position.

Tour en l'air The dancer jumps and makes one or more complete turns before landing.

Below This dancer in *The Sleeping Beauty* performs an attitude with one foot raised on its point.

Position One of five positions of the feet that are used in all ballet movements. The positions are:

1 The heels are placed together

2 The heels are separated

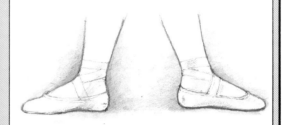

3 The feet are crossed together

4 The feet are crossed but apart

5 The front heel is placed against the big toe of the back foot

Famous Ballets

English Name*	Original Name	Composer	Original Choreographer	First Performance
Ballets with original music				
Agon	Agon	Stravinsky	Balanchine	New York 1957
Apollo	Apollon Musagète	Stravinsky	Balanchine	Washington 1928
Billy the Kid	Billy the Kid	Copland	Loring	Chicago 1938
Cinderella	Zolushka	Prokofiev	Zakharov	Moscow 1945
Coppélia	Coppélia	Delibes	Saint-Léon	Paris 1870
Daphnis and Chloe	Daphnis et Chloe	Ravel	Fokine	Paris 1912
Fancy Free	Fancy Free	Bernstein	Robbins	New York 1944
La Fille Mal Gardée	La Fille Mal Gardée	Hérold	Dauberval	Bordeaux 1828
The Firebird	L'Oiseau de Feu	Stravinsky	Fokine	Paris 1910
Giselle	Giselle	Adam	Coralli & Perrott	Paris 1841
Jeux	Jeux	Debussy	Nijinsky	Paris 1913
The Nutcracker	Casse-Noisette	Tchaikovsky	Ivanov	St Petersburg 1892
Orpheus	Orpheus	Stravinsky	Balanchine	New York 1948
Parade	Parade	Satie	Massine	Paris 1917
Petrushka	Petrushka	Stravinsky	Fokine	Paris 1911
Pulcinella	Pulcinella	Pergolesi & Stravinsky	Massine	Paris 1920
The Rite of Spring	Le Sacre du Printemps	Stravinsky	Nijinsky	Paris 1913
Rodeo	Rodeo	Copland	de Mille	New York 1942
Romeo and Juliet	Romeo i Dzhuletta	Prokofiev	Lavrovsky	Brno 1938
The Seven Deadly Sins	Les Sept Péchés Capitaux	Weill	Balanchine	Paris 1933
The Sleeping Beauty	La Belle au Bois Dormant	Tchaikovsky	Petipa	St Petersburg 1890
Spartacus	Spartak	Khachaturian	Jacobson	Leningrad 1956
Swan Lake	Le Lac des Cygnes	Tchaikovsky	Reisinger	Moscow 1877
			Petipa & Ivanov	St Petersburg 1895
La Sylphide	La Sylphide	Schneitzhoeffer	Taglioni	Paris 1832
		Ljøvenskjold	Bournonville	Copenhagen 1836
The Three-Cornered Hat	El Sombrero de Tres Picos	Falla	Massine	London 1919
Ballets with existing music				
Afternoon of a Faun	L'Après-Midi d'un Faune	Debussy	Nijinsky	Paris 1912
Les Sylphides	Les Sylphides	Chopin	Fokine	Paris 1909
Enigma Variations	Enigma Variations	Elgar	Ashton	London 1968
The Fantastic Toyshop	La Boutique Fantasque	Rossini & Respighi	Massine	London 1919
Mayerling	Mayerling	Liszt	Macmillan	London 1978
Piano Concerto No 2	Ballet Imperial	Tchaikovsky	Balanchine	New York 1941
Pierrot Lunaire	Pierrot Lunaire	Schoenberg	Tetley	New York 1962
Pineapple Poll	Pineapple Poll	Sullivan	Cranko	London 1951
Serenade	Serenade	Tchaikovsky	Balanchine	New York 1934
Le Spectre de la Rose	Le Spectre de la Rose	Weber	Fokine	Monte Carlo 1911

*Several ballets are so well known by their original name that they do not have an English name.

Popular Music

Popular music is music which has tremendous impact on people. It is packed with the personality of its performers and the music is very much the creation of those who sing and play it. Popular music covers a wide range of styles, among them jazz, rock, soul, country and pop music. All have achieved massive popularity, particularly in America and Europe, where they originated. But popular styles are arising everywhere as young people create their own music, rather than keep within the boundaries of traditional music.

No kind of music is more powerful in its appeal than popular music. Singers and groups that rise to the top of their profession can play to audiences so huge that they fill football stadiums and their records sell in millions. What makes popular music different from other kinds of music and gives it such enormous impact?

The ingredients of a good piece of popular music are simple. There is very often a catchy tune with a 'hook' – a short phrase that lingers in your memory. The hook can be so strong that if you hear it again in a different context – say in an opera or a symphony – you immediately think of the popular tune. Then there is the beat of the music: a good popular piece will get your foot tapping or make you want to dance. Finally, there are the words or lyrics, for most popular pieces are songs. These can be amusing or sad or be about anything at all, but good lyrics are instantly memorable.

Simple though these essentials of popular music are, they are by no means easy to achieve – especially as the pieces are short. The music and words must get across to the audience immediately and they must be performed with great style so as to involve the listeners. The personalities of the performers – whether singers or players – are very important in popular music.

One could say that any kind of music that people like is popular. Performances of folk music do attract large audiences, and famous operas and symphonies fill opera houses and concert halls, yet these kinds of music are not what we usually call popular music. Folk singers and musicians continue a long tradition of music by performing music that is handed down from earlier generations. Classical musicians perform music written by composers. In popular music, the singers and players either create the music themselves or, if the music has been written by others, place their own identity firmly upon it.

Popular Styles

Popular music is nothing new. When you sing a song like *Greensleeves*, *The Coventry Carol* or *Yankee Doodle*, you are singing the popular music of centuries past. Like today's popular music, such songs have remained favourites because they have a good tune, an

Styles of popular music are influenced by advances in technology. Frank Sinatra could sing softly to an audience using a microphone. Now television puts music across, as in this Arctic video featuring Ultravox.

102

infectious beat or unforgettable words.

In the last century or so, a wide range of styles of popular music has developed in Europe and North America. They include the musical, jazz, blues, country music and rock music. Modern communications – radio, records, cinema and television – have brought popular music to millions and ensured its continuing popularity.

Although one fashionable style of music makes up the records of the hit parade and much of the music played on radio and television, the other older kinds of popular music still exist. You can go to performances of old musicals and hear the various different kinds of jazz played live here and there. And there are also recordings of past performers and films of musicals, many of which are made available again on records and video. Popular music is not just the latest fad at the top of the charts. With its tremendous variety and individuality, it is an important form of music that is very much alive.

Popular Songs

Songs are the basis of popular music, and in Europe popular songs date back to the Middle Ages. Singers called troubadours and minstrels would stroll the streets, rather as buskers do today, offering to sing the songs that people wanted to hear. They also sang at

the homes of the rich and powerful to entertain lords and ladies and their guests.

From about 1800, popular songs became part of more formal entertainment in Europe and North America. There were pleasure gardens where people went to hear songs and have a good time. These gave way to song and supper rooms, where people ate and drank while singers performed, rather like night clubs today. These rooms developed into the music hall or vaudeville, which was a show in a theatre which people could enjoy listening to and join in the songs of the day. And if people did not want to go to the music hall, they sang these songs at home around a piano.

In some ways, these early popular songs were similar to today's pop songs. They usually had a good tune that was repeated several times to a set of verses. Sometimes there was an introduction before the main tune, and often a refrain sung to the same words at the end of the tune. The lyrics were sentimental, cheerful or stirring. But always, as in *Daisy Daisy* and *Don't Dilly Dally*, the songs were easy and enjoyable to sing. Unlike today's popular songs, which are usually written by the people who perform them, the songs were composed by songwriters or were sometimes taken from folk music. One of the best songwriters of the last century was Stephen Foster, who wrote songs like *Beautiful Dreamer* and *Camptown Races* that are still often sung today.

The Musical

Songwriters were professional musicians who could produce fine pieces of music and poetic lyrics. Influenced by opera, they began to create musical shows in which the songs were strung together with a story line. The singers spoke their lines between the songs. This kind of entertainment was at first called an operetta or light opera, and then a musical comedy or simply a musical. Gilbert and Sullivan had enormous success in the late 1800s with their operettas, which had absurd or light-hearted love stories and are still very popular today.

This tradition of comedy and romance has continued in musicals up to the present day. The stories have often been taken from successful plays or books, *West Side Story* and *Kiss Me Kate* being very loosely based on Shakespeare's *Romeo and Juliet* and *The Taming of the Shrew*, for example. Many stage musicals have also been filmed but the cinema industry created its own kind of film musical with spectacular sets and dancing, above all in the films of Fred Astaire and Gene Kelly. All these musicals, whether stage or film, produced many excellent popular songs that were the hits of the day. Singers and bands everywhere performed and recorded them and singers nowadays return to musicals for material again and again.

However, musicals are very expensive to mount and fewer are now performed. New musicals have marvellous sets and costumes and a modern sound that is more rhythmic than the musicals of the past. Old musicals are also revived in new productions.

Below A scene from the film version of the stage musical *West Side Story*. The film musical was remarkable for the way in which it used real locations for the songs and dancing.

Famous Stage Musicals

Title	Music	Lyrics	First Performance	Best-known Songs
Annie Get Your Gun	Irving Berlin	Irving Berlin	New York 1946	There's No Business Like Show Business Anything You Can Do I Can Do Better
Anything Goes	Cole Porter	Cole Porter	New York 1934	I Get A Kick Out Of You
The Arcadians	Lionel Monckton	Arthur Wimperis	London 1909	The Pipes Of Pan
Bitter Sweet	Noel Coward	Noel Coward	London 1929	I'll See You Again
Cabaret	John Kander	Fred Ebb	New York 1966	Cabaret
Carousel	Richard Rodgers	Oscar Hammerstein	New York 1945	June Is Busting Out All Over
The Desert Song	Sigmund Romberg	Otto Harbach & Oscar Hammerstein	New York 1926	One Alone The Desert Song
Evita	Andrew Lloyd-Webber	Tim Rice	London 1978	Don't Cry For Me Argentina
Grease	Jim Jacobs	Warren Casey	New York 1972	Summer Nights
Guys And Dolls	Frank Loesser	Frank Loesser	New York 1950	Luck Be A Lady If I Were A Bell Sit Down You're Rocking The Boat
Hair	Galt MacDermot	Gerome Ragni & James Rado	New York 1967	Aquarius
The King And I	Richard Rodgers	Oscar Hammerstein	New York 1951	I Whistle A Happy Tune
Kiss Me Kate	Cole Porter	Cole Porter	New York 1948	Brush Up Your Shakespeare So In Love Too Darn Hot
Lady Be Good	George Gershwin	Ira Gershwin	New York 1924	Lady Be Good Fascinating Rhythm
A Little Night Music	Stephen Sondheim	Stephen Sondheim	New York 1973	Send In The Clowns
The Mikado	Arthur Sullivan	W. S. Gilbert	London 1885	Three Little Maids From School A Wandering Minstrel I Willow, Tit-Willow
My Fair Lady	Frederick Loewe	Alan Jay Lerner	New York 1956	The Rain In Spain On The Street Where You Live I Could Have Danced All Night
Oklahoma	Richard Rodgers	Oscar Hammerstein	New York 1943	Oh What A Beautiful Morning The Surrey With The Fringe On Top Oklahoma
Rose Marie	Rudolf Friml & Herbert Stothart	Otto Harbach & Oscar Hammerstein	New York 1924	Rose Marie
Show Boat	Jerome Kern	Oscar Hammerstein	New York 1927	Old Man River Why Do I Love You?
The Sound Of Music	Richard Rodgers	Oscar Hammerstein	New York 1959	My Favourite Things Climb Every Mountain
South Pacific	Richard Rodgers	Oscar Hammerstein	New York 1949	Some Enchanted Evening I'm Gonna Wash That Man Right Out Of My Hair
The Student Prince	Sigmund Romberg	Dorothy Donnelly	New York 1924	Drinking Song Serenade
The Threepenny Opera	Kurt Weill	Bertolt Brecht	Berlin 1928	Mack The Knife
West Side Story	Leonard Bernstein	Stephen Sondheim	New York 1957	Maria Tonight America I Feel Pretty

Note: Most of these stage musicals have also been made into films.

Famous Film Musicals

Title	Music	Stars	Date	Best-known Songs
Easter Parade	Irving Berlin	Fred Astaire Judy Garland	1948	We're A Couple Of Swells
Forty-second Street	Al Dubin & Harry Warren	Warner Baxter Bebe Daniels Ruby Keeler Dick Powell	1933	You're Getting To Be A Habit With Me
Meet Me In St Louis	Hugh Martin & Ralph Blane	Judy Garland Margaret O'Brien	1944	The Trolley Song The Boy Next Door
On The Town	Leonard Bernstein & Roger Edens	Gene Kelly Frank Sinatra	1949	New York, New York
Les Parapluies de Cherbourg (The Umbrellas Of Cherbourg)	Michel Legrand	Nino Castelnuovo Catherine Deneuve	1964	I Will Wait For You
Top Hat	Irving Berlin	Fred Astaire Ginger Rogers	1935	Top Hat, White Tie And Tails Cheek To Cheek
Seven Brides For Seven Brothers	Gene de Paul & Johnny Mercer	Howard Keel Jane Powell	1954	Bless Yore Beautiful Hide
Singin' In The Rain	Nacio Herb Brown	Gene Kelly Debbie Reynolds Donald O'Connor	1952	Singin' In The Rain You Were Meant For Me
The Wizard Of Oz	Harold Arlen	Judy Garland	1939	Over The Rainbow
*Yellow Submarine	The Beatles	The Beatles	1968	Eleanor Rigby When I'm 64 Lucy In The Sky With Diamonds

*This is a cartoon film of the Beatles

Above The title song from the film musical *Top Hat*. Fred Astaire is in the foreground.

Left A recent revival of the stage musical *Guys And Dolls*, originally produced in 1950. Modern production techniques, especially lighting and dancing, enhanced the old songs and made this revival a great success.

Marches, Barrelhouse and Ragtime

One great feature of the popular music of America and Europe is its driving beat. The music is played and sung with tremendous rhythmic zest and power, giving it a beat that lifts the music and propels it along. Often called swing or groove, this rhythmic drive is a special and valuable quality that makes listening and dancing to music highly enjoyable. Musicians and singers who can swing have a great musical gift.

This way of playing developed in North America in about 1900. Music with a beat was already popular: there were dances, such as the waltz, and also marches. The tuneful marches of John Philip Sousa were and still are particularly famous. This music was essentially European; the pieces were composed in several sections and played by orchestras or bands with a light or solid beat as in Europe. There was not yet the bounce

and spring in the rhythm that the twentieth century has given to music.

This quality came to America from Africa. It is present in the folk music of Africa and was brought to America by black people transported from Africa to work as slaves on the cotton fields of the south. Their rhythmic heritage, combined with the melody and harmony of European music, has created much of the popular music of this century, which has spread from America to Europe and elsewhere. In the United States, the black people sang and played guitars, creating a vocal and instrumental style that is the basis of blues and rock music. In the West Indies and South America, the people also played percussion instruments, producing the lively rhythms of Latin American music (see page 64).

At the end of the 1800s, a new kind of black music sprang up in the United States. Pianists in drinking houses began to play a strongly rhythmic music known as barrelhouse piano and also as boogie-woogie. It contains repeated bass patterns

Below John Philip Sousa poses with his band, which he conducted in his tuneful and ever popular marches.

Left Jelly Roll Morton (piano) and the Red Hot Peppers, one of the bands that pioneered traditional jazz in New Orleans. Jelly Roll, whose real name was Ferdinand Morton, was a fine pianist who combined barrelhouse and ragtime piano styles.

played by the left hand to give the music terrific drive, over which tunes and phrases are laid by the right hand. Another feature of this music is that the pianist can improvise as he or she plays. For this reason, boogie-woogie pieces have a simple harmony (see page 151), often consisting of the harmony used in blues repeated as many times as necessary. Boogie-woogie remained popular into the 1930s and is still heard today.

Another black piano style became very popular in about 1900. Unlike barrelhouse piano, it is composed music similar in structure to dances and marches. But it features a strong marching left-hand rhythm with melodies played in the right hand. The music is called piano rag or ragtime and it is renowned for its syncopation, which is a way of playing notes off the beat so that the music bounces along. In fact, this quality gave ragtime its name, which came from 'ragged time' (meaning uneven rhythms).

Ragtime was also played by bands and it became a craze in North America and Europe, lasting until the 1920s. Music with a stronger beat then began to oust ragtime, beginning with livelier kinds of rags called stomps and leading to a style that was to remain popular for decades – jazz.

Scott Joplin is the best-known composer of ragtime. He achieved lasting fame with *Maple Leaf Rag* in 1899 and wrote many fine rags over the next ten years, including *The Entertainer*. Joplin desired more respectability than his reputation as the King Of Ragtime gave him, so he wrote an opera called *Treemonisha* using ragtime styles. It was finished in 1911, but never performed publicly in Joplin's lifetime because people would not take it seriously. Following a revival of interest in ragtime in the 1960s, *Treemonisha* was given its first performance in 1972 and recorded three years later.

Ragtime and Boogie-Woogie Pianists

Eubie Blake	Jelly Roll Morton
Cow-Cow Davenport	Joshua Rifkin
James P. Johnson	Jimmy Yancey
Meade Lux Lewis	

Jazz

Jazz is a very broad kind of music. It has gone through five stages of development since it began in the early years of this century. These are usually called traditional jazz, swing, modern jazz, free jazz and jazz-rock. The first three kinds of jazz were very popular in North America and Europe in their time, and some jazz musicians were as famous as pop stars are now. The various kinds still have enthusiastic followings today, and you can still hear jazz music played either by the original musicians in person or on records or by younger musicians who can perform in these styles.

All five forms of jazz sound quite unlike each other, yet they have two things in common. One is improvisation – the musicians make some or all of the music up as they play. The second vital ingredient of jazz is a driving beat. This is important because it urges the musicians along as they improvise – forcing them to play with ever more passion and daring as they create the music. It is the resulting feeling of suspense and surprise that makes jazz so different from other kinds of popular music and so appealing to its devotees.

Traditional Jazz

Jazz was born in the city of New Orleans in the United States during the early years of this century. It sprang up as black people got together in bands that often played at parades and funerals in the streets of the city. They used instruments like cornets, clarinets and trombones left over from the Civil War to create the bright, strident sound of traditional jazz. White musicians also began to play traditional jazz and a white band called The Original Dixieland Jazzband made the first jazz record in 1917. However it was black musicians who created and advanced jazz.

In traditional jazz, a trumpet or cornet leads the band with a clarinet playing high above and a trombone beneath. A rhythm section of tuba or string bass, a guitar or banjo, and drums keep the beat going. A piano or saxophone may be added.

The music is usually happy and lively, the bands playing well-known tunes often

Left Traditional jazz lives on in New Orleans, where it is still played in street parades.

The trumpet player **Louis Armstrong** was the first great jazz musician. He was born in New Orleans in 1900 and advanced traditional jazz in the 1920s. He created sections in the music in which he could improvise on his own, backed by the rhythm section, instead of playing with all the musicians all the time. In this way, Armstrong created a style of solo improvisation that allowed jazz musicians to be much more free and daring as they played.

Louis Armstrong was also a great jazz singer and his gravelly voice became famous throughout the world. He was nicknamed Satchmo, short for satchel-mouth.

Swing

Swing or big band jazz developed in the late 1920s as traditional bands became bigger and it had its heyday in the 1930s and 1940s, a period known as the swing era. Instead of one trumpet and trombone, there are three or four of each, and a section of saxophones instead of the clarinet. The rhythm section is much the same as in traditional jazz but it plays with a far more powerful beat.

However, there are too many musicians for everyone to improvise together. So swing music is written by a composer or arranger, who is sometimes the bandleader. Each piece usually has sections in which a player plays a solo improvisation. The music, in which the brass and saxophone sections often answer one another, is loud and exciting. The big bands of the swing era include those of Count Basie, Benny Goodman, Artie Shaw, Tommy Dorsey, Glenn Miller and Woody Herman. They had famous vocalists, among them Billie Holliday, Frank Sinatra and Ella Fitzgerald. These singers could sing and swing like jazz musicians. Several big bands had a more orchestral approach to jazz and produced a much greater range of sounds, notably those of Duke Ellington, Stan Kenton and Gil Evans. Swing and big

containing several sections like rags. They also play blues which have the sad feeling of blues singers, who sometimes sing with the bands. The musicians each play their part in their own particular way, changing the rhythms and notes and inserting their own phrases. However, although traditional jazz musicians improvise together in this way, they do not stray very far from the original tune so that it can still be recognized.

Above Jazz has spread from the United States to many other countries. Trumpeter Humphrey Lyttleton leads a British band in the mainstream jazz style of the 1930s, a development of traditional jazz.
Below right Benny Goodman and his orchestra, pictured in the heyday of the swing era.

Famous Traditional Jazz Musicians

Trumpet or Cornet	Trombone	Clarinet
Louis Armstrong	Kid Ory	Sidney Bechet
Bix Beiderbecke	Jim Robinson	Barney Bigard
Bunk Johnson	Jack Teagarden	Johnny Dodds
Joe 'King' Oliver		George Lewis
Nick La Rocca		Jimmy Noone

Piano	Drums
Lil Hardin	Baby Dodds
Earl Hines	Zutty Singleton

Note: Many of these musicians also recorded music in later jazz styles.

Famous Traditional Jazz Tunes

Basin Street Blues	Struttin' With Some Barbecue
Livery Stable Blues	Tiger Rag
Muskrat Ramble	Way Down Yonder In New Orleans
St Louis Blues	When The Saints Go Marching In

Note: These tunes all date back to the early years of jazz and are played by all traditional jazz bands.

band music can be enjoyed on records and in performances by new bands that recreate the sounds of the original bands.

Jazz was also played by small groups of musicians, who were often members of the big bands. They used simple arrangements of tunes that gave them much more opportunity to improvise.

Left The jazz singer Billie Holliday.

Duke Ellington was the finest composer in jazz music as well as a great jazz pianist. He was able to write music for his own orchestra throughout his career. This enabled Ellington to compose music that suited his particular performers and took advantage of their sounds and styles of playing. In this way, Ellington created one of the most individual and human sounds in all instrumental music.

Famous Musicians of the Swing Era

Trumpet	Trombone	Clarinet
Bunny Berigan	Tommy Dorsey	Benny Goodman
Buck Clayton	Dicky Wells	Woody Herman
Harry Edison		Artie Shaw
Roy Eldridge		
Harry James		
Cootie Williams		

Alto Sax	Tenor Sax	Baritone Sax
Benny Carter	Bud Freeman	Harry Carney
Johnny Hodges	Coleman Hawkins	
	Ben Webster	
	Lester Young	

Piano	Vibraphone	Drums
Count Basie	Lionel Hampton	Jo Jones
Duke Ellington		Gene Krupa
Art Tatum		Buddy Rich
Fats Waller	**Guitar**	
Teddy Wilson	Django Reinhardt	

Note: Most of these musicians continued to make records after the swing era was over.

Modern Jazz

Although it is called modern, this type of jazz actually began in the 1940s and was very popular until the 1960s. Unlike the jazz of the swing era, modern jazz is mainly a music for small bands — usually a trumpet and/or a saxophone with a rhythm section of piano or guitar, double bass or bass guitar, and drums. It also features far more improvisation with little composed or arranged music. For this reason, the pieces are usually very simple, consisting of a tune played by the whole band, then solo improvisations by members of the band, followed by the tune again to end the piece. The tune may be a standard (a well-known popular song or jazz tune) but often the tune is written by a member of the band. There may also be a singer but this is not usual.

This kind of jazz can still be heard in jazz clubs, and there are several different styles. The first was bop or bebop, which was developed by Charlie Parker and Dizzy Gillespie. Unlike the straight-forward music of the swing era, bop is complicated and requires brilliant musicians. But it is a powerful and very exciting music. From bop, two main kinds of modern jazz grew up. One

is cool jazz, which is tuneful and thoughtful, as in the music of Gerry Mulligan and Dave Brubeck. The second is hard bop, which is simpler than bop but hard-driving energetic music. Miles Davis spearheaded this development, just as he has been at the forefront of most other advances in modern jazz. This style of jazz became wilder, especially in the intense improvisations of John Coltrane.

Unlike many other kinds of music, jazz became simpler as it developed. In bop and other early modern jazz styles, the musicians use the harmony of the tune as a basis for their improvisation. The sequence of harmonies that goes with the tune is repeated over and over again by the bass and piano or guitar, while the solo musicians improvise their own lines over these harmonies. If you can hear this happening, the improvisation will make sense. In later modern jazz styles, musicians use scales of notes instead of a repeated harmonic sequence. This allows them greater freedom in improvisation.

Free Jazz and Jazz-Rock

Free jazz developed in the late 1960s with the music of saxophonist Ornette Coleman and pianist Cecil Taylor. In free jazz, all rules disappear. There can be any number of musicians playing all kinds of instruments, and there need be no tune nor even any beat. All the music is totally improvised, a feat

Miles Davis is the most creative performer in all jazz and one of the finest musicians of the twentieth century. He plays the trumpet with an intensely emotional sound as well as great rhythmic power, displaying astonishing powers of instant musical invention. Ever since 1945, when he became one of the founders of modern jazz alongside Charlie Parker, Miles Davis has refused to confine himself to one style of jazz and has led almost every advance in jazz.

This photograph shows Charlie Parker (left) and Miles Davis during the be bop period in the late 1940s. The original thinking that Miles Davis has brought to jazz was evident in his very first recordings with Parker, which were made when he was only 19 years old.

Left John Coltrane was a master of the tenor saxophone and introduced the soprano saxophone to modern jazz.

Famous Modern Jazz Musicians

Trumpet	Trombone	
Clifford Brown	Bob Brookmeyer	
Miles Davis	J. J. Johnson	
Dizzy Gillespie		
Clark Terry		
	Tenor Sax	
Alto Sax	John Coltrane	**Baritone Sax**
Paul Desmond	Stan Getz	Gerry Mulligan
Lee Konitz	Sonny Rollins	John Surman
Charlie Parker	Wayne Shorter	
	Guitar	
	Charlie Christian	
Piano	John McLaughlin	**Drums**
Dave Brubeck		Art Blakey
Bill Evans	**Bass**	Kenny Clarke
Errol Garner	Ray Brown	Elvin Jones
Keith Jarrett	Charlie Mingus	Max Roach
Thelonius Monk	Jaco Pastorius	
Oscar Peterson		

Blues

Blues is basically a kind of North American folk music (see page 65). It was created by the poor black country people of the United States during the 1800s as they sang about their lives and troubles. But in this century, blues has spread from its humble origins and permeated almost all forms of popular music, strongly influencing the ways in which singers and musicians perform.

The reason for the tremendous appeal of blues is that it is a very natural form of music; it puts over feelings – whether of joy or sorrow – easily and with great power. Both blues singers and players do this by using a strong beat and by 'bending' notes. They change the pitch of a note as they hit it, sliding slightly up or down to create a tension that emphasizes the feeling in the song or music. Blues is also very simple. A sung blues usually has just three lines in each verse, in between which instruments, often a guitar, or maybe a chorus of singers answer. This call-and-response pattern gives additional power to the music and it is also used in instrumental versions of blues.

which requires musicians who are very sensitive to each other's playing. At its best, free jazz is music of raw and intense feeling.

As free jazz developed, jazz generally lost its popularity, audiences preferring the excitement and directness of rock music. However, without abandoning improvisation, several jazz musicians added features of rock music to their playing – notably its strongly rhythmic beat and electric instruments such as the electric guitar and synthesizer. Miles Davis again pioneered this style of jazz, and the group Weather Report continued it to great success.

Right The blues singer Bessie Smith.

Below The jazz-rock band Weather Report features Jo Zawinul on keyboards and Wayne Shorter on saxophones.

Top Muddy Waters developed rhythm and blues in Chicago in the 1950s.

Above The Rolling Stones in their early days. Vocalist Mick Jagger is playing the maracas.

Famous Blues Singers and Performers

Big Bill Broonzy	Ma Rainey
Blind Lemon Jefferson	Bessie Smith
Robert Johnson	Joe Turner
B. B. King	T. Bone Walker
Huddie Leadbetter (Leadbelly)	Muddy Waters

Rhythm and Blues

It is impossible to write blues down — the note-bending and rhythm of the beat are styles that people can only learn from hearing blues artists. Early in the 1900s, blues records began to circulate in America and blues came to cities. More people heard blues and it began to take grip on popular music. It strongly affected jazz; blues singers often sang with jazz bands — as they still do.

Bands that specialized in blues sprang up in the 1930s, giving rise to rhythm and blues. This style of popular music is raw and powerful, played with a driving beat and sung with a rough throaty voice — not for nothing are many blues singers known as blues shouters. Electric guitars and often a harmonica and saxophone also feature strongly, answering the singer and playing riffs (repeated phrases) to drive the beat even harder.

Rhythm and blues became immensely popular in the 1950s and has maintained its appeal ever since. One reason is that British groups such as The Rolling Stones and The Who, influenced by their American idols, produced a blues sound that appealed to the large white audience in Europe and America.

Rock Music

In the mid-1950s, a revolution occurred in popular music. This was rock and roll, which exploded on to the music scene with such force that its sounds are still with us today. For about twenty years, dance music played by the swing bands and sentimental songs, often from musicals, had been popular with the record-buying and radio-listening public in North America and Europe. Rhythm and blues was still favoured mainly by black people in America, and modern jazz had become too involved to have great appeal.

Then suddenly there appeared a mixture of rhythm and blues and country music, the popular music that developed from white folk music. It had less of the raw power of rhythm and blues, but the country influence gave the music an energetic rocking and rolling beat. With its direct, simple lyrics and tunes, rock and roll became an immediate hit

Elvis Presley was the first superstar of the rock era. He stunned live audiences with his wild movements and defiant image, setting a style that many later rock performers were to emulate. But his voice had tremendous presence too and also captivated people on record, leading to a string of hits in the late 1950s and early 1960s. These included *Heartbreak Hotel* (1956), *Hound Dog* (1956), *Love Me Tender* (1956), *All Shook Up* (1957), *Jailhouse Rock* (1957) and *Are You Lonesome Tonight?* (1960).

Presley then made many films before appearing live again in 1968. He later retired into seclusion and died in 1977 from the effects of drugs. He was only 42 years old.

with the public. It created a superstar in Elvis Presley and launched many performers, notably Buddy Holly in United States — whose popularity has long survived his death in 1959 — and Cliff Richard in Britain, still going strong in the 1980s.

Right Rock and roll star Chuck Berry, here performing the shuffling duck-walk for which he is renowned.

Classic Rock and Roll Hits

Title	Singer/Band	Date
Rock Around The Clock	Bill Haley And The Comets	1955
Tutti Frutti	Little Richard	1955
Roll Over Beethoven	Chuck Berry	1956
Blueberry Hill	Fats Domino	1956
Blue Suede Shoes	Carl Perkins	1956
Hound Dog	Elvis Presley	1956
Be Bop A Lula	Gene Vincent	1956
Great Balls Of Fire	Jerry Lee Lewis	1957

Progressive to Punk

The impact of rock and roll led to a wide range of styles of popular music that are known as rock music. Rock groups, composed basically of one or two electric guitars, bass guitar and drums, often with a keyboard instrument and a saxophone, have dominated popular music ever since. Members of the group may sing or a vocalist may front the band.

Often influenced by rhythm and blues, rock groups have developed their own individual approach to music. The groups usually write their own music and lyrics to express their ideas. The group strives to make its own kind of sound and the resulting music is often very personal and has a strong identity. The group that pioneered this direction in rock music was The Beatles, who produced some of the best songs in all music. They developed a variety of ways to present these songs. The Beatles could put over a song simply and strongly just by singing and playing it straight. But they also made great use of recording techniques to add other instruments to their line-up and get all kinds of different effects and sounds on their records.

This elaborate kind of rock music is often known as progressive rock. It developed in the late 1960s and was really intended for listening rather than dancing. Progressive groups such as Pink Floyd and Genesis produced records of music that was brilliantly performed and often intense and dramatic in feeling, while their live performances were spectacular shows.

Other rock groups preferred to keep their music less complex. Bands such as Cream concentrated on the musical ability of their players and went in for jamming or extended improvisation. This led to a style of rock known as heavy metal, which is loud music strongly featuring the electric guitar, as with Led Zeppelin and Black Sabbath. Many groups went in for simple and direct songs, especially in the rebellious punk rock movement of the late 1970s, notably with The Clash. Another very simple but very individual style of rock music is reggae, which originated in the West Indies. This is sparse and uncluttered music; the approach is often laid back with every note and word used to maximum effect. The best-known

The Beatles were the most famous rock group of the 1960s. They were Paul McCartney (bass guitar), John Lennon (guitar), George Harrison (guitar) and Ringo Starr (drums). The Beatles were a British group and hailed from Liverpool. Their songs were mostly written by Lennon and McCartney, and have marvellous tunes with words that range from being witty to profoundly moving. Helped by their record producer, George Martin, the Beatles maintained an approach to rock that was always fresh and inventive.

Among the Beatles' many hits were *Please, Please Me* (1964), *Can't Buy Me Love* (1964), *A Hard Day's Night* (1964), *Yesterday* (1965), *Eleanor Rigby* (1966), *Michelle* (1966), and *All You Need Is Love* (1967). Their best-known albums include *Revolver* (1966) and *Sergeant Pepper's Lonely Hearts Club Band* (1967).

The Beatles broke up in 1970. Paul McCartney went on to form Wings and continued to write songs. John Lennon also produced good songs, notably *Imagine* (1971), before he was murdered in 1980.

Twelve Famous Rock Albums

Title	Group or Artist	Date
Pet Sounds	The Beach Boys	1966
Sergeant Pepper's Lonely Hearts Club Band	The Beatles	1967
Electric Ladyland	Jimi Hendrix	1968
Beggars Banquet	The Rolling Stones	1968
Wheels Of Fire	Cream	1968
Tommy	The Who	1969
Hot Rats	Frank Zappa And The Mothers of Invention	1969
The Rise And Fall Of Ziggy Stardust	David Bowie	1972
Catch A Fire	Bob Marley And The Wailers	1972
Tubular Bells	Mike Oldfield	1973
Rumours	Fleetwood Mac	1977
The Clash	The Clash	1977

reggae group was Bob Marley And The Wailers. Other later rock groups such as Fleetwood Mac and Police continued to develop rock music in a personal way.

Rock music has also produced many famous individual musicians as well as groups. Among the best known are the guitarists Jimi Hendrix and Eric Clapton, and

Frank Zappa, who is a superb composer as well as a fine guitarist. Mike Oldfield became a star with albums on which he played most of the instruments himself. There are also some singers who create a complete artistic style of their own. Foremost among these has been David Bowie, who has continually explored new and thought-provoking ways of presenting himself.

Many of the pioneering rock groups have now broken up and some of the people are dead. However their music lives on in their recordings and in its influence on today's popular music.

Left Punk rock group The Clash in dramatic pose.

Above Stylish rock performer David Bowie.

Soul and Tamla Motown

At about the same time as rock and roll exploded on to the music scene, another kind of popular music was born. It too has its roots in black American folk music. This is soul music, an enduring style that was founded in the late 1950s by the great blind singer and performer Ray Charles. Soul comes from gospel, the music of the black churches in the United States. Gospel songs are performed with tremendous exuberance and fervour, the singers and congregation clapping on the off beat (the second and fourth beats in each bar) to drive the beat along and shouting the words in repeated call-and-response patterns to create mounting excitement.

Ray Charles used these features of gospel music to produce a joyful, earthy music sung in a rasping, throaty voice with great expression and a strong rhythmic drive. Other singers, often with church backgrounds, took up the style and it became known as soul music. A vocal group often answers and backs the singer. The soul style of singing can be applied to any song, including well-known standard songs and slow ballads, and it has become the main kind of black popular music. Much of soul's success was due to the singers and vocal groups promoted by Tamla Motown, a record company in Detroit, which had hit after hit in the 1960s. From Tamla Motown, there emerged several great popular singers, notably Diana Ross, Michael Jackson and Stevie Wonder.

Folk Roots

The southern United States has a legacy of folk music that arrived with the white pioneers and settlers from Britain and Europe. In North America, their music developed a very lively style and came to be known as hillbilly or country music. Its main instrument is the violin, and the guitar, banjo and mandolin are prominently featured, the singers often accompanying themselves on these instruments.

Above The blind singer and pianist Ray Charles, who has been the king of soul music for 30 years.

Right Diana Ross (left) and the Supremes.

Giants of Soul Music

James Brown	Aretha Franklin
Solomon Burke	Wilson Pickett
Ray Charles	Otis Redding
Sam Cooke	Tina Turner

Famous Tamla Motown Artists

The Jackson Five
Gladys Knight and the Pips
Martha and the Vandellas
Smokie Robinson and the Miracles
Diana Ross and the Supremes
The Temptations
Stevie Wonder

Above The original Carter family from Virginia, who were pioneers of country music. The trio were, from left to right, Maybelle Addington (guitar and vocal), Alvin Carter (vocal) and Sara Carter (autoharp). Alvin was Sara's husband and Maybelle her cousin.

Right Country music star Johnny Cash.

Like the blues in black folk music, the country music of the whites spread with the rise of radio and records and it became widely popular. The recordings made from 1928 by the Carter family from Virginia greatly helped to popularize country music, and so too from 1925 did the *Grand Ole Opry* radio show broadcast from Nashville, Tennessee. Both the Carter family and the *Grand Ole Opry* are still going strong, the latter now housed in the 3,000-seat Ryman Auditorium in Nashville, which has long been the centre of country music.

During the 1930s, country music came to embrace the cowboy songs known as western swing, and today country music is also known as country and western. It still features the traditional instruments of its folk origins but drums are now often added and the guitars may be electric. In addition, the singing sound of the pedal steel guitar is used to give country music a unique flavour. The songs, which may be traditional or original, are generally relaxed and sung with an easy swing. Country music is almost entirely played by white performers.

Folk-Rock

In the mid-1960s, another folk-based style of music arose by combining features of both white and black folk music. Called folk-rock, it was strongly influenced by Woody Guthrie, the folk song pioneer who wrote several well-known songs, including *This Land Is Your Land*. Bob Dylan sang in the style of white folk music but added the pounding beat of rock to create folk-rock. He composed his own songs, leading a generation of singer-songwriters who wrote and performed their own work. Several American and British groups and performers have developed folk-rock, some playing rock versions of traditional folk songs while others have created their own style and material.

Famous Country Music Artists

Roy Acuff	Brenda Lee	Kenny Rogers
Glen Campbell	Bill Monroe	Earl Scruggs
Johnny Cash	Dolly Parton	Hank Williams Senior
Tennessee Ernie Ford	Charley Pride	Bob Wills
Emmylou Harris	Jim Reeves	Tammy Wynette
Kris Kristofferson	Marty Robbins	

Singer-Songwriters and Folk-Rock Groups

Joan Baez	Carole King
The Byrds	Ralph McTell
Crosby, Stills, Nash and Young	Joni Mitchell
Fairport Convention	Simon and Garfunkel
Bob Dylan	Steeleye Span

Bob Dylan began his musical career in the early 1960s, singing his own and traditional folk songs and playing guitar and harmonica. He became famous when he began to perform with a strong rock beat, putting over his simple tunes and hard-hitting lyrics with great power. Dylan's work created the style known as folk-rock and he greatly influenced rock musicians, notably The Beatles. Among his best-known songs are *Blowing In The Wind* (1963) and *Mr Tambourine Man* (1965), and his most important albums include *Bringing It All Back Home* and *Highway 61 Revisited*, both recorded in 1965.

Pop

Popular music is often called pop music for short, but the term 'pop' can mean a style of music which is different from other kinds of music that are very popular, such as rock and soul music. Pop is music performed by singing stars and groups that is usually light and entertaining. The songs may be new or old. Pop has no particular style of its own and may make use of the styles of rock, soul, folk or country music presented in such a way as to have as wide an appeal as possible. For this reason, some pop is known as MOR, meaning music that is 'middle of the road' in style.

Singers and performers come and go rapidly in the world of pop, but some hit it off with the public and become stars, remaining at the top year after year. Presentation is very important in pop, and stars give spectacular television shows and live concerts; some appear in films as well.

Pop Stars and Groups	
Abba	Diana Ross
Michael Jackson	Bruce Springsteen
Elton John	Rod Stewart
Barry Manilow	Barbra Streisand
Johnny Mathis	Stevie Wonder

The Triumph of Technology

Popular music has always been dependent on technology. The development of radio and records carried popular music into homes and ensured its future as styles came and went. The use of microphones has enabled singers to develop individual styles of singing that have great appeal, and sound systems have allowed performers to put their music across to huge audiences at concerts.

Today, technology is at the heart of popular music and it shows in several important ways. Modern recording techniques, for example, enable bands and singers to produce spectacular albums that are technically much more advanced than their live appearances. Technology has also created disco music, which developed as people began to dance to records played on high-quality sound systems in discotheques. Disco is renowned for its strong, insistent beat, which makes the music good for dancing. Allied to this style is funk, a bouncy rhythmic way of playing that features driving bass lines.

Another application of technology is a style often called electropop because it features electronic instruments. This style

Stevie Wonder is one of the most talented stars in popular music. Born blind in 1950, he made his first single at the age of 12 singing and playing harmonica. He then had his first hit – *Fingertips Part Two* – a year later. He has since explored a wide range of popular music styles, writing songs with good tunes and lyrics. On his records he often plays most of the instruments himself – he is a superb performer on the guitar, bass guitar, drums and keyboards. Stevie Wonder's best-known songs include *You Are The Sunshine Of My Life* (1973), and his most highly-regarded album is *Songs In The Key Of Life* (1976).

has been developing since the late 1970s, when synthesizers became widespread, and now many groups produce sounds that are mostly or even totally generated by electronic and computer-driven instruments. Electropop is one of the few developments in popular music that began outside North America and Britain. In 1976, it produced one of the most original sounds in popular music with the album *Oxygène* by the French musician Jean-Michel Jarre, and the first electronic bands to gain fame were the German groups Tangerine Dream and Kraftwerk. This kind of music has been mainly limited to records and film soundtracks, but progress in computer technology will make electronic music easier to perform live and should bring it to a wider audience.

A further and very important technological development to affect popular music is video, which is more than just a promotion device. The choice and production of visual images in a pop video can be just as creative as writing and performing the music. The music must now be seen as well as heard, a revolutionary development that is very likely to affect popular music greatly far into the future.

Above The French musician Jean-Michel Jarre brought the electronic sounds of the synthesizer to a mass audience with his hit album *Oxygène*. He plays all the instruments himself.

Left To bring a record by a singer or group to the attention of the public, a video of the music is a necessity. This promotes the singer or group on television, especially on pop programmes and cable channels. Making a music video usually requires the musicians to mime to a recording of the music. Here the camera closes in on Miles Davis as he plays the music.

121

The History of Music

While we may never know exactly how people made music in the past, we can trace the ways in which music has developed from its beginnings to give the wealth of music throughout the world today. It is a fascinating story because the music we have now depends very much on the music that people made in the past, even many centuries ago. Furthermore, it is a human story: one that is to do with past civilizations and the movements of people around the globe.

The origins of music go back to prehistory, possibly even to a time before our ancestors began to use language. Yelling and chanting in a musical way could have helped early people to face real or imagined dangers around them. The sounds would have had instant meanings, signifying warnings or giving reassurance in rituals, for example. This aspect of musical meaning is still with us – in whistled signals and in languages such as Chinese that employ different tones of voice to give sounds different meanings. Ritual chants are part of many religions.

Musical instruments have prehistoric origins too. The oldest known instruments are some mammoth bones dating back about 35,000 years that were found in Siberia. The bones have marks that show where to hit them in order to get a resonant sound, and some have holes and could be blown like a flute.

All kinds of natural materials were used to make music in prehistoric times. Wind instruments were made from stems like bamboo and the hollowed horns of animals. Drums and percussion instruments have their origins in hollow logs, skins that could be stretched on frames or over pits or containers, and bracelets that jangled. String instruments most likely came about by twanging the stretched string of a hunter's bow. In these ways, all the basic kinds of acoustic instruments came into being many thousands of years ago.

Music in the Ancient World

The first civilizations sprang up in the Middle East some 10,000 years ago as people began to settle and farm. For about 5,000 years we have no record of the music of these peoples but they must have begun to make instruments using natural materials. The first pictures and descriptions date back to about 3000 BC in ancient Mesopotamia, which was situated around the Tigris and Euphrates rivers in present-day Iraq. They tell us of instruments such as harps and lyres and also the double pipe, which was a pair of reed pipes played by one musician.

Right These trumpets, which were found in the tomb of the Egyptian king Tutankhamun, are more than 3,000 years old. They can still be played.

Far left This wall painting from ancient Egypt shows women playing a double reed pipe (left), lute (centre) and harp (right).

Below This harp, with a soundbox fashioned like a bull's head, comes from Ur in ancient Sumer and dates back to about 2600 BC.

These and other instruments, including flutes, lutes and percussion instruments like rattles, castanets and tambourines were played in ancient Egypt from about 2500 BC onwards. With the advent of the Bronze Age, metal instruments began to appear. Two metal trumpets, one of bronze and gold and the other of silver, were found in the tomb of the Egyptian king Tutankhamun, who died in 1352 BC.

What kind of music was played in these ancient civilizations and what was its purpose? The music probably consisted of simple melodies played or sung by all the people together in unison. However, religious songs or chants would have been performed with a chorus answering a singer or groups of singers answering each other, as still happens in some churches today. There may have been a drone – a constant low note over which the melody was played or sung. Ancient pictures show us that music was used to mark special occasions like processions and feasts as well as religious ceremonies, such as funerals.

Above This drawing engraved on the wall of a cave depicts what some experts think could be a man disguised as a bison playing a musical bow like that shown on page 59. It was made by prehistoric people in France about 16,000 years ago.

123

Ancient Greece

Much of our knowledge and appreciation of art and science was founded by the Greeks from about 1000 BC onwards. Music was treated as both art and science in ancient Greece. The Greeks considered music, dance and poetry to be arts that enhance life, and they were taught from childhood and studied extensively.

The philosopher Pythagoras, using knowledge gained from Mesopotamia and Egypt, developed the theory of music in about 500 BC. He showed that notes which sound pleasant together are produced by strings or pipes whose lengths are in simple proportions. If one string or pipe is exactly two-thirds or three-quarters the length of another, for example, they give two notes at intervals that we call fifths (such as C and G) or fourths (such as C and F).

This discovery was very important in music. It led to a series of seven-note scales called modes, which are like scales of white notes on the piano and include our major and minor scales. By singing or playing melodies using these notes, we get tunes with a variety of feelings. Many of our folk songs are built around Greek modes. The Greek theorists went on to find all the twelve notes of the chromatic scale (the black and white keys on the piano), thus providing a basis for all Western music that was to follow.

Below This medieval illustration shows how the theory of Pythagoras relates the sizes of bells to their musical notes.

The Greeks Had A Word For It

Many of the words we use in music come from ancient Greek, including the word music. It comes from *mousike*, which meant the arts of music, poetry and dance. Other Greek words in music include: cymbal from *kymbalon*, originally a hollow vessel; guitar and zither from *kithara*, a lute or lyre; harmony from *harmonia*, which meant fitting together; rhythm from *rhythmos*, a measure; and *orchestra*, which was the Greek name for the space in front of the stage of a theatre that was used by the chorus in a play.

The Greeks also developed musical instruments, producing panpipes and lyres in which the pipes and strings could be tuned to the notes of their scales. They wrote music down from about 400 BC, using letters of the alphabet rather as we give notes the letters A to G.

Eastern Music

The civilizations of the East also made important advances in music in ancient times. The beginnings of Indian music took place from about 1500 BC with the chanting of sacred verses in temples. These were performed using three notes at first, and then later sung using a wider range of notes. Rather like the Greeks, from these beginnings came a music based on scales of notes as well as belief in the importance of music, poetry and dance to life.

More is known about music in ancient China. There, other kinds of instruments developed, notably the zither, chimes and bells, which were made by chipping stones and suspending them on a frame to be struck by a stick. There was also the sheng, a kind of mouth organ consisting of several reed pipes and a container into which air was blown to sound the pipes.

In about 250 BC, the Chinese created a standard pitch for music, rather as we use devices like tuning forks to tune instruments today. They used a pitch pipe, a bamboo pipe of a fixed length that always sounded the same note, though for some reason it was known as the huang-chung, meaning 'yellow bell'. From the use of standard-

East, Egypt and Sicily. They then gave way to the Romans, who expanded their empire over most of Europe, the Middle East and North Africa.

The Romans were not great creators and they took over Greek music as they absorbed Greek art and science. However, the Romans enjoyed music of all kinds and some of the emperors were reputed to be good musicians. They enjoyed spectacular shows too and saw music as a form of entertainment, mounting huge concerts with hundreds of performers.

The desire for loud music spurred the development of the first keyboard instrument, the organ. This was invented by Ctesibius, a Greek engineer at Alexandria in about 220 BC. He had the idea of mounting a group of pipes on a chest into which air was forced by water pressure. Sliders containing holes were then pushed in and out of the chest to force air into the pipes and sound them. Eventually, these sliders were sprung and worked by levers like a keyboard, while extra ranks of pipes were added to increase the volume.

This instrument was called the hydraulis, meaning 'water pipe'. Greek vases show that the players of reed pipes used to bind their cheeks so that they could blow harder and make a loud noise. The hydraulis could compress air to blow the pipes very strongly and reports say that it could be heard over many kilometres.

However, many people deplored the Roman spectacles, which became increasingly cruel, and came to associate music with vulgarity. This trend away from enjoyment in music was increased by Roman persecution of the Jews and Christians. The psalms of the Bible were originally sung to traditional melodies accompanied by instruments. But playing instruments was now discouraged. To preserve the faith, religious music was 'purified' in this way, divesting it of associations with the Romans and thereby with entertainment. It began a division into two kinds of music – music that appeals to the mind and music that is entertaining. This division, now between classical music and popular music, is still very much with us in the West today. With the fall of the Roman Empire in the AD 400s and the rise of Christianity, music was set towards a new course in Europe.

Above This Roman mosaic portrays the hydraulis or water organ, the first keyboard instrument, and a cornu, which was a large horn that curved over the player's head.

length pipes, the Chinese found out about intervals in the same way as Pythagoras and they too concocted scales as a basis for their music. However, they mainly used only five notes to give a pentatonic scale, for example C D F G A. This was because the number five was thought to have a special significance, and Chinese music has been pentatonic ever since.

The Influence of Rome
The Greeks led the ancient world until about 200 BC, extending their rule as far as India and dominating Persia (Iran), the Middle

A Golden Age in Asia

In Europe, the period from about AD 400 to 1000 is called the Dark Ages. The continent descended into barbarity and music was of little importance. However in Asia – in the Arab lands and to the East in India, China and Indonesia – music continued to advance and attained a golden age. Instruments developed rich and brilliant sounds to delight the ear, while the melodies swooped and soared in sinuous patterns to express musical feelings. None of the notes were written down – indeed, much of the music was improvised. The music and its style of performance were handed down from one generation to the next, and it can be heard in much the same form in these parts of the world today (see *Music Around the World*).

In India, the scales of notes used as the basis of the music developed and became more complex. Each piece or raga was improvised in sections around a particular scale and in complex rhythms to produce an appropriate mood or feeling in the people playing and listening. The scales and forms of the ragas had developed by about AD 700.

Chinese music also developed in complexity, especially in its presentation and form. There were ballets with singing, large bands of musicians and instrumental pieces in several movements that portrayed events such as battles. The bright and varied sounds of the Chinese instruments in full cry must have been very impressive. It certainly made its mark on the Japanese, who borrowed Chinese instruments and music theory in about AD 800 and used them to develop their own music.

Indonesia created its own scales and people made music mostly by striking objects to give a unique sound unlike any other music, even today. Instruments like xylophones were made with pieces of bamboo or blocks of wood, and chimes and gongs with metal. In about AD 200, Indonesians emigrated to Africa and it is possible that they took the xylophone with them. There it was transformed into the marimba, an instrument now common in African music.

The Arab lands became Muslim during the 600s and developed a rich music often using Greek scales in which melodies were

performed by orchestras of instruments playing in unison against percussion rhythms. Several of the instruments we use today began to take their final form, and these found their way to other parts of the world as the Muslim religion spread with conquest. The guitar and rebec, an ancestor of the violin played with a bow, came to Europe via Spain and the sitar, tambura and tabla entered India from Persia (Iran).

The Rebirth of Music in Europe

While music was evolving towards a brilliant golden age in the East and Arab lands, in Europe music was reduced to extreme simplicity. But Asian music then reached a peak and could not grow much more. It has changed little since and still basically consists of a line of melody formed from a particular scale of notes. The scale remains the same during a piece and there is no change of harmony. Expression comes from the shape or contours of the melody, which may produce feelings of excitement or relaxation, for example.

In Europe, however, the very simplicity with which music was now reborn allowed it to grow and develop without pause. It has since taken a totally different direction from Asian music, mainly because harmony was able to evolve.

During the Dark Ages, from AD 400 to about 1000, Christianity spread throughout Europe. The church decreed that its music should be chants sung to slow-moving and even-flowing melodies based on the Greek scales. It was called plainsong, and no instruments were allowed to sully its purity. This kind of singing still exists in the Catholic church, especially in the orthodox churches which have retained the early decrees.

Left This Indian miniature shows a raga being played to celebrate spring. It was painted in the 1600s, but classical Indian music developed its basic form about a thousand years earlier.

The Beginnings of Harmony

Plainsong was sung in unison with all the voices singing the same notes. From this bare melody, music then began to develop the basic element of harmony. Instead of everyone singing the same notes, the voices split into two or more groups. One sang the original plainsong melody, while the others sang it at a fixed interval of a fourth, fifth or octave so that all the voices rose and fell together. This practice, called organum, spread widely from about 900. At about the same time, instruments were allowed to accompany plainsong and the organ entered the church.

This music was not written down. The very simplicity of plainsong allowed it to be remembered easily as it passed from one generation to the next. However, music began to be sung in which the other vocal lines were less fixed to the plainsong. The upper line above the plainsong began to be embellished and soon it became a separate melody, rather like a descant sung above a hymn tune.

The next step was to create music in three or four parts that move much more independently but always sound notes that are in harmony with each other. The organ

or other instruments accompanying the singers could help them to sing the right notes, but remembering the different parts and singing the notes at the right time so that they fitted together correctly was more difficult. Fortunately, another development occurred to make this possible. This was notation – a way of writing music down on paper.

Music Notation

The writing of music developed over a long period. In about 900 a Flemish monk called Hucbald devised a system that used the letters T and S to denote changes of tones and semitones in a melody (see page 153). Another monk, Odo of Cluny, later produced a notation using letters of the alphabet similar to our use of the letters A to G. But more practical was a system using neumes,

which were marks above the words of the song that indicated whether the sounds should rise or fall in pitch. Eventually, lines were drawn across these marks and a letter was marked on one of the lines to define the pitch of the notes. This was the beginning of the stave and clef signs that we use in music today.

The system was brilliantly explained in

Left A minstrel and juggler together with neumes, an early way of writing music. The words are those of a song and the marks above them show how the notes rise and fall in pitch.

Far left Guido d'Arezzo (left) explaining his system of writing music.

An Everlasting Song

The song *Sumer Is Icumen In (Summer is A-Coming In)* is a remarkable piece of music that was composed by an English monk in the 1200s. Its English words show that it was a secular (popular) song, although it had alternative Latin words for church use.

The song is a round to be sung in six parts. Four people sing the main words, each starting in turn when the previous singer gets to the point marked by a cross. The other two singers repeat two lower parts over and over again at the same time. The resulting parts do not clash but blend in a flow of harmony. *Sumer Is Icumen In* is still sung today and it demonstrates how advanced music had become in Europe eight centuries ago.

Above The joy of making music is evident in this medieval picture of minstrels.

music. With a system of writing music, composers could develop new ways of putting music together. The first known composers were Léonin and Pérotin, who lived in France in the late 1100s and 1200s. They wrote pieces in several parts based on plainsong melodies, often slowing down the plainsong so that it became little more than a skeleton on which the other parts were built.

Music of the People

In this way, the church laid the foundations of Western music, steering it towards a composed music of separate parts producing a flow of harmony. But what of secular music – the music of the people? Little is known until the end of the Dark Ages, but during this time bards kept legends alive by singing.

From about 1000, troubadours became famous throughout Europe. They were singers who sang to royal and noble audiences, entertaining them with songs of love and daring exploits, even giving whole plays with songs. There were also travelling entertainers who wandered from place to place singing, juggling and performing acrobatics for a living.

These people developed songs with music in set sections, making it easy to put words to the music and also to dance to it. Some sang alone but many played instruments such as early forms of the violin, guitar and lute.

about 1030 by the Italian monk Guido d'Arezzo, who went on to invent the method of using the sounds *do*, *re*, *mi* etc to teach the notes of the scale.

By about 1200, marks indicating time values such as crotchets and quavers had appeared, and the basic system of writing music that we have today was in use.

This was a very important development in

A New Art

From about 1300, a new form of music arose that was much freer than the religious music based on plainsong. It was called *ars nova*, which is Latin for 'new art'. Composers still wrote polyphonic music (music in several separate parts), but these parts were much more independent and not tied to the plainsong. The various lines could even have different words to be sung at the same time. In the most advanced pieces, which were called motets, we have the beginning of music as an art in itself rather than a means of enhancing words of devotion and poetry. Composers delighting in their new-found freedom, produced motets of all kinds with a wide range of expression, including even political views. They also began to write musical settings of the words of the mass, as well as songs and dances.

The new music began in France and spread throughout Europe, other countries adding their own contributions. In Italy, for example, the form known as canon developed, in which a melody is played or sung against itself, like a round. The Italians called this *caccia*, which means a hunting song,

from the way the music chases itself. In such ways, the music was cleverly wrought yet also highly expressive, paralleling great advances taking place at that time in other arts, notably painting and architecture. It was primarily vocal, though instruments could accompany the voices, playing the same parts. The earliest keyboard music, probably for the organ, dates from the 1300s and includes motets with words.

The First Great Composers

The polyphonic style developed over the next two centuries. Its masters included Vitry, Machaut, Dunstable, Dufay and Des Près and these men can be considered the first great composers. Their music developed true counterpoint, in which the various parts or musical lines each have a full identity of their own as if they are separate melodies, yet combine together to give a greater whole. The ways in which the parts interweave can be highly exhilarating and very moving, as in madrigals, which were imaginative settings of poems (often amorous) in as many as six parts.

Instrumental music also developed at this time. The new, composed polyphonic music could be played on keyboard instruments

Below left The early composers Guillaume Dufay (left) and Gilles Binchois, who lived in the 1400s.

Below right These four paintings from a Spanish musical manuscript of the 1200s depict tuned bells (top left), a viol and lute (top right), early forms of the guitar (bottom left) and pipes and drums (bottom right).

Right The portative organ was a small pipe organ that could be carried.

Below This painting of the 1500s shows a group of people singing a madrigal.

and also by small bands called consorts. These contained families of instruments such as recorders, viols and lutes for indoor music, and more raucous instruments such as sackbuts and shawms (early forms of the trombone and oboe) for outdoors. The invention of printing aided the performance of composed music greatly as people who were amateur musicians and singers could begin to perform motets, madrigals and other pieces.

The 1500s

The polyphonic style came to its height in the 1500s in the work of composers such as Victoria, Byrd, Palestrina and Lassus. It tended to become increasingly complex, as in the famous motet *Spem In Alium* by Tallis, which was written in 1573 for eight choirs and has 40 separate parts! Not all people favoured such intricate music, especially as it obscured the words. Popular songs became simple tunes often accompanied by the lute, and choral music in churches was simplified so that everyone could sing the same words together even if they were singing different notes in separate parts. This became important in the 1500s as churches in some countries began to use their own languages instead of Latin.

This simplification allowed composers to develop the use of harmony in their music. Previously the notes used in all the parts of a piece were the notes of one of the ancient Greek scales. Although various harmonies were produced by the different parts in polyphonic music, sticking to one scale gave the music a static quality. In modern terms, the music never changed key. In the 1500s, European music began to move away from the Greek scales and towards the major and minor scales that are used in music today. By doing so, it could begin to make use of different keys and introduce a movement of harmony that is fundamental to our appreciation of music.

This development finally made European music totally different from music elsewhere. The music of Asia and Africa never developed the use of changing keys and so retained its ancient, timeless, trancelike quality. Western music was set well on the road to music that has a sense of continual movement and contrasts.

Famous Pieces of Early Music

Pérotin (Perotinus Magnus)	*Sederunt Principes (Gradual For The Feast Of St Stephen)*	c 1200
Machaut	*La Messe De Notre Dame*	1364
Dunstable	*Veni Sancte Spiritus*	1431
Dufay	*Mass: Se La Face Ay Pale*	c 1450
Josquin Des Près	*El Grillo*	c 1520
Tallis	*The Lamentations Of Jeremiah The Prophet*	c 1560
Palestrina	*The Song Of Songs*	1584
Byrd	*My Ladye Nevells Book*	1591
Victoria	*O Magnum Mysterium*	1592
Dowland	*Lachrimae*	1604

The Birth of Opera

The importance placed on words in music produced a completely new kind of music in Europe. This was opera, which was born in Italy at the beginning of the 1600s. The first opera that is still performed is *Orfeo*, composed by Monteverdi in 1607. The story, as in many early operas, is about a legend and concerns Orpheus and his descent into the underworld. The music is simple, consisting of recitative (accompanied speech) and arias, which are basically songs. But the very simplicity of the music allows the words and actions of the opera to come across with power and intensity, supporting the singers in their roles.

However, opera was nothing new in the East. In China, it had already become a fully-fledged form, similar to European opera in the use of speech and song and descriptive music played by an orchestra, however different the actual music may have sounded. In Japan, a style of drama known as noh theatre had developed that combined acting with music. These kinds of music are described in *Music Around the World*.

In Europe, opera developed during the next two centuries. In France, it was combined with ballet in the opera-ballets of Rameau and Lully, which were often spectacular entertainments. In Britain and Germany, Purcell, Handel and Gluck wrote dramatic operas. Opera singers started to become famous and were feted, rather like popular singers today.

In religious music, the new emphasis on words led to the development from about 1600 of large-scale vocal works that told Bible stories – rather like opera but without action. This was the beginning of the cantata and oratorio, which came to a height with the vocal works of J. S. Bach and Handel in Germany and Britain in the 1700s.

Top The opera *Dido And Aeneas* by Purcell.

Above Lully's opera *Alceste* being performed at Paris in 1674.

Right The Italian composer Claudio Monteverdi, a pioneer of opera.

Early Operas

Composer	Title	First Performance
Peri	*Dafne*	Florence 1598
Monteverdi	*Orfeo*	Mantua 1607
	The Coronation Of Poppaea	Venice 1642
Lully	*Alceste*	Paris 1674
	Armide	Paris 1686
Purcell	*Dido And Aeneas*	London 1689
Handel	*Julius Caesar*	London 1724
	Xerxes	London 1738
Rameau	*Castor And Pollux*	Paris 1737
Gluck	*Orpheus And Eurydice*	Vienna 1762

Baroque Music

From about 1650, instrumental music began to come to the fore. The quality of instruments improved, especially in the violins and other string instruments made by the Amati and Stradivari families in Italy. New instruments were invented, including the piano in Italy in 1709. The orchestra, which had begun to develop in the opera house, gained its basic form of a body of strings plus other instruments, and techniques of organ and harpsichord playing advanced greatly. Furthermore, public concerts of music began to take place. Composers, given new opportunities for music making and a wide range of new sounds to exploit, responded enthusiastically, masters such as Vivaldi and Telemann turning out hundreds of instrumental compositions.

The diversity of instruments and the ability of players spurred the imagination of composers and new kinds of instrumental pieces developed. From simple compositions – suites of dances, sets of variations on themes and fantasias that freely embroider a melody – large-scale forms in which the musical structure is more involved started to emerge. These were principally the sonata and concerto, in which composers began to write music in contrasting sections or movements and for contrasting groups of players within the orchestra or for a solo musician and orchestra. In character, the music was still contrapuntal (written in separate, interweaving lines), and the polyphonic music of previous centuries came to a magnificent climax in the fugue, a form in which the separate parts are complete in their own right but related so that they constantly imitate one another as they interlace to create a perfect musical whole.

Composers were now concerned with building their musical ideas into finely wrought musical structures, an art similar in spirit to the elaborate, involved architecture of the 1700s. This is known as baroque architecture and so the music of this period is often known as baroque music. Though solid in structure, it may nevertheless be tuneful and graceful and by no means heavy and serious. Baroque music is noted for its joyful exuberance and dancing rhythms. This is

evident in the music of the greatest composers of this period – Domenico Scarlatti, Corelli, Handel and above all J. S. Bach, whose extraordinary technical ability enabled him to pour out both instrumental and vocal music with immense emotional power. Strangely, Bach's music was not well known in his lifetime and some of his greatest works were not even performed. It was through the efforts of Mendelssohn a century later that Bach became and has remained so justly renowned.

Above J. S. Bach, the greatest composer of the baroque period.

Famous Pieces of Baroque Music

Corelli	Violin Sonata No 12 (La Folia)	1700
	Christmas Concerto	1712
J. S. Bach	Toccata and Fugue in D minor	c 1710
Vivaldi	The Four Seasons	1725
Telemann	Suite in A minor for Recorder	c 1730
Domenico Scarlatti	Cat's Fugue	1738
Handel	Arrival of the Queen of Sheba	1749

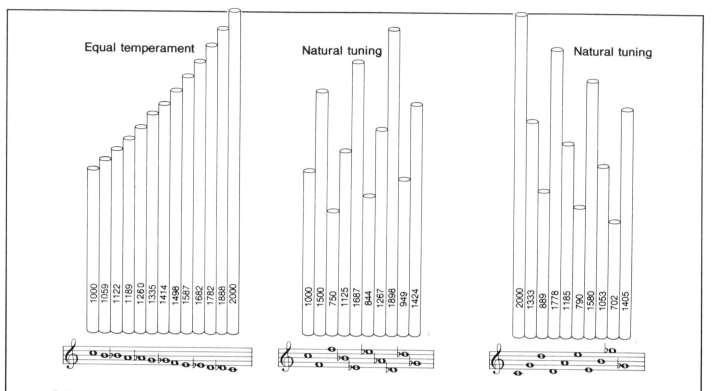

Equal Temperament

Before about 1700, instruments were tuned to different notes according to the methods developed in ancient times. These were based on the natural principle that two notes an octave apart (for example C and C below) are produced by strings or pipes whose lengths are in the ratio 2:1 – that is, one is exactly twice the length of the other. Furthermore, two notes a fifth apart (for example C and F below) are in the ratio 1.5:1 – the first string or pipe is exactly half as long again as the second. Starting from one note at a standard pitch (say C), the pitches of other notes can be found by using these principles. F (a fifth below C) can be found from C and then G (a fifth above C), followed by B flat (a fifth below F) and D (a fifth above G) and so on.

This system of tuning worked well before about 1600, because the music did not change key and was restricted to seven different notes (the notes of the ancient Greek scale in use – for example, A B C D E F G). But from about 1600, composers began to write music that changed key. Instead of using just the seven notes of the scale, all twelve semitones available in the octave were required so that sharps and flats could be used to change key. This began to cause severe problems, especially with keyboard instruments. As the music changed key, it went out of tune.

The reason was that tuning by natural principles produces notes that get successively more and more out of tune. Using this system, it is impossible to get all twelve semitones in tune. If C and G are correct, then C sharp and G sharp will be slightly out and vice-versa. The tuning system was therefore changed by tempering (adjusting) the pitch of the notes so that all twelve semitones are equal intervals. This system, which we use today, is therefore called equal temperament. The interval of an octave remained at 2:1 but the interval of a fifth was very slightly flattened from 1.5:1 to 1.498:1, and this brought all twelve semitones into tune. Once equal temperament had been adopted by about 1700, composers could safely write music in all keys. Music began to develop the flow of harmony that characterizes Western classical and popular music today.

Above The lengths of the pipes above the notes represent the pitches of the notes produced by equal temperament and natural tuning, starting with an arbitrary length of 2000 for middle C and 1000 for the C an octave above. The pitches of the notes produced by natural tuning get farther and farther away from those produced by equal temperament, in which two notes a semitone apart are always in the ratio 1.0595:1.

The two examples of natural tuning show how the pitch of G flat is reached from the C above and below by natural tuning, producing two different pitches (1424 and 1405 respectively). In equal temperament, the pitch is 1414, the interval of six semitones always having a ratio of 1.414:1.

The Classical Era

In building their musical structures, baroque composers developed methods of starting the music in a 'home' key and then moving to other keys and back again, thus causing the harmony to move in set patterns from one section of the music to the next. Pieces began to be identified by their home key, like J. S. Bach's famous *Toccata and Fugue in D minor*. Bach in fact wrote two sets of preludes and fugues called *The Well-Tempered Clavier* in all 24 major and minor keys to demonstrate his mastery of the new harmonic movement. This method of composition was then further developed in the music composed from about 1750 to 1830, a time known in music as the classical era.

At the beginning of this period, composers depended on princes, dukes and bishops for their living and these masters demanded a formal, elegant style of music to reflect their status. Composers, principally Haydn and Mozart at Vienna in Austria, responded by developing the symphony and string quartet and also by refining the concerto and sonata.

The complex interweaving lines of the polyphonic age mostly disappeared, replaced by simple contrasts of instrumental sound carrying strong themes and tuneful phrases from one key to another. The players in various sections of the orchestra – and fingers on the keyboard – were now often sounding and playing notes to form chords, thus creating a stronger flow of harmony as the music moved into different keys and back again.

Instrumental music of the middle and late 1700s is renowned for its elegance; it is beautifully composed but often of less emotional power than much other music. However, composers of this time were able to express great feeling in their vocal works – for example in Haydn's oratorios and especially in Mozart's operas, in which the music supports the drama or comedy far more strongly than ever before.

However, the development of the use of harmony at this time was to serve composers well in the years to come, giving them a means of achieving greater expression in instrumental music.

Left The Esterházy Palace at Eisenstadt in Austria, the home of the noble Esterházy family who employed Haydn.

Left The great Austrian classical composer Mozart, who was a musical prodigy. He began composing when he was only six years old and fully developed the classical forms of music during his short life. He died at the age of 35.

Below A scene from Mozart's last opera *The Magic Flute*, which expresses the spirit of freedom.

Right The great German composer Ludwig van Beethoven, who became deaf towards the end of his life. The utter power of Beethoven's music could well be due to his deafness: unable to perform, he concentrated his creative energies totally on composition, not resting until each work was as perfect as he could make it.

Below Schubert, in spectacles at the piano, entertains people at a musical evening.

Famous Works of the Classical Era

Haydn	String Quartet No 77 in C major	1797
	(The Emperor Quartet)	
	The Creation	1798
Mozart	Eine Kleine Nachtmusik	1787
	(A Little Night Music)	
	Symphony No 40 in G minor	1788
Beethoven	Symphony No 5 in C minor	1808
	Piano Concerto No 5 in E flat major	1809
	(The Emperor Concerto)	
Schubert	Symphony No 8 in B minor	1822
	(The Unfinished Symphony)	
	An Sylvia (Who Is Sylvia?)	1828

Beethoven and Schubert

From about 1800, a great change took place. The scene was still Vienna, where Beethoven and Schubert brought the classical era to its height. Composers were no longer the servants of the church, royalty or nobility; they were independent people able to write whatever music they chose and to take any direction that they wished. The public, in attending concerts and opera houses and buying music to perform, could now support composers. Previously, composers had written music virtually to order for immediate consumption and had consequently developed great facility. Vivaldi wrote more than 450 concertos, J. S. Bach nearly 300 cantatas, Haydn about 80 string quartets and Mozart 41 symphonies, for example. Now composers could concentrate more energy on single works to make them as individual and original as possible, expecting performances to continue during their lifetime and thereafter. Beethoven and Schubert each wrote nine symphonies, for example – though sadly neither were to hear their last works, Beethoven because of deafness and Schubert through his tragic early death.

Beethoven and Schubert developed the classical instrumental forms of Haydn and Mozart, writing symphonies, sonatas, string quartets and, in Beethoven's case, concertos but now with great emotional intensity. Beethoven produced works of immense dramatic power, using silent pauses, for example, to create suspense as well as blasts of orchestral sound to thrill audiences – thus founding the instrumentation of the modern symphony orchestra.

Schubert's music, on the other hand, is poetic and lyrical; it has great beauty. This is particularly true of his many songs or lieder, a form that Schubert created by making the piano accompaniment as important as the voice.

Classical Music

The forms that were developed during the classical era have since served composers so well and are still played so much today that all European composed music is known generally as classical music, even though it may not always be music in such classical forms as the symphony.

The complexity of instrumental works such as symphonies and string quartets demanded that all the musicians play exactly together. The music was first performed at a strict unchanging tempo so that everyone kept together. This gave instrumental music a bland quality, so orchestras and ensembles began to speed up and slow down here and there to give the music more variety and expression. Conductors became necessary to direct orchestras and with this development, classical music finally abandoned the rhythmic excitement present in the beat of folk and popular music.

The Romantic Movement

From about 1820 through to the end of the century, the music composed in central Europe was mainly romantic in spirit. This does not mean that it was inspired by or portrayed love and romance, though this was sometimes true, for example in Schumann's music. The romantic movement, which occurred in other arts such as painting, aimed to use art to express individual feelings and ideas and portray life and landscape. Formal qualities were less important, and so the forms brought to a peak in the classical era were not much used by later composers. Exceptions included Brahms and later Bruckner and Mahler but their symphonies are imbued with romantic qualities such as lyricism, grandeur and intense drama which can make them very moving.

To enable them to create a wider range of expression in music and to portray subjects in sound, composers needed more resources to produce greater contrast and variety in their music. They did this by developing harmony, introducing new sounds previously considered unpleasant to the ear, and by shifting key unexpectedly. They also extended the range of tone colours that instruments could provide by expanding the orchestra and finding new ways of combining instruments.

The drama and poetry in the music of Beethoven and Schubert foreshadowed the

Left Frédéric Chopin, the great romantic composer, by the painter Delacroix.

romantic movement, of which Chopin and Berlioz were the first great composers. Although they came immediately after Beethoven and Schubert, their music sounds completely different and was revolutionary at the time. Chopin was a great harmonic innovator as well as a prodigious pianist. He was able to take advantage of the recent development of the grand piano to create a new style of piano music of intense expression, later raised by Liszt to a formidable level. Berlioz developed orchestral music in a succession of grand works. He and others, particularly Schumann and Mendelssohn, expressed romantic ideals, often in descriptive music, using the sounds of instruments to paint scenes and reflect moods, as well as in songs.

Famous Pieces of Romantic Music

Chopin	*Revolutionary Study*	1829
Berlioz	*Fantastic Symphony*	1830
Mendelssohn	*Hebrides Overture*	1830
Schumann	*Carnaval*	1835
Liszt	*Les Préludes*	1848
Brahms	*Piano Concerto No 1 in D minor*	1858
Bruckner	*Symphony No 4 in E flat major* (The Romantic Symphony)	1874
Rachmaninov	*Piano Concerto No 2 in C minor*	1901
Mahler	*Symphony No 5 in C sharp minor*	1902
Richard Strauss	*Alpine Symphony*	1915

Grand Opera

These developments in romantic music took place in France and Germany. Grand opera, in which the expression of emotion reaches its greatest height in music, was swept onwards and upwards by the romantic movement. It advanced in Italy and France in the operas of Rossini, Donizetti, Bellini, Gounod and Bizet, which can be high-spirited as well as serious, and attained a climax of dramatic power in the operas of Verdi in Italy and Wagner in Germany (see the table of operas on page 92).

These opera composers developed a style of music that always carries the action forward, shifting mood and pace as necessary but never letting up as the plot unfolds. Verdi could fashion a seamless flow of melody to achieve this purpose, while Wagner developed harmony to the point at which it is in constant motion, continually shifting key to produce a restless, ever-evolving music that can be sustained for several hours. In doing so, Wagner not only advanced opera but all music by stretching the flow of harmony among keys to its limits. To go much further, it would be necessary to abandon the use of keys altogether.

Above A scene from *The Valkyrie*, the opera by Wagner (left). This is one of the great cycle of operas, known as *The Ring Of The Nibelung*, based on German legends.

Below The opera *La Traviata* by Verdi (right) is based on the tragic love story *The Lady Of The Camellias* by Alexandre Dumas.

Nationalist Music

Romantic instrumental music and opera continued into the twentieth century, notably in the operas of Puccini and Richard Strauss as well as in instrumental works by Strauss and Rachmaninov. But alongside it from about 1850 onwards, there grew a desire to put national qualities into music. Many composers did this by utilizing the melodies and dance rhythms of the folk music of their countries, thus creating several distinct national schools. The composers worked in the classical tradition, producing symphonies or concertos, for example, or in the romantic idiom, often writing music that was descriptive of their homelands. But whatever its form, they gave their music a fresh, invigorating sound in conferring a national identity upon it.

The nationalist composers came from outside central Europe, which had dominated music for so long. The various schools

included Elgar, Vaughan Williams and Holst in Britain; Grieg in Norway: Albéniz, Granados and Falla in Spain; Villa-Lobos in Brazil; Smetana, Dvořák and Janáček in Czechoslovakia; Sibelius in Finland; and Kodály and Bartók in Hungary. There was also a strong Russian school of composers who created enduring music that is particularly colourful and vital. Greatest among these is Tchaikovsky, though his music was more central European. Other composers, more Russian, include Borodin, Mussorgsky and Rimsky-Korsakov.

Left Much of the music written by the Finnish composer Jean Sibelius has associations with his country, depicting the landscape of Finland with its many lakes or Finnish legends.

Left Edvard Grieg's music has a Norwegian character that comes from the folk music of Norway. Its charm reflects the beauty of the fiords.

Left The Hungarian composer Béla Bartók often used the rhythms of Hungarian folk dance in his music. He travelled around his country collecting folk songs.

Famous Pieces of Nationalist Music

Smetana	*Má Vlast (My Country)*	1894
Grieg	*Four Norwegian Dances*	1881
Dvořák	*Slavonic Rhapsodies*	1878
Borodin	*In The Steppes Of Central Asia*	1880
Tchaikovsky	*1812 Overture*	1880
Rimsky-Korsakov	*Russian Easter Festival Overture*	1888
Sibelius	*Finlandia*	1899
Vaughan Williams	*Norfolk Rhapsody*	1906
Albeniz	*Iberia*	1909
Kodály	*Dances of Galánta*	1933

Music in North America

While Europe had been developing classical music over a period of about a thousand years, music was of course evolving and spreading elsewhere in the world. The folk music of Asia and the East was well established early on with its basic tradition of a single line of melody swooping and soaring, often over percussive rhythms or a drone. No flow of harmony developed to create musical forms and express feelings as in Europe. The contours of the melody line give the music its form and feeling.

In Africa, folk music evolved with a rhythmic drive unequalled elsewhere in the world, the players setting drum and percussion rhythms against one another to create a complex rhythmic interplay of sounds. The African peoples thus developed a response to the rhythmic flow of the music whereas Asian music principally exploits melodic flow and European music harmonic flow.

So, at this point in the history of music about a century ago, three of the four main regions of the world had created three basic kinds of music. Each had separately used as a foundation one of the three fundamental elements of music: harmony, melody and rhythm. There had been little cross-influence as few people travelled and heard the music of other continents. Some instruments had spread outside their origins; the mouth organ came from China and the banjo from Africa to the West in the 1800s, for example.

A new kind of music combining the separate traditions could only spring up where different peoples came together, and this happened in America from about 1800. The arrival and spread of white pioneers and settlers across North America subjugated the American Indians so that America never developed a kind of music that is truly American in origin. The white people brought their own folk music and also religious music, such as hymns, with its simple but strong harmony. The importation from Africa of black people forced to work as slaves brought the powerful African sense of rhythm into contact with European harmony. This meeting began a new American music unlike any that existed elsewhere and which was eventually to make a vital contribution to the music of the world.

The Origins of Popular Music

From the work songs of the black people and European hymns, spirituals and blues developed. Spirituals were songs for people to sing together, often with great religious fervour and rhythmic vigour, and they evolved into the gospel music of the black churches. Blues on the other hand were individual songs about life. The singers took the major and minor scales that provided the harmony of the music but flattened some of the notes, called blue notes, to give

Below This painting, made in the United States in the early 1800s, shows black people dancing to the music of a banjo and drum. The driving rhythm that black people brought to America from Africa gave rise to popular music.

Right The revolutionary American composer Charles Ives who as well as being a composer had a successful career in insurance.

the music a unique melodic flavour.

In this way, music with a strong harmonic flow and powerful rhythmic drive began to emerge and develop. It grew into all the styles of popular music – ragtime, jazz, rock, soul and so on – which are described in the previous chapter. So great has been the appeal of this music that with the development of records, radio and television in this century, it has spread throughout the world.

Into the Twentieth Century

As the rise of popular music got under way in North America at about the turn of the century, a crisis had developed among composers in Europe. Romantic music had almost reached the limit of key movement. But even though it moved restlessly from one key to another, the music was still tonal, meaning that the harmony still contained the major and minor chords that had existed for so long (and which still exist, for example in popular music). This music could not develop much further without destroying tonality, a step that composers were reluctant to take. But in seeking new ways of writing music, composers had no particular direction in which to go. Several new paths lay ahead and among the first to take them was a great American composer, Charles Ives.

Ives sought to create a totally North American music. He rejected the European tradition and took elements of the music he heard around him, which he put together in a completely new fashion. Ives composed music in which two or more separate things may be going on at once. The music may be in two or more keys and different harmonies and rhythms may be played together – even totally different tunes may be heard at the same time. The result can be mysterious, invigorating and humorous but also, to many ears, dissonant and cacophonous.

Ives was not a professional composer and was isolated from developments in Europe, which later made many of his discoveries independently. He did not create a school of American composition and subsequent advances in classical music were still made by European composers. However, several of the greatest of these composers did go to live in the United States.

Music at the Crossroads

Before about 1900, composers had followed more or less the same path in developing the art of music. There had been the baroque period, then the classical era, followed by the romantic movement. But now composers found themselves at a crossroads as they looked for ways of progressing beyond romantic music.

Firstly, there was a late romantic period with the music of Mahler and Richard Strauss, which took tonality to its limits. Further progress would destroy the sense of key and take away the major and minor chords that had sustained composers for some three centuries. Strauss drew back from this step after almost breaking with tonality in his early music.

New Kinds of Tonality

Other composers came up with several alternative ideas to such a break. Some, including Scriabin and Rimsky-Korsakov in Russia, developed new kinds of scales that gave an exotic flavour while still keeping a sense of key. In France, Debussy used whole tone scales (such as C D E F sharp G sharp A sharp) to create a completely new sound without a sense of key and he also went back to the ancient Greek scales or modes. However, Debussy's main achievement was to pioneer impressionist music, in which sounds are produced mainly for the sensations that they evoke. He conjured up new kinds of harmonies and fresh sounds from the orchestra and the piano, using them to create impressions of subjects and moods, often of breathtaking beauty. Debussy was followed by Ravel, also a master of the orchestra and piano, though Ravel tended to compose in classical forms whereas Debussy could allow his music to move freely.

This music was mainly tonal – it still contained major and minor chords though the harmony flowed in different and unexpected ways. This is also true of the music of several twentieth-century composers, notably Satie, Weill, Prokofiev, Walton, Copland, Britten and Shostakovich, who produced music in both classical and new forms that was fresh without being revolutionary.

Serial Music

A complete break with the past was made by Schoenberg, who in 1921 introduced a totally new type of music known as twelve-note or serial music. Using keys and producing tonal harmony of major and minor chords, composers select notes from the chromatic scale (the twelve semitones in an octave). Some notes are more important than others, one of them giving the home key for example. Schoenberg's idea was to compose music in which all twelve notes are treated equally. He therefore based each piece on a theme or series containing only twelve notes, these being the twelve notes of the chromatic scale. The music is made by repeating the series in all kinds of different ways – reversed, inverted (upside-down) and so on. In doing so, Schoenberg rejected the tonal major and minor harmonies. Any

Below The ballet *Petrushka* by Stravinsky broke new ground in 1911 with its introduction of bitonality, which combines melodies or harmonies in two different keys. Stravinsky went on to explore this method of composition, notably in the ballet *The Rite Of Spring*. The music for these ballets is so important that it is often played alone without dancing.

other groups of notes could sound as the various forms of the series were combined together, so totally new atonal harmonies resulted. Schoenberg was followed by Berg and Webern, who developed the serial method of composition. With Berg, it gained intense dramatic power while Webern's music has an icy precision. However, to many people, the atonal harmony makes the music sound unpleasant and it has never become popular.

Fresh and Vivid Sounds

Three great composers of this century found other ways forward. These were Stravinsky, Bartók and Varèse, though Stravinsky took up serial music in his last years and gave it his own personal sound. Stravinsky exploded on to the musical scene with the three ballets described on page 98, which contained several revolutionary musical ideas. In *Petrushka*, for example, Stravinsky expressed the half-human, half-puppet nature of Petrushka by writing his music in two keys at once. In *The Rite Of Spring*, the music is made savagely rhythmic by using bars of uneven and irregular lengths. Bartók composed music that was often in classical forms such as string quartets and concertos, but in which the various themes develop in unusual and highly logical ways. Such intellectual procedures not only advanced music but greatly excited the musical imagination of these composers and their music can be exciting, colourful, mysterious, dramatic; it is never dull.

In his middle years, Stravinsky turned to the music of the past for his inspiration, interpreting it in his own way. This music is known as neoclassical, meaning a reviving of classical styles. Varese, on the other hand, was always an experimenter in sound. He produced totally new concepts, such as *Ionisation* (1931), a work for percussion instruments only, and helped to pioneer a music of the future – electronic music.

Pioneering Works of the Turn of the Century

Debussy	*Prelude To The Afternoon Of A Faun*	1894
Richard Strauss	*Salome*	1905
Ives	*The Unanswered Question*	1906
Scriabin	*The Poem Of Ecstasy*	1908
Stravinsky	*Petrushka*	1911
	The Rite Of Spring	1913
Bartók	*Allegro Barbaro*	1911
Schoenberg	*Pierrot Lunaire*	1912

Above The French composer Claude Debussy pioneered impressionist music, producing fresh sounds of great beauty from the piano and the symphony orchestra.

Above Arnold Schoenberg, the Austrian composer who created serial music, a revolutionary method of composition that is very formal.

Above Picasso's drawing of the Russian composer Igor Stravinsky who explored new methods of composition in ballet music.

Modern Music

During this century, with the rise of popular music and a wealth of classical music of the past to claim people's attention, modern music has become a minority interest. However, this has allowed composers to develop their music in all kinds of directions and the forty years since World War II have seen swifter and greater changes in classical music than ever before. All have had one purpose in common – a desire to create musical sounds that are completely new and have never been heard before. Several styles of modern music now exist. However different and strange they may sound compared with the music of the past, all of them, especially in live performance, are in their own way capable of providing just as strong a musical experience.

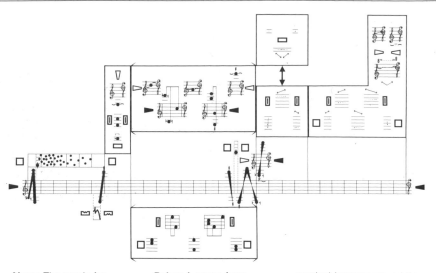

Above The music for *Zyklus*, a percussion work composed by Stockhausen in 1959, uses new and graphic ways of notating music to represent musical sounds. It can also be played upside-down.

Below A scene from Stockhausen's opera *Donnerstag*, first performed in 1981. Here the hero Michael – played by trumpeter Markus Stockhausen (the composer's son) – makes a musical journey around the world, encountering different peoples. The opera combines electronic and acoustic sounds that bombard the audience from all directions.

Above The French composer Pierre Boulez, who has become a brilliant conductor as a result of conducting his own works.

Above The American experimental composer John Cage, whose works include one that consists of silence. In such pieces, Cage challenges our ideas of the very nature of music.

Organization or Chance?

Serial music was taken to great extremes in the 1950s by Boulez and Stockhausen. As well as the pitch of the notes, their duration and volume were also determined by mathematical procedures that resulted in music of immense complexity. A whole variety of unusual composing techniques was also employed by Messiaen, among them imitations of birdsong, the incorporation of Indian music and ways of grouping the rhythms of the music into structures.

Composers such as Cage went in the reverse direction to such complexity of organization and invented music in which the choice of notes was to some degree left to chance. Various methods were found to show the performers how to play the music. For example, the music could be written in separate sections for the performer to play in any order. Composers also developed different ways of writing music, often using diagrams to indicate the effects they wanted rather than using conventional notation to write out the music exactly, as in the music of Penderecki for example.

Such methods have produced all kinds of new sounds from conventional instruments, which are often grouped together in unorthodox ways. Composers have also stretched the sound-making possibilities of individual instruments to their limits. Cage, for example, introduced the prepared piano in which objects are inserted between the strings to change the sounds.

Electronic Sounds

New sounds have also been provided by technology. The development of the tape recorder enabled composers to record sounds and then manipulate them, transforming and combining the sounds in various ways to assemble a new piece of music on tape. At first, normal sounds were recorded and transformed to produce a style known as concrete music. Then, from the early 1950s, sounds produced by electronic means were used and electronic music was born. Pieces were composed that exist only as recordings on tape, but many composers have also produced works in which the tapes are played with performing musicians. Stockhausen has been the main figure in the development of electronic music. He has also investigated ways of altering the sound of instruments with electronic devices as well as employing spatial effects in which the sounds come to the listener from different directions.

Minimal Music

In the mid-1960s, a new movement began in North America in reaction against the complexity and resulting unpopularity of modern music. It is called minimal music and has produced music of great simplicity and immediate appeal in the work of Terry Riley, Steve Reich and Philip Glass. Basically, the music is built up of short phrases that are constantly repeated, but subjected to a process of gradual change. The music, utterly different from anything before, is generally rhythmic and often trancelike in its effect.

Music in the Future

Modern music is in these ways possibly undergoing a confused period of transition from which a strong new direction will emerge. The development of the computer is likely to have a great effect on modern music and may prove to be its salvation. Computers now exist that can be programmed to produce any kind of sound. With such an instrument, composers and creative musicians have a greater means for using sound to move and entertain us than has ever existed before. The sound of music is likely to change greatly, but its effect on people should remain as powerful as ever.

Pioneering Works of Modern Times

Messiaen	Quatuor Pour La Fin Du Temps (Quartet For The End Of Time)	1941
	Turangalîla	1947
Cage	Sonatas And Interludes	1948
	Music Of Changes	1951
Stockhausen	Kontra-Punkte	1953
	Gesang Der Jünglinge (Song Of The Youths)	1956
Boulez	Le Marteau Sans Maître (Mallet Without Master)	1954
Varèse	Poeme Électronique (Electronic Poem)	1958
Penderecki	Threnody For The Victims Of Hiroshima	1960
Riley	In C	1964
Reich	Drumming	1971

The Mechanics of Music

What makes music work? How do we hear music, and how do musicians put notes together to create music? Music may be a gift, but not all musicians are born with the ability to make music. To be musical, most people have to learn about music – though this can bring out a natural talent for music. But however musical you are, learning how music works will give you a broad basis of musical knowledge that increases enjoyment of music, both in listening and playing.

To make music, it helps to have a good musical ear, which means a good sense of pitch. A few people have such a good musical ear that they can play instruments or compose music without learning anything about music. They hear the music in their heads and can play the notes or write them down without making mistakes. These people are said to have perfect pitch, and while it is an enviable ability that only few possess, it is not necessary to have perfect pitch to be a great musician.

Many people instead have a sense of relative pitch, which can be gained by training the ear to recognize notes. If one note is given or known, then a person with relative pitch can correctly hear other notes by gauging how much higher or lower in pitch they are than the given note. Most good musicians develop relative pitch with practice.

A good sense of time is also necessary in music and this too can be natural or developed with practice. However, there is more to music than sensing which note is which and when to play it. To know how music works, it is necessary to know what happens when we produce and hear sounds. It is also important to understand how these sounds are put together to create music.

Producing and Hearing Music

To produce any sound, whether music, speech or noise, something has to vibrate rapidly. The surface or the air inside a musical instrument vibrates to give sound. When you speak or sing, the vocal cords inside your throat vibrate. And when objects strike or rub against each other to produce a noise, their surfaces vibrate.

As this vibration occurs, it sets up vibrations in the surrounding air. These vibrations travel outwards through the air,

Left This home music computer can be programmed to play music. The notes are entered by using the computer keyboard and the music appears on the screen. A knowledge of music is required to program a music computer, but a keyboard may also be connected to the computer and played in the normal way.

producing sound waves. When the waves strike your ears, they cause the eardrum in each ear to vibrate too. Signals then travel along nerves from the eardrums to the brain and you hear the sound. You can tell the direction of the sound because the sound waves strike one ear just before the other.

Pitch and Frequency

When you hear a musical sound, for example by pressing a key on a piano or singing a note, it has a certain pitch. The pitch of the sound is how high or deep it sounds. On the keyboard, the notes get higher in pitch to the right and deeper in pitch to the left. Your voice has a certain range of pitch, depending on your age and sex. This is because of the size of your vocal cords. Men have longer vocal cords than women or children and so possess deeper voices. Generally, the bigger an instrument is, the deeper it can sound.

The reason that a musical sound has a certain pitch is that the sound waves vibrate at a particular rate called the frequency. This is the number of vibrations in a second. The faster the vibration, the higher the pitch. We can hear sounds which vibrate from about 20 times a second up to as much as 20,000 times a second. Frequency is measured in units called hertz (Hz for short), so that a sound with a frequency of 1,000 Hz vibrates at a rate of 1,000 times a second.

To produce musical notes, either a string, a column of air, the surface of an instrument or a loudspeaker vibrates. In instruments, the pitch given out depends on three things: the length, tension and weight of the vibrating medium. The longer it is, the deeper the pitch that is produced. Tension means the tightness of a stretched string or surface, and a greater tension gives a higher pitch. Weight causes pitch to vary so a thin string gives a higher note than a thick string of the same length and tension.

Loudness or Volume

The loudness or volume of the sound depends on the strength of the sound waves. The vibrations are stronger in a loud sound than a soft sound. Playing or singing with more force therefore gives a louder sound. But it does not change the pitch, unless you also happen to produce a harmonic.

Tuning Up

Most musical instruments produce the notes of the chromatic scale, which are the notes given by the black and white keys on a piano or organ. The pitch of each note is determined by equal temperament (see page 134). So that all the notes are in tune with each other when instruments play together, the pitch of one note is adjusted to a standard pitch called concert pitch. This pitch has a frequency of 440 Hz for the A above middle C, and it is to this note that an orchestra tunes before a concert starts. The musicians adjust their instruments so that this note and then all the other notes are in tune, though players sometimes have to make small adjustments as they play to keep in tune.

A piano tuner also uses concert pitch to tune the A above middle C and then tunes the other notes in relation to it. It is possible to tune instruments using electronic tuning devices that indicate whether any note is sharp, flat or in tune.

Above The sound waves that come from a high-pitched and soft instrument such as a violin (right) are close together and of low energy or strength. The waves pass the ear at a high rate or frequency, giving a high-pitched note. Deep and loud sounds, such as those produced by a tuba (left), have sound waves that are farther apart and of high energy. They have a low frequency, giving a low-pitched note.

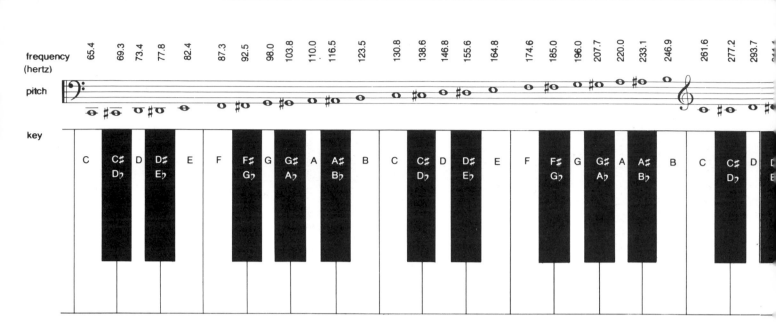

frequency (hertz)	65.4	69.3	73.4	77.8	82.4	87.3	92.5	98.0	103.8	110.0	116.5	123.5	130.8	138.6	146.8	155.6	164.8	174.6	185.0	196.0	207.7	220.0	233.1	246.9	261.6	277.2	293.7

Tone

The tone quality of an instrument is the kind of sound that it produces. The tone of a violin makes it sound different from a flute or a trumpet, for example. The reason that different instruments have different tones is that they are played in different ways. But how does the actual sound itself differ?

Even though you hear just one note at one pitch, a musical sound does in fact contain several notes at different pitches. You hear only the note at the lowest pitch because it is much louder than the other notes, which are usually higher harmonics that are produced at the same time as the main note. The number and strength of these other notes make one instrument sound different from another. If they are comparatively numerous and loud, though still not strong enough to be heard separately, they give a rich, bright sound – as in a violin or trumpet. If the higher notes are few and quiet, the tone is mellow and round, as in the flute and clarinet. In bells and chimes, the higher notes are very strong and you may be able to hear them separately.

The way in which the sounds change in volume and tone as they are produced is also very important in enabling our ears to tell one instrument from another. Synthesizers imitate instruments and produce new sounds by generating harmonics electronically and mixing them together to create a musical sound with a particular tone.

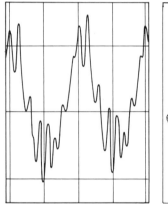

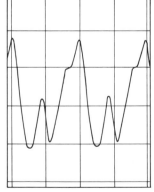

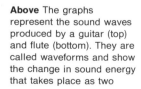

Above The graphs represent the sound waves produced by a guitar (top) and flute (bottom). They are called waveforms and show the change in sound energy that takes place as two waves reach the ear. Sounds with different tones have different waveforms. A bright sound, such as that produced by the guitar, has a jagged waveform. The flute has a mellow tone, which results in a smooth waveform. Understanding waveforms is important in creating electronic and computer music.

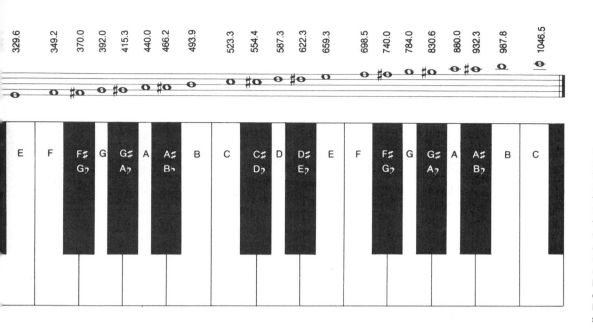

329.6 349.2 370.0 392.0 415.3 440.0 466.2 493.9 523.3 554.4 587.3 622.3 659.3 698.5 740.0 784.0 830.6 880.0 932.3 987.8 1046.5

| E | F | F♯ G♭ | G | G♯ A♭ | A | A♯ B♭ | B | C | C♯ D♭ | D | D♯ E♭ | E | F | F♯ G♭ | G | G♯ A♭ | A | A♯ B♭ | B | C |

Left The notes produced by a keyboard instrument and their frequencies. The range covers four octaves from the C two octaves below middle C to the C two octaves above middle C. The piano and other acoustic keyboard instruments have a wider range than this. Electronic keyboards may have fewer octaves, but the range can be changed by pressing a switch.

Harmonics

If you watch someone playing a fanfare on a bugle, you will see that the musician gets different notes just by blowing. What happens is that the column of air inside the bugle can vibrate as a whole, or as two halves, three thirds, four quarters and so on, depending on the lip pressure. As the air column breaks up into smaller vibrating sections, the pitch of the note gets higher. A set of notes called harmonics, overtones or partials can be obtained.

These harmonics are produced on all brass instruments, and they can be obtained on other instruments as well by using special fingering. On string instruments like the violin, guitar and harp, harmonics have a delicate, ethereal sound.

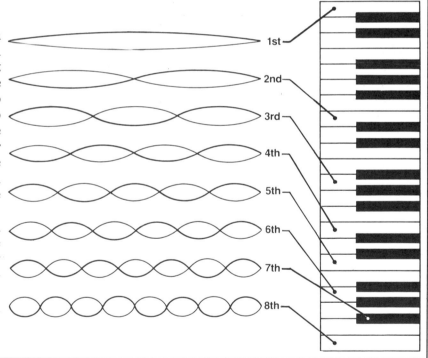

1st
2nd
3rd
4th
5th
6th
7th
8th

Acoustics

The sound that you hear when an instrument is played or a person sings depends greatly on your surroundings. Unless you are outside, some of the sound waves bounce off the walls and ceiling before reaching your ears. For this reason some sound waves take longer to reach you than others. The notes you hear are actually longer than those produced by the musician or singer because

they take some time to die away.

This effect is called reverberation or echo, and in the right amount it improves the sound quality of the music. If there is too little reverberation, the music sounds dry and thin. But if there is too much, it becomes thick and muddy and it is difficult to hear all the notes being produced. When a concert hall is built, the architect has to consider its acoustics (the amount of reverberation that will occur). The acoustics depend on the shape of the hall and the materials used, and designing the hall so that the music sounds good in every seat is not easy. Sometimes, electronic devices are used to improve the reverberation. This is often done in recording and broadcasting studios so that the engineers can control the sound quality.

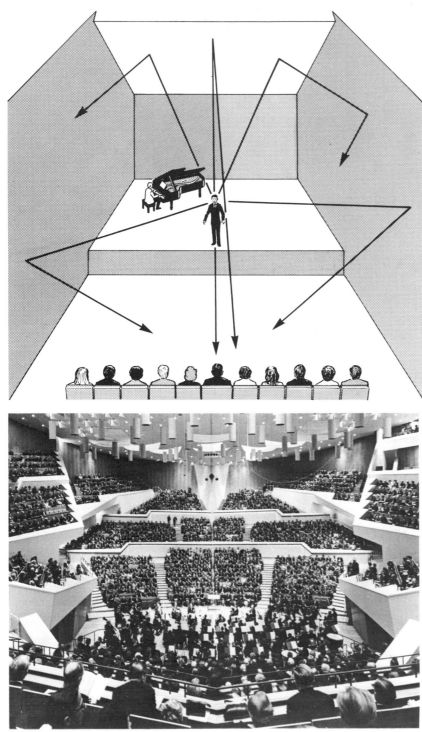

Below The sound waves from a performer bounce off all surfaces before reaching the ear, affecting the acoustics or sound quality of a hall. Modern concert halls, like this hall in Berlin, are designed to have good acoustics.

The Elements of Music

When people create music, however simple or complex, it is normally made up of three fundamental elements: melody, harmony and rhythm. It is to the use of these elements that we mainly respond when we hear music. For example, we may find the melody of a tune beautiful, the harmony of a dirge sad and the rhythm of a dance lively. Musicians put these elements together in different ways to create music that is satisfying both to themselves and to their listeners.

Melody
A melody is basically a group of musical notes played one after the other. You can take an instrument and pick out a few notes to create a melody. In fact, composers often 'hunt' for melodies in this way. However, a good melody is more than just a random collection of notes. It must have a particular character of its own so that it is unlike other melodies, and it should have a good 'shape' so that it feels complete when it is played. The ability to compose a good and original melody is rare and musicians who can do so are very fortunate.

A melody can vary from a short tune to a long line of notes, as in Asian music and popular music such as jazz and rock in which a melodic line may be improvised by a musician. However, the melody is usually made up of short phrases assembled together, often by repeating a phrase in different ways. It is the short phrase that makes a melody distinctive, especially if it is catchy or instantly memorable. The composer or player puts the various phrases together so that they answer one another and form a complete melody.

Using Scales In creating melody, most music makes use of scales. A scale is a sequence of notes that rises or falls one octave. The black notes on the piano form a scale of five notes – F sharp, G sharp, A sharp, C sharp and D sharp – before the first note (F sharp) is reached again. This five-note scale is called a pentatonic scale and it is common in the folk music of many countries. Tunes can be written using just these five notes; for example, *Auld Land Syne* is just one well-known pentatonic tune; it starts on C sharp.

However, most melodies in classical and popular music use major and minor scales, which have seven notes each a tone or semitone apart. The white notes from C to C above give a major scale, while the scale from A to A above is a minor scale. These scales have different characters because they contain different sequences of tones and semitones, the major being often happy or cheerful while the minor is sad or mysterious. In creating melodies, musicians choose notes from the scales to give the music particular feelings.

Keys These scales can start on any note, and the first note of the opening scale gives the key of the melody. The melody usually either stays in this scale or returns to it at the end, giving a sense of returning home and completing the melody as the melody ends. But instead of saying that the melody uses a particular scale, we say that is it in a certain home key – for example, G major or B minor, meaning that the melody begins and ends with a major scale beginning on G or a minor scale beginning on B. In folk music, melodies tend to stick to the same scale throughout but in classical and popular music, they often move into different keys.

Harmony

Harmony is the sound that occurs when two or more musical notes are played or sung at the same time. Any number of notes can sound together but most combinations do not sound pleasant, as you can find out by pressing several keys at random on a piano. But if you take any group of five white keys and play the first, third and fifth keys only, then a pleasant harmony results. The three notes form chords (combinations) called triads that are the basis of harmony. This works for any five black keys too, though the chords may be slightly different.

When musicians make music, they combine the different notes that make up the music to give a pleasant harmony. Usually the harmony accompanies a melody and it is often formed by combining notes that are in the same scale as the notes of melody. The

melody normally has the highest notes and the other notes go beneath the melody and harmonize with it. As the notes combine, triads and other chords occur that are made up of notes in the scale in use at that time. Major and minor scales give major and minor chords that have similar sensations – major chords are happy and cheerful whereas minor chords sound sad and mysterious.

Above This music of this band, the Guest Stars, makes full use of the three fundamental elements of music – melody, harmony and rhythm. The melody or tune of a piece is sung or played by a melodic instrument such as the saxophone. The guitar and keyboards may play chords that give a harmony to the melody. The notes played by the bass guitar are the basis of the harmony. The drums and percussion are rhythm instruments and play a lively rhythm that drives the music along.

Chord Symbols

In popular music, songs are often sung and tunes played with a simple accompaniment on the piano or guitar. The accompaniment provides a harmony to the melody of the song or tune, but many musicians do not bother to write out the harmony in full. Instead they use chord symbols, which are signs that indicate the harmony to be played. The players read or remember the symbols and play music that gives the chords indicated by the symbols. This is not a strict system and it allows the musicians a lot of freedom in choosing which notes to play.

The symbols are placed above or below the notes of the song or tune and consist of a letter often followed by 'm' or a number – for example F, Am or G7. The letter indicates the notes of a triad chord in a major key, or a minor key if it is followed by m. F therefore indicates an F major triad (F A C), and Am indicates an A minor triad (A C E). The number indicates an extra note above the first or root note, so that G7 signifies the harmony G B D F (F being seven notes above G).

Major and Minor Scales and Keys

A major scale is made up of notes in a fixed sequence of tones (T) and semitones (S). The order is always TTSTTTS when ascending, as in the G major scale.

There are three kinds of minor scales, but the main one (the melodic minor) has the sequence TTSTTST when descending, as in the B minor scale.

Major and minor scales can start with any of the twelve notes in the octave, so there are twelve of each kind. The use of one of these scales to open and close a melody places it in a certain key given by the first note of the scale. To save writing the sharps or flats of notes in the scale every time they occur in a melody, the sharps or flats are put at the beginning of the music in the key signature. These are the twelve major and minor keys.

Above This keyboard music by J. S. Bach is composed in four-part counterpoint, and Bach has written it so that the different parts show clearly. Because each hand has to play two different parts, it is difficult to play.

Sharps/Flats In Key Signature	Major Key	Minor Key
None	C major	A minor
1 sharp	G major	E minor
1 flat	F major	D minor
2 sharps	D major	B minor
2 flats	B flat major	G minor
3 sharps	A major	F sharp minor
3 flats	E flat major	C minor
4 sharps	E major	C sharp minor
4 flats	A flat major	F minor
5 sharps/7 flats	B major/C flat major	G sharp minor/A flat minor
5 flats/7 sharps	D flat major/C sharp major	B flat minor/A sharp minor
6 sharps/6 flats	F sharp major/G flat major	D sharp minor/E flat minor

The use of harmony emphasizes these feelings. And as a melody moves into different keys, various sequences of chords occur to produce a flow of harmony. The changing chords give sensations of restlessness, suspension, and particularly of resolution, which occurs at the end of a melody or phrase as the final harmony is reached and the music sounds complete. A change of harmony that produces a resolution is called a cadence; a very common cadence is the 'Amen' at the end of a hymn, for example.

The use of harmony is a very powerful way of giving a piece of music a particular character. A melody or repeated phrases within a melody can be given different kinds of harmony to vary the effect of the music, and sequences just of chords following one another without a melody can create tremendous atmosphere in music.

Counterpoint

Playing chords beneath a melody is just one way of producing harmony. Another way is to play or sing one or more extra melodies that produce harmony with the first melody. This method of making music is called counterpoint. A simple method of counterpoint is used to create a round, in which voices singing the same melody enter one after the other. But most counterpoint has several separate melodies proceeding at the same time. As this is difficult to produce, counterpoint is mainly limited to classical music.

Melody, Harmony and Counterpoint

These three constituents of music can be illustrated by showing how they are used in the first part of the following well-known tune, which is variously known as *God Save The Queen*, *God Save America* and *My Country 'Tis Of Thee*. Ask someone to play the music for you if necessary.

The melody is made up of three phrases. The second phrase is similar to the first with the notes only slightly changed. The third phrase is an answering phrase that completes the melody. The whole melody uses notes in the scale of G major.

This music gives the melody with its standard harmony. There are no sharps or flats apart from the G major key signature, showing that the harmony uses notes in this key.

This music gives the melody again, but this time with a very unusual harmony that makes it sound dramatic and mysterious. A lot of sharps and flats shows that the harmony moves through several different keys, ending in E minor instead of G major.

In this version, the melody is harmonized with three other melodies to produce counterpoint. Each of the three extra melodies is also tuneful on its own, yet all four combine to give a good flow of harmony.

Music Terms

Accidental A sign such as a sharp, flat or natural that changes the pitch of a note. It acts only for the bar containing the accidental.

Bass Any sound that is deep in pitch, as opposed to treble.

Chord Any combination of notes that sound together at the same time.

Clef The sign which indicates the pitch of the lines in the staff. Two clefs are commonly used: the treble clef and bass clef.

Flat The sign which lowers the pitch of a note by one semitone. A double flat, lowers a note by two semitones. Also, a note that is flat is a note that is slightly below the correct pitch.

Interval The difference in pitch between any two notes.

Major In a major key or scale, the first and third notes are four semitones apart, for example C and E. A major chord is basically formed by the first, third and fifth notes of a major scale.

Minor In a minor key or scale, the first and third notes are three semitones apart, for example C and E flat. A minor chord is basically formed by the first, third and fifth notes of a minor scale.

Natural The sign which cancels the effect of any sharp or flat.

Octave An interval of 12 semitones – that is, between any note and the next note having the same letter-name, for example between C and the next C (above or below).

Semitone The smallest interval normally used in music. Any two notes next to each other on an instrument are usually a semitone apart.

Sharp The sign which raises the pitch of a note by one semitone. A double sharp raises a note by two semitones. Also, a note that is sharp is a note that is slightly above the correct pitch.

Staff or Stave The five lines on which music is written.

Tempo The speed at which a piece or section of music goes.

Tone An interval of two semitones. Also the sound quality of an instrument or voice.

Treble Any sound that is high in pitch, as opposed to bass.

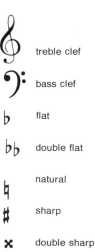

treble clef

bass clef

♭ flat

♭♭ double flat

♮ natural

♯ sharp

𝄪 double sharp

Rhythm

The rhythm of music is the way in which it moves in time. We often use the word rhythm to indicate the feeling of beat or drive that music may have, saying that music has a lively rhythm or is strongly rhythmic. However, rhythm is not only the beat in music. It also means the organization of the notes and rests (silences) in the music into various lengths or durations. The time values of notes and rests are in simple proportions, as shown in the table.

In most music, the notes and rests are grouped into sections called bars that usually each have the same length in time. Within each bar, the various instruments or voices may produce notes of several different time values. These all mesh together to give a feeling of a regular pulse or beat, as in a march for example. The number of beats in the bar is called the metre, and it is usually 2, 3, 4, 6, 8 or 12. The speed at which the beat goes is called the tempo of the music.

In popular music, music for dancing and marching and folk music, the singers and musicians keep the beat going at a constant tempo. They often play or sing in a way that drives the beat forward, making the music lively and energetic. In classical music, musicians and singers tend to speed up and slow down, often under the direction of a conductor. In fact, people do not always perform the time values of the notes with total accuracy; they tend to change the durations slightly to keep together or to drive the music along. Only computer music is totally accurate and the accuracy can make it sound mechanical.

Below Buddy Rich, the jazz drummer, propels the music of his band with driving rhythms.

Time Signatures

At the beginning of a piece of music, two numbers are given to indicate the time signature, such as 4/4 or 3/8. The top number indicates the number of beats in each bar. The bottom number indicates whether each beat is a crotchet, quaver or so on, using the numbers given below. The time signature 4/4 therefore indicates that each bar contains four beats each equal to a crotchet, and 3/8 three beats each equal to a quaver. Normally this number of beats will be heard but in 6 or 12 beat signatures, such as 6/8 and 12/8, there are basically two or four main beats, in this case each containing three quavers.

Right A page from the orchestral score of *The Rite Of Spring* by Stravinsky. The three bars shown each have a different time signature – 7/4, 3/8 and 4/8. This produces irregular rhythms that are a strong feature of the music.

Time Values

The longest time value commonly used is the semibreve, and all other time values are divisions of this value. The number indicates how many of the notes or rests equal a semibreve.

Time Value	Symbol		Number
	Note	Rest	
Semibreve	𝅝	▬	1
Minim	𝅗𝅥	▬	2
Crotchet	𝅘𝅥	𝄽	4
Quaver	𝅘𝅥𝅮	𝄾	8
Semiquaver	𝅘𝅥𝅯	𝄿	16
Demisemiquaver	𝅘𝅥𝅰	𝅀	32
Semidemisemi-quaver	𝅘𝅥𝅱	𝅁	64

A symbol with a dot after it indicates a time value that is half as long again as the symbol without a dot.

Reading and Writing Music

Many people who make music throughout the world, especially singers and performers of folk music, have little if any knowledge of key signatures, harmony, time values, time signatures and so on. They know instinctively or from experience how to make their music and do not need to read music in order to make music. But classical music and to some extent popular music is either so complex or so varied that performers need to be able to read music that has been written down for them. They may learn the music so that they can perform it from memory, which makes a performance easier.

In classical music, composers like to write down their music so that it can be read accurately. As well as giving the pitch and time value of each note, the musician has to understand marks that indicate how the notes are to be played – whether loud or soft, short or smooth – and directions, often in Italian, that indicate such matters as tempo and expression.

Being able to read music is of course essential to anyone who wants to write music. A composer usually starts by sketching out a piece of music, often composing a melody line first and then filling in harmony or counterpoint. Some people work at the piano as they do this, wanting to hear the music and testing out different ideas. But others compose in their heads and write the music down on paper straightaway. All composers can hear in their heads the sounds of instruments or voices performing the music as they compose it. They finally write a score in which all the separate parts for the instruments and voices are written one above the other. From this, the composer or a copyist writes out individual parts for each performer.

Songwriters in popular music do not need to go to quite so much trouble as classical composers; the words, melody line and chord symbols for the harmony (see page 151) are sufficient. The singer and group can then work on this music to build the song into a good number. Sometimes an arranger will take the music and arrange it for an orchestra and singer, using the same methods as a classical composer.

In putting all the elements of music together to create a piece of music, both composers and songwriters have to work very hard. However, the music does not necessarily spring straight into their heads. They may use musical devices or systems to help them develop the piece from an initial phrase or idea. Many songs have set patterns of harmony that a writer may use, just as a composer may choose to work in classical forms such as the symphony or fugue. Manipulation of a musical idea by playing a phrase backwards, writing a melody upside-down, changing time values of notes or experimenting with different harmonies, can give a composer inspiration that may lead to a fine piece of work. In the end, the method does not really matter; it is the result that you hear which is important.

Below The American song writer George Gershwin composing at the piano. Many composers work at the piano as they like to hear the actual sounds of the music.

Italian Musical Directions

Accelerando (Accel.) Get faster.
Adagio Slow.
Agitato Agitated.
Allegretto Fairly fast.
Allegro Fast.
Andante Medium speed (literally 'at a walking pace').
Animato Lively.
Arco Play with the bow.
Cantabile Song-like or flowing in style.
Con Brio Spirited.
Crescendo (Cresc.) Get louder.
Da Capo (D.C.) Play again from the start.
Dal Segno (D.S.) Go back to the sign.
Diminuendo (Dim.) Get softer.
Espressivo With expression.
Forte (f) Loud.
Fortissimo (ff) Very loud.
Glissando (Gliss.) Play with sliding notes.
Grave Slow.
Grazioso Gracefully.
Largo Slow.
Legato Smoothly, with long notes.
Lento Slow.
Maestoso Majestically.

Meno or **Meno Mosso** Slower.
Mezzo Forte (mf) Moderately loud.
Mezzo Piano (mp) Moderately soft.
Moderato At a moderate speed.
Molto Much or very.
Non Troppo Not too much, not exaggerated.
Pianissimo (pp) Very soft.
Piano (p) Soft.
Più More.
Pizzicato (Pizz.) Pluck the string.
Poco A little.
Prestissimo Very, very fast.
Presto Very fast.
Rallentando (Rall.) Slow down.
Ritardando (Rit.) Get slower.
Ritenuto (Rit.) Get slower.
Sforzando (sf or **sfz)** Play the note or chord strongly.
Sostenuto Sustained notes.
Sotto Voce Whispered.
Staccato Short, detached notes.
Tremolo (Trem.) Repeat the note or notes rapidly (literally 'trembling').
Vivace Lively.

Below The British composer Benjamin Britten at work. He is writing his music away from the piano, but not because he cannot play the piano. He is able to write down the notes that come into his head and prefers to work in silence.

Recording and Broadcasting

Throughout the world, there is now hardly a home that does not possess a radio, television set, record player or tape player, and these machines can bring us all kinds of music. With them we can hear virtually any kind of music we choose. And with the latest digital sound equipment and hifi video, we can experience music in our own homes with a realism that may be greater than we would get in a concert hall.

In this century music has become by far the most popular of the arts. While this is a reflection of the power that music has to move people, its enormous popularity is due mainly to recording and broadcasting.

The power of recording and broadcasting to bring all kinds of music to everyone has also affected the course of music itself. The phenomenal rise of popular music in this century has taken place with the growth of records and radio. These means of sound reproduction have enabled budding musicians and singers to hear and learn styles of popular music, and have then spread their music far and wide as they became famous. This process, now aided by high-quality television and video, is likely to continue influencing music greatly.

Left A pop music show in a television studio contrasts with a recording studio in the early days of sound recording. Then the musicians had to crowd together in front of a horn that picked up the music. The sound quality was not good, but modern computer technology can greatly improve the quality of old records.

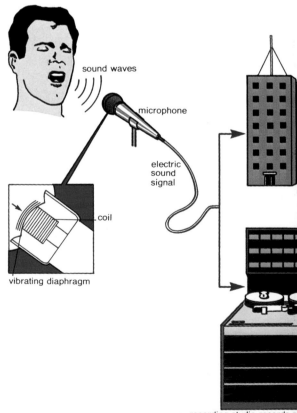

sound waves

microphone

electric sound signal

coil

vibrating diaphragm

recording studio records s

Sound Reproduction

The various processes of sound reproduction all begin and end in the same way. They start with a microphone that detects the sound waves which come from a musical instrument or singer, and they end with a loudspeaker that reproduces the original sound.

A microphone is rather like an electrical ear. It contains a small plate called a diaphragm that vibrates in the same way as the ear drum does when struck by sound waves. The rate of vibration of the diaphragm is the same as the frequency of the sound wave, and the strength of the vibration depends on how loud or soft the sound is. Like the ear, devices connected to the diaphragm produce electrical signals as it vibrates. The ear sends its signals directly to the brain, while the signals from the microphone begin a long journey to the listener in the home.

The electrical signals that come from the microphone vibrate at a certain rate that comes from the pitch of the sound and at a particular strength that comes from the volume of the sound. They are therefore an electrical copy of the original sound waves. Modern technology can do all kinds of things with electrical signals, and the signals that come from the microphone next enter several processing chains.

The signals may be broadcast directly to homes by radio or television or they may be recorded, usually on magnetic tape. The recording may be broadcast, or it may be copied to manufacture discs or tapes for sale to the public. In the home, a radio, television set, disc player, or tape player produces the electrical signals again and feeds them to a loudspeaker. This is where the chains end. The signals cause the loudspeaker to vibrate at the same rate and relative volume as the original sound that entered the microphone. From the loudspeaker, a copy of the original music emerges.

Below The chain of processes that reproduce sound. The sound waves enter a microphone, which produces electric signals. The signals are then either broadcast by radio or television or recorded on cassette tapes or discs, which may be either records or compact discs. Radio and television sets and tape and disc players reproduce the electric signals, and these are then amplified to drive earphones or loudspeakers. Sound waves identical to those that entered the microphone reach the ears.

The best quality radio reproduction is given by FM radio broadcasts received on a stereo radio tuner.

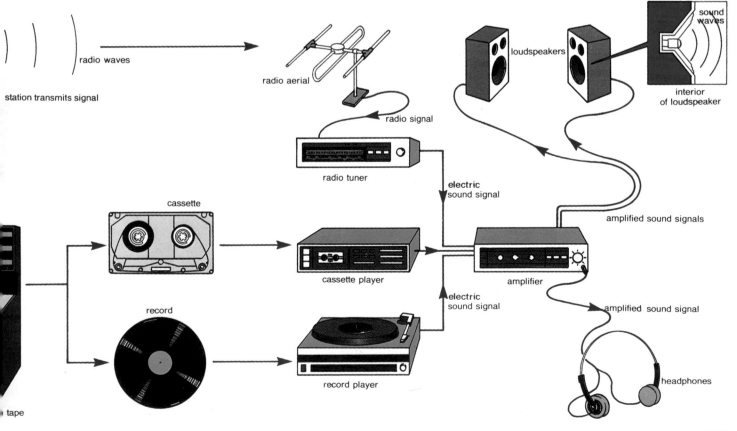

radio waves

station transmits signal

radio aerial

radio signal

radio tuner

loudspeakers

sound waves

interior of loudspeaker

amplified sound signals

electric sound signal

cassette

cassette player

amplifier

electric sound signal

amplified sound signal

record

record player

headphones

tape

159

Analog and Digital

When you listen to music from a radio, television set, disc player or tape player, you are listening to a copy of the original music. But as the sound of the music is changed into electrical signals by a microphone, and the signals are then processed and finally changed back into sound by the loudspeaker in your set or player, they are degraded in quality. The sound that you hear is not quite as good as the original.

The microphones used in recording and broadcasting are very good indeed, and loudspeakers of very high quality can reproduce sound very accurately. The problem of quality lies in the way the signals are processed. There are two basic methods: analog and digital. They work on different principles, digital reproduction giving the better results.

Analog Systems

An analog system uses devices like tape recorders and gramophone records to copy the sound waves. The tape contains invisible magnetic patterns that are copies of the vibrations in the sound waves, as are the wiggles in the groove of a record. These copies are called analogs of the sound waves and the system is imperfect: it cannot produce an exact copy of the original sound waves. The music that results is not quite lifelike, mainly because it cannot get as loud or as soft as the original. Furthermore, an analog system produces noise which may be heard as a hiss, though noise reduction units lessen this problem. Finally, dirt and scratches may produce poor quality and crackles as tapes and records are played.

Digital Systems

Digital systems are based on computers. The signal that comes from the microphone is immediately processed by a computer that measures the sound waves thousands of times a second. It then produces a stream of digits or numbers that measure the strength of the signal. The numbers are then recorded in code on tape and the codes can then be transferred to discs known as compact discs. The compact disc player contains a computer that decodes the numbers and converts them into an electrical signal that goes to the loudspeaker. Because the numbers do not change during the chain of processing, the signal that results is virtually an exact copy of the original signal from the microphone and the sound that results is very lifelike. Furthermore, there is no hiss and no crackling of any kind; the background is totally silent.

It is possible to get gramophone records that are described as being digital recordings. In fact, the record itself is analog but the original recording is made using digital techniques. The record is superior to older all-analog records, but not as good as an all-digital compact disc.

Below Both analog and digital recording methods begin with a microphone (1), which produces an electric signal (2) that varies in energy at exactly the same rate as the sound waves being recorded. In a gramophone record (3), the signal produces a groove that curves at this rate. In a tape recording, a magnetic pattern (4) that varies at the same rate is produced. The pick-up in the record player and play-back head in the tape player produce a copy of the electric signal (8), which goes to a loudspeaker (9) to reproduce the original sound. Both records and tapes are analog recordings.

In digital recording, a converter measures the electric signal at small intervals (5), producing a set of numbers in the form of electric code signals that are first recorded on tape. These codes are transferred to a compact disc, where they are recorded in the form of microscopic pits on the surface of the disc (6). A laser beam in the disc player reads the disc to produce the code signals (7), which are then converted to an electric signal (8) that drives a loudspeaker (9).

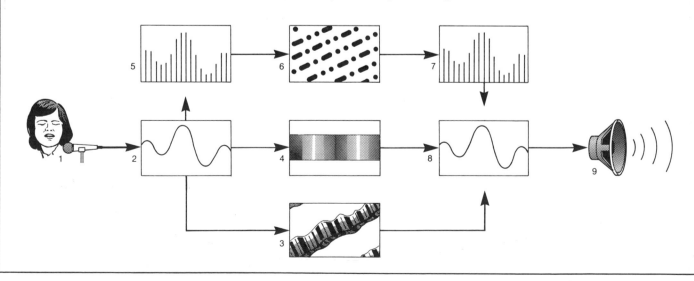

In the Studio

A recording or broadcasting session is an exciting occasion when players and singers aim to produce their very best. It usually takes place in a special studio containing the recording or broadcasting equipment. However, sometimes engineers set up their equipment at a concert to capture the music live. A live recording or broadcast can be exhilarating because an audience is present. However, studio recording does enable the performers to make several versions of the music and choose the best one. Furthermore, musicians can use all the special facilities of the studio to create sounds and effects that are not possible in live performance.

In the studio or at the concert, engineers set up microphones to capture the sound of the music. With classical music, just one or two microphones may be used to get the overall sound of the performers. In popular music and much classical and other music, the engineers use several microphones, possibly one for each performer. The microphones are all connected to a device

Above An orchestra records the music for a feature film starring Sophia Loren. The conductor can look at the screen to make sure that the music is being played at the right point in the film.

Mono, Stereo and Quad

Record and tape players, radios and television sets with only one loudspeaker produce mono or monophonic sound. This means that the music comes from one source and there is no separation of the instruments or voices. Stereo or stereophonic sound comes from two loudspeakers. The instruments and voices are spread out in front of the listener between the two speakers, just as music comes from different directions to both ears at a concert.

Quad or quadraphonic sound is produced in a sound reproduction system that uses four loudspeakers positioned all around the listener. The sound comes from all directions, an exciting experience. Several quad systems, all analog, appeared in the 1970s and disappeared after a few years as quality was low. However, digital techniques could reproduce quadraphonic sound of high quality and it is possible that quad may make a comeback.

called a mixer in the control room of the studio. This mixes the signals from the microphones together to produce a pair of signals. These go to two loudspeakers in the control room, and the engineers operate the mixer to spread the sounds from the microphones between the speakers to give a good stereo sound.

Broadcasting

These signals may then be broadcast, possibly mixed to one signal for mono radio and television using one loudspeaker. The electrical signal goes to a transmitter, where it is changed into a radio signal. The aerial of the radio or television set picks up this signal, and electronic devices inside the set change it back into an electrical signal that drives the loudspeaker.

161

Recording

In recording, either to make records and tapes or for broadcasting later, the electrical signals from the microphones are recorded on tape using either analog or digital methods (see page 160). The stereo signal from the mixer may be recorded on tape, using two separate tracks, one for the left speaker and one for the right. This is common in broadcasting, but to make records or tapes, the signals from the microphones are usually first recorded in separate tracks on a wide tape using a multitrack tape recorder. The musicians and engineers can then mix the signals together later to produce a stereo master tape. This has several advantages. The sound of each instrument or voice can be enhanced and carefully balanced against the others, and extra parts such as vocals can be added later by a process called over-dubbing.

Below Making a record – the studio (1), control room (2), multitrack recorder (3), mix down (4), master tape (5), disc cutter (6), disc manufacture (7, 8) and packing (9).

Right A recording studio in action.

Making Tapes and Discs

The stereo master tape produced by the engineers and musicians in the studio now has to be used to make tapes and discs for sale to the public. The tapes are produced as cassettes for playing in tape decks and cassette players. Discs are of two kinds: gramophone records for record players and compact discs for compact disc players.

Tapes

Cassette tapes are direct copies of the master tape. When a tape is made on a tape recorder, electrical signals from a microphone or another recorder go to the recording head. This produces magnetic signals that are captured on the tape as it moves past the head. However, because it would take too long to manufacture cassette tapes at normal playing speed, copies of the master tape are played at very high speed into the cassette copying machines. The cassettes record the speeded music at high speed too, so that the music is copied in a short time. When played at normal speed, the cassettes reproduce the music correctly.

Records

Gramophone records are made from a master disc that is produced with the master tape. The tape is played into a cutting machine similar to a record player. The machine has a cutting head like the stylus or needle on a record player. The master tape is played on a high-quality tape recorder that feeds electrical signals to the cutting head. The head vibrates and cuts a groove in a special rotating disc. This is the master disc.

Copies of the master disc are made and used to manufacture plastic gramophone records by a moulding process. The records are either 18 cm (7 inches) in diameter, which play at 45 rpm (revolutions per minute), or 30 cm (12 inches) in diameter which play at 33 or 45 rpm. The maximum playing time is about 30 minutes per side.

Compact Discs

Compact discs are also made from a master tape. However in this case, the tape is digital and contains magnetic codes that represent the numbers produced by the computer in the studio. A master disc is made from the tape in a special machine that records the codes in the form of tiny pits along a spiral track in the surface of the disc. Unlike a gramophone record, the spiral track begins at the centre of the disc. A laser in the machine fires a beam to cut the pits in a light-sensitive layer on the disc.

From this master disc, the compact discs are manufactured from plastic in a similar way to gramophone records. However, they are then given a silvery coating of aluminium followed by a clear plastic coating for protection. The discs are 11 cm ($4\frac{1}{2}$ inches) in diameter and revolve at a speed that varies from 500 rpm at the beginning of the disc to 200 rpm at the end. Music is recorded on only one side but may last for over an hour.

Below Compact discs receive a transparent plastic coating to protect them from damage. Total cleanliness is strictly observed in the factory to prevent dirt and dust ruining the discs.

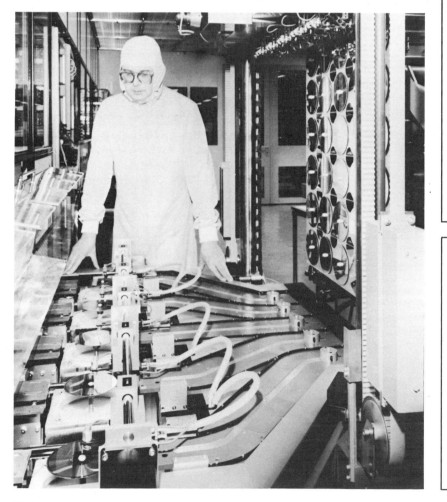

Home Recording

It is possible to make your own recordings of music at home or anywhere else, but remember that recording is usually not allowed at concerts. You can record with a cassette player, but the quality will not be very good. To make a good recording, you need a high-quality tape recorder, preferably a multitrack, reel-to-reel model, and good microphones.

You can record music directly with a good recorder. Drawing the curtains helps to cut down outside noise and may improve the acoustics of the room. If you have a multitrack recorder, you can record each part separately by listening to the other parts with earphones as you build up the music. But you will need another recorder, such as a good cassette player, to produce the finished tape.

Note that recording music composed by other people and taping discs, tapes and broadcast music may infringe copyright and could be against the law, especially if the recordings are sold to other people.

Right Recording a song with a four-track cassette recorder. A rhythm track is recorded first, here using a drum machine (1), connected to a mixer, which is in turn connected to the four-track recorder. The bass part (2), keyboard or guitar (3) and vocal (4) are then recorded on the other three tracks, using earphones to listen to the tracks that have already been recorded. The final stereo tape is made by feeding the four tracks back into the mixer and connecting the mixer to a stereo cassette recorder (5), which is connected to an amplifier and two loudspeakers.

Music and Video

The sound quality of the music produced by a television set is of poor quality, mainly because the loudspeaker in the set has to be small. However, hifi video recorders and video disc players can give high quality sound to match the superb colour pictures of modern television and video. This development brings a full enjoyment of opera, musicals and popular music shows into the home.

Hifi video recorders are video cassette recorders with special recording and playback heads that give stereo sound of

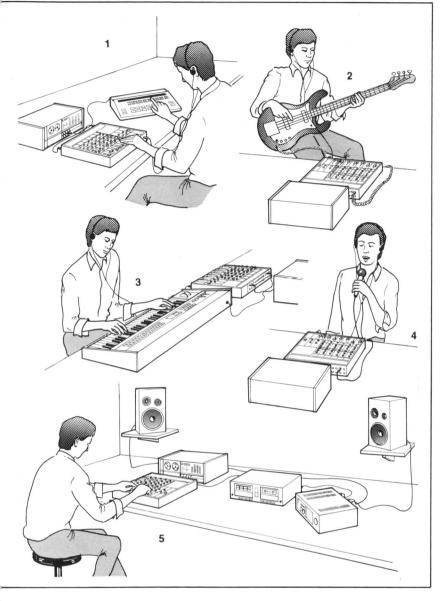

Playing Tapes and Discs

All tape players work in basically the same way. They contain a playback head over which the tape in the cassette passes. The magnetic patterns on the tape produce an electrical signal in the head. This goes to an amplifier, which strengthens the signal so that it is strong enough to drive a loudspeaker and produce the music. The tape usually has two tracks to give two signals for stereo sound.

A record player or gramophone has a cartridge or pick-up containing a stylus or needle that is lowered into the groove on the gramophone record. Two tracks of stereo sound are recorded in the two sides of the groove. As the record turns, the stylus vibrates and the cartridge converts the vibrations into two electric signals. These signals then go to an amplifier and speakers to give stereo sound.

A compact disc player is much more automatic in operation. The compact disc is slotted into the player and may disappear inside. The control panel gives information about the music on the disc, and can be operated to choose any section. Inside, a small laser fires a beam of light at the surface of the disc as it rotates, following the spiral track of pits in its surface. The beam is reflected back, but is interrupted by the pits. In this way, the codes represented by the pits are converted into light signals. A detector

excellent quality. They can play special hifi video music tapes as well as record television programmes broadcast with stereo sound. To hear the sound, the hifi video recorder is connected to the amplifier and speakers of a home music system.

A video disc player does not record but plays stereo sound and colour pictures from digital discs similar to compact discs. The quality of both sound and pictures is superb. The player is connected to a television set and a home music system.

Right A hifi video recorder.

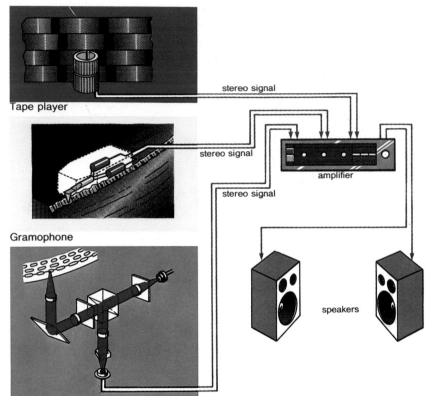

Tape player

stereo signal

Gramophone

stereo signal

amplifier

stereo signal

Compact disc player

speakers

Above The three methods of stereo sound recording. A cassette tape actually contains two stereo pairs of tracks, one pair for each side of the cassette.

then changes the light signals into electric code signals, and the computer in the player converts the codes into electric sound signals. From the player, these signals go to an amplifier and loudspeakers to reproduce the music.

Home Music Systems
To get the best-quality music from tapes and discs, a music system is needed. This contains several different units. To play tapes or discs or to listen to broadcast music, the system has a cassette deck, FM stereo radio tuner, a record deck (turntable and tone-arm) or a compact disc player. A full system would have all of these units, none of which contain their own amplifier and loudspeakers. They are therefore all connected to a separate amplifier, which in turn is connected to two loudspeakers.

The best home systems are called hifi (high fidelity) systems. All the units are separate (though often mounted together in a rack) and of very high quality, and the system is expensive. However, high-quality music centres consisting of one cabinet containing all the units required plus two separate loudspeakers can be bought for less.

The Music Business

Most people who make music do so without any thought of financial reward. They may be performers of traditional music or amateur music makers in classical or popular music, However, music is a big business, in which recording and broadcasting play an important part, and to many people — not all of them musical — it is a living.

Popular Music
The most lucrative field in music is popular music. Singers and groups who make it to the top and stay there earn fortunes. However, they depend on the services of a wide range of professional music people. There are managers and agents who look after the financial affairs of performers and arrange concerts, recordings, travel, publicity and so on. There are the people who work for record companies, such as the A&R man (artists and repertoire manager) who decides which singers and groups to record, record producers who work with the singers and groups and make decisions about the music, the engineers and technicians who operate the equipment, and the session musicians — very capable musicians who play for all kinds of performers on records. Then there are music publishers, who make money for a composer or performer from the music itself, both by selling sheet music and earning royalties from recordings and broadcasts of the music. And there are the people who work in the music press, and people in the music departments of radio and television stations.

All these people depend for their living on the desire of the public to buy records and tapes (audio and video), tickets for concerts, music magazines and newspapers and to listen to or watch music on radio and television. It is a highly competitive business, and one often concerned more with making money than the quality of music.

Classical Music
Poles apart from the popular music business is the world of classical music. In addition to composers and performers, this also has its managers, agents, record companies, publishers and specialist press and broadcasting

organizations. However, public support cannot keep orchestras, opera companies and so on going – the music costs more to produce than paying customers can provide. So, financial help and subsidy has to come to the aid of people who work in classical music.

Record companies may support classical recordings with money from the profits of popular records. State subsidy is provided in many countries, in which government departments aided by music advisers allocate funds that come from taxes to organizations and individuals. Firms may give money too, though this private sponsorship tends to go to prestigious projects that are in less need of support than others possibly more deserving on musical grounds. Jazz and folk music are other forms of music that may also be dependent on support.

Commercial Music

There is also a third and thriving kind of music industry – a commercial industry that provides music for any purpose. People from both the popular and classical sides of the music business may also work in the commercial music industry. It involves the production of music such as theme tunes and background music for films, television and radio shows; music for jingles or commercials; and music for the background tapes played in public buildings.

Left The distribution of royalties to composers, song writers and music publishers is a complicated business requiring powerful computers. It is done by national agencies that receive money from radio and television companies and other users of music.

Above A disc jockey usually operates the equipment that plays records and tapes while talking to the listeners.

Left The press office of a major record company is a hive of activity.

Music Makers

This is an A to Z glossary of famous people — composers, performers, groups and instrument makers — who are creating music now or have created music in the past. The various pieces of music that are given are not their complete output, but a selection of compositions or recordings that represent them at their best. All the compositions mentioned can be heard, either on records, in broadcasts or at concerts. In the case of popular performers and groups, the albums chosen have their original titles.

A

Abba Swedish pop group formed in 1973 and named after the first names of its four members — Agnetha Fältskog (1950–), Bjorn Ulvaeus (1945–), Benny Andersson (1946–) and Anni-Frid Lyngstad (1945–). Hits include *Waterloo* (1974) and *Money, Money, Money* (1976).

Abbado, Claudio (1933–). Italian conductor. Principal positions: La Scala, Milan; Vienna Philharmonic Orchestra; London Symphony Orchestra.

Adam, Adolphe (1803–1856). French composer of many stage works, the best-known being the ballet *Giselle* (first performed at Paris in 1841).

Adler, Larry (1914–). American harmonica (mouth organ) virtuoso resident in Britain. Milhaud and Vaughan Williams composed works for him.

Albéniz, Isaac (1860–1909). Spanish classical composer known for music in Spanish national style. Works include *Iberia* (1909) for piano.

Albinoni, Tommaso (1671–1750). Italian composer of many concertos and operas. The famous *Adagio in G minor for Strings and Organ*, often ascribed to Albinoni, was in fact mainly written by his biographer, Remo Giazotto (1910–) in this century.

Amati A family of renowned Italian violin makers who made violins from about 1550 to the early 1700s.

Ansermet, Ernest (1883–1969). Swiss conductor who in 1918 founded the Orchestre de la Suisse Romande in Geneva, and gave the first performances of many important works, especially music by Stravinsky.

Armstrong, Louis (1900–1971). American jazz trumpeter and singer, who founded the solo style of improvisation in jazz in the

1920s. Armstrong's bands included the Hot Five and Hot Seven. Among his best-known records are *Potato Head Blues* (1927) and *West End Blues* (1928). See page 109.

Arne, Thomas (1710–1778). British composer, known for the masque *Comus* (1738), and also several operas and songs, including *Rule Britannia* (1740).

Ashkenazy, Vladimir (1937–). Russian-born classical pianist and conductor, resident in Iceland from 1968.

B

Bach, Carl Philipp Emanuel (1714–1788). German classical composer. Son of J. S. Bach, he served King Frederick the Great of Prussia for many years and helped to develop the classical forms of the sonata, concerto and symphony.

Bach, Johann Christian (1735–1782). German classical composer. Son of J. S. Bach, he is known for his operas, songs and piano concertos.

Bach, Johann Sebastian (1685–1750). German classical composer, considered the greatest composer of the baroque era, combining a mastery of counterpoint and superb melodic gift with a formidable command of musical expression. Bach worked as an organist and composer mainly at Weimar (1708–17) and Leipzig (1723–50). As well as a total of 295 cantatas, his major works include the six *Brandenburg Concertos* (1721), *The Well-Tempered Clavier* (Book 1 – 1722; Book 2 – 1744), *St John Passion* (1723), *St Matthew Passion* (1729), *Chromatic Fantasia and Fugue* (1730), *Christmas Oratorio* (1734), *Mass in B minor* (1738), *Italian Concerto* (1735), *Goldberg Variations* (1742), *The Musical Offering* (1747) and *The Art of Fugue* (1748–50).

Baker, Janet (1933–). British mezzo-soprano, performing in lieder and opera.

Barber, Samuel (1910–1981). American classical composer, best known for *Adagio for Strings* (1936).

Barenboim, Daniel (1942–). Israeli classical pianist and conductor born in Argentina.

Bartók, Béla (1881–1945). Hungarian classical composer, resident in America from 1940. Bartók studied Hungarian folksong, which appears in his work, but also composed abstract music and operas. His major works include the opera *Bluebeard's Castle* (first performed at Budapest in 1918), the ballet *The Miraculous Mandarin* (Cologne, 1926), the piano pieces *Mikrokosmos* (1926–37), the orchestral works *Music for Strings, Percussion and Celesta* (1936) and *Concerto for Orchestra* (1943), six string quartets, three piano concertos, and two violin concertos.

Basie, Count (1904–1984; real name William Basie). Jazz pianist and band leader of swing era. Basie featured several great jazz soloists, notably tenor-saxophonist Lester Young (1909–1959), in his fiercely rhythmic band. Albums include *The Atomic Mr Basie* (1957).

Beach Boys American rock group formed in 1961, and originally comprising Brian Wilson (1942–), Dennis Wilson (1944–), Carl Wilson (1946–), Mike Love (1941–) and Alan Jardine (1942–). Their albums include *Surfin' USA* (1963) and *Pet Sounds* (1966).

Beatles British rock group, first formed in 1956 as *The Quarrymen* and comprising John Lennon (1940–1980), Paul McCartney (1942–), George Harrison (1943–) and Ringo Starr (1940– ; real name Richard Starkey). Originally the group comprised Lennon, McCartney, Harrison, Pete Best (1941– , guitar) and Stuart Sutcliffe (1940–1962, drums). The Beatles broke up in 1970. See page 116.

Beecham, Sir Thomas (1879–1961). British conductor, renowned for his wit, who founded the London Philharmonic Orchestra in 1932 and Royal Philharmonic Orchestra in 1946.

Top left Vladimir Ashkenazy conducts a concerto from the piano.

Left Django Reinhardt with the Quintet of the Hot Club of France.

Beethoven, Ludwig van (1770–1827). German classical composer, resident in Vienna, Austria. Greatest exponent of classical forms such as sonata, concerto and symphony. Beethoven began to go deaf in about 1800 and lost his hearing completely by 1824. His major works include nine *Symphonies* – No 1 in C major (1800), No 2 in D major (1802), No 3 in E flat major (*Eroica*, 1803), No 4 in B flat major (1806), No 5 in C minor (1808), No 6 in F major (*Pastoral*, 1808), No 7 in A major (1812), No 8 in F major (1812), No 9 in D minor (*Choral*, 1824); five *Piano Concertos* – No 1 in C major (1795), No 2 in B flat major (1798), No 3 in C minor (1800), No 4 in G major (1806), No 5 in E flat major (*Emperor*, 1809); and the *Violin Concerto in D major* (1806). The best known of Beethoven's 35 *Piano Sonatas* are the *Pathétique* sonata in C minor (1798), the *Moonlight* sonata in C sharp minor (1801) and the *Appassionata* sonata in F minor (1805). Beethoven wrote only one opera, *Fidelio*, first performed in Vienna in 1805.

Berg, Alban (1885–1935). Austrian classical composer, who made lyrical use of Schoenberg's twelve-note system. His major works include the operas *Wozzeck*, first performed at Berlin in 1925, and *Lulu*, first performed unfinished at Zurich in 1937; *Lyric Suite* (1926) and *Violin Concerto* (1935).

Berio, Luciano (1925–   ). Italian classical composer, active in several styles. His works include *Circles* (1960) and a series of *Sequenzas* (1958–75) for solo performers.

Berlin, Irving (1888–   ; real name Israel Baline). Russian-born songwriter, resident in America from 1893. Songs include *Alexander's Ragtime Band* (1911), *Cheek to Cheek* (1935), and *I'm Dreaming Of A White Christmas* (1942). Shows include *Annie Get Your Gun* (first performed in New York in 1946) and *Call Me Madam* (New York, 1950). Films include *Top Hat* (1935) and *Easter Parade* (1948).

Berlioz, Hector (1803–1869). French classical composer who pioneered romantic music and modern orchestration. His major works include *Fantastic Symphony* (1830) and the symphony *Harold In Italy* (1834); the choral works *Requiem* (1837), *The Damnation of Faust* (1846) and *The Childhood of Christ* (1854); the overture *Roman Carnival* (1844); and the operas *Benvenuto Cellini* (first performed at Paris in 1838), *The Trojans* (Karlsruhe, 1890) and *Beatrice And Benedict* (Baden-Baden, 1862).

Bernstein, Leonard (1918–   ). American composer and conductor, principally of New York Philharmonic Orchestra. Best known for the musicals *On The Town* (first performed in New York in 1944), which is based on the ballet *Fancy Free* (1944), *Candide* (New York, 1956) and *West Side Story* (New York, 1957).

Berry, Chuck (1926–   : real name Charles Berry). American rhythm and blues singer who influenced the Beatles and other rock bands of the 1960s. His hits include *Maybellene* (1955), *Roll Over Beethoven* (1956) and *Sweet Little Sixteen* (1958).

Bizet, Georges (1838–1875). French classical composer, known mainly for the operas *Carmen* (first performed at Paris in 1875) and *The Pearl Fishers* (Paris, 1863). Other works include the suites *Children's Games* (1871) and *L'Arlésienne* (1872).

Boccherini, Luigi (1743–1805). Italian classical composer who developed chamber music, his works including more than 200 string quintets and quartets.

Boehm, Theobald (1794–1881). German inventor who devised the modern key systems of most woodwind instruments, making them much easier to play and enabling good performers to get much more from them.

Borodin, Alexander (1833–1887). Russian classical composer, best known for the opera *Prince Igor* (first performed at St Petersburg in 1890) and his *String Quartet No 2 in D major* (1881). Borodin's themes are used in the musical *Kismet* (New York, 1953).

Boulez, Pierre (1925–   ). French classical composer who has advanced serial and computer music. His major works include *Le Marteau Sans Maître* (Mallet Without Master – 1954), *Pli Selon Pli* (1962) and *Répons* (1983). Boulez is also highly regarded as a conductor of 20th-century music, and is director of IRCAM (the music research centre in Paris).

Bowie, David (1947– : real name David Jones). British rock singer who has pioneered several styles in rock music. Albums include *The Rise And Fall Of Ziggy Stardust And The Spiders From Mars* (1972), *Aladdin Sane* (1973), *Diamond Dogs* (1974) and *Young Americans* (1975).

Brahms, Johannes (1833–1897). German composer of great works in the classical tradition. These include four *Symphonies* – No 1 in C minor (1876), No 2 in D major (1877), No 3 in F major (1883), and No 4 in E minor (1885); two *Piano Concertos* – No 1 in D minor (1858) and No 2 in B flat major (1881); and the *Violin Concerto in D major* (1878). Other well-known works include *Academic Festival Overture* (1880), and *Variations On A Theme By Haydn* (*The St Anthony Chorale* – 1873).

Bream, Julian (1933–). British classical guitarist, also renowned as a lute player.

Britten, Benjamin (1913–1976). British classical composer, notably of operas which include *Peter Grimes* (first performed in London in 1945), *Albert Herring* (Glyndebourne, 1947), *Billy Budd* (London, 1951), *Gloriana* (London, 1953), *The Turn Of The Screw* (Venice, 1954), *A Midsummer Night's Dream* (Aldeburgh, 1960), and *Death In Venice* (Aldeburgh, 1973). Other major works include *Les Illuminations* (1939), *Serenade For Tenor, Horn And Strings* (1943), *Young Person's Guide To The Orchestra* (1946), *Spring Symphony* (1949) and *War Requiem* (1961).

Brubeck, Dave (1920–). American jazz pianist and leader of quartet formed in 1951 with alto-saxophonist Paul Desmond (1924–1977). Albums include *Jazz Goes To College* (1954) and *Time Out* (1959).

Bruch, Max (1838–1920). German classical composer, best known for his *Violin Concerto No 1 in G minor* (1868).

Bruckner, Anton (1824–1896). Austrian classical composer of large-scale orchestral works. These include ten symphonies (numbered 0 to 9) and religious works.

Buxtehude, Dietrich (1637–1707). Danish classical composer and organist who influenced J. S. Bach and Handel.

Byrd, William (1542–1623). English classical composer of masses, motets, anthems, madrigals, songs and instrumental music for keyboards and viols.

C

Cage, John (1912–). American experimental composer who has investigated many different ways of making music. These include the production of sounds not normally thought of as musical, such as those of the prepared piano (a piano containing objects to change its tone, a Cage invention); extraneous noises, such as those of radio sets; and prolonged silence. Cage's music may be totally written or preconceived, or it may consist of directions that leave much or all of the performance to chance.

Callas, Maria Meneghini (1923–1977; real name Maria Kalogeropoulou). American-born soprano of Greek descent known for operatic roles.

Caruso, Enrico (1873–1921). Italian tenor famed for operatic roles; one of the first singers to gain success through records.

Casals, Pablo (1876–1973). Spanish cellist, known for his interpretation of J. S. Bach's cello suites.

Cash, Johnny (1932–). American country singer. Albums include *Ride This Train* (1960) and *Bitter Tears* (1964), based on the folklore of the American West.

Chabrier, Emmanuel (1841–1894). French composer of light classical music. His best-known works are the orchestral rhapsody

España (1883) and the comic opera *Le Roi Malgré Lui* (which was first performed at Paris in 1887).

Chaliapin, Feodor Ivanovich (1873–1938). Russian bass, known for roles in Russian opera.

Charles, Ray (1930– ; real name Ray Charles Robinson). American popular singer and organist, blind from the age of six, who pioneered soul music. Hits include *I've Got A Woman* (1955), *What'd I Say* (1959) and *Georgia On My Mind* (1960). See page 118.

Chopin, Frédéric François (1810–1849). Polish classical composer and pianist, resident in France from 1831, who wrote and performed imaginative piano works of great virtuosity. These include two piano concertos, three piano sonatas, four ballades, four scherzos, ten polonaises, 19 waltzes, 19 nocturnes, 25 preludes, 27 studies and 55 mazurkas.

Clapton, Eric (1945–). British rock guitarist, a member of the groups Yardbirds (1963–1966) and Cream (1966–1968). Albums include *Layla* (1970), *461 Ocean Boulevard* (1974) and *There's One In Every Crowd* (1975).

Clash British rock group, foremost in punk movement, formed in 1976 and comprising Mick Jones, Joe Strummer, Paul Simenon and Topper Headon. Albums include *The Clash* (1977), *London's Calling* (1980) and *Combat Rock* (1982).

Coltrane, John (1926–1967). American jazz musician, known for his intense improvisations on the tenor and soprano saxophones. Albums include *Giant Steps* (1959) and *My Favorite Things* (1960).

Copland, Aaron (1900–). American classical composer of works that often incorporate elements of jazz or American folk music. His major works include the ballets *Billy The Kid* (first performed at Chicago in 1938), *Rodeo* (New York, 1942) and *Appalachian Spring* (Washington, 1944); and the orchestral works *El Salón México* (1936) and *Concerto for Clarinet and Strings* (1948).

Corelli, Arcangelo (1653–1713). Italian classical composer who established the sonata and concerto grosso as musical forms.

Couperin, François (1668–1733). French classical composer, known mainly for more than 200 harpsichord pieces with descriptive titles.

Coward, Noël (1899–1973). British songwriter and playwright. Songs include *I'll See You Again* (1929) and *Mad Dogs And Englishmen* (1931). Shows include *Bitter Sweet* (first performed in London in 1929).

Cream British rock group formed in 1966 with Eric Clapton (1945–), Jack Bruce (1943–) and Ginger Baker (1939–). Broke up in 1968. Albums include *Disraeli Gears* (1967) and *Wheels Of Fire* (1968).

Cristofori, Bartolommeo (1655–1731). Italian harpsichord maker who invented the piano in 1709.

Curzon, Clifford (1907–1982). British classical pianist, known for interpretation of Schubert's music.

Czerny, Carl (1791–1857). Austrian classical composer, best known for his piano studies.

D

Davies, Peter Maxwell (1934–). British classical composer, best known for works with a theatrical character such as *Eight Songs For A Mad King* (1969) and *Vesalii Icones* (1969), and the opera *Taverner* (first performed in London in 1972).

Davis, Miles (1926–). American jazz trumpeter who pioneered modern jazz and jazz-rock styles. Albums include *Birth Of The Cool* (1949), *Miles Ahead* (1957), *Kind Of Blue* (1959) and *In A Silent Way* (1969). See pages 112–3.

Debussy, Claude (1862–1918). French classical composer who developed impressionist music. His major works include the orchestral pieces *Prélude À L'Après-Midi D'Un Faune* (Prelude To The Afternoon Of A Faun – 1894), *Nocturnes* (1899), *La Mer* (The Sea – 1905) and *Images* (1912); the piano works *Suite Bergamesque* (1905), *Children's Corner* (1908) and *Préludes* (Book 1 – 1910; Book 2 – 1913); one string quartet (1893); the opera *Pelléas et Mélisande* (first performed at Paris in 1902) and the ballet *Jeux* (Games – Paris, 1913)

Delibes, Léo (1836–1891). French classical composer, best known for the ballets *Coppélia* (first performed at Paris in 1870) and *Sylvia* (Paris, 1876), and the opera *Lakmé* (Paris, 1883).

Delius, Frederick (1862–1934). British classical composer of impressionist music. His best-known works include the opera *A Village Romeo And Juliet* (first performed at Berlin in 1907), the choral works *Sea Drift* (1904), *A Mass of Life* (1909) and *Requiem* (1916), and the orchestral works *Brigg Fair* (1907) and *On Hearing The First Cuckoo In Spring* (1912).

Diaghilev, Sergei (1872–1929). Russian impresario who created the Ballets Russes in 1909 and subsequently commissioned important music by Stravinsky, Ravel, Debussy, Falla and Satie.

Dohnányi, Ernö (1877–1960). Hungarian classical composer, best known for *Variations On A Nursery Song* (1914).

Domingo, Placido (1941–). Spanish tenor, known for leading roles in opera.

Donizetti, Gaetano (1797–1848). Italian opera composer. His major works include *L'Elisir D'Amore* (The Elixir Of Love, first performed at Milan in 1832), *Lucia Di Lammermoor* (Naples, 1835), *La Fille Du Régiment* (The Daughter Of The Regiment, Paris, 1840) and *Don Pasquale* (Paris, 1843).

Dowland, John (1563–1626). English classical composer, known mainly for his lute music and songs.

Dufay, Guillaume (c 1400–1474). Flemish classical composer who pioneered polyphonic music, notably in his church music and songs.

Dukas, Paul (1865–1935). French classical composer, known mainly for the orchestral piece *L'Apprenti Sorcier* (The Sorcerer's Apprentice, 1897) and the ballet *La Péri* (first performed in Paris in 1912).

Dunstable, John (c 1390–1453). English classical composer of motets, church music and songs.

Dvořák, Antonin (1841–1904, pronounced Vorjak). Czech classical composer, resident in the United States from 1892 to 1895. Dvořák's works, which often contain elements of folk music, include nine *Symphonies*, which are now numbered No 1 in C minor (1865), No 2 in B flat major (1865), No 3 in E flat major (1873), No 4 in D minor (1874), No 5 in F major (1875), No 6 in D major (1880), No 7 in D minor (1885), No 8 in G major (1889) and No 9 in E minor (*From The New World*, 1893). Symphonies 5 to 9 are sometimes given their old numbers, which are 1 (now 6), 2 (now 7), 3 (now 5), 4 (now 8) and 5 (now 9). Other notable orchestral works are the *Slavonic Dances* (1878 and 1887), *Violin Concerto in A minor* (1880) and *Cello Concerto in B minor* (1895). Dvořák also composed 14 string quartets, of which the *American* quartet (1893) is well known, and 10 operas, the best-known being *Rusalka* (first performed at Prague in 1901).

Dylan, Bob (1941– ; real name Robert Zimmerman). American popular singer and composer who pioneered the folk-rock style in the mid-1960s. See page 120.

E

Elgar, Edward (1857–1934). British classical composer, best known for the orchestral work *Enigma Variations* (1899) and the oratorio *The Dream of Gerontius* (1900). Other well-known works include the five *Pomp And*

Circumstance marches (1901–30), from the first of which comes the song *Land Of Hope And Glory*, the overture *Cockaigne* (1901) and the *Cello Concerto* (1919).

Ellington, Duke (1899–1974; real name Edward Kennedy Ellington). American jazz composer and pianist who pioneered orchestral composition in jazz with his own orchestra from 1923. Ellington's best-known shorter pieces include *Mood Indigo* (1930), *It Don't Mean A Thing* (1932) and *I Got It Bad* (1941), and among his large-scale works are *The Tattooed Bride* (1948), *Harlem* (1950) and *Such Sweet Thunder* (1957). Billy Strayhorn (1915–1967), who collaborated with him from 1939 to 1967, composed Ellington's theme tune *Take The A Train* (1940). See page 111.

Evans, Geraint (1922–). British baritone noted for his operatic roles.

Evans, Gill (1912– ; real name Ernest Gilmore Green). Canadian jazz composer and arranger, resident in the United States. Renowned for his orchestral albums with Miles Davis, notably *Miles Ahead* (1957) and *Sketches Of Spain* (1959).

F

Falla, Manuel de (1876–1946). Spanish classical composer of works in Spanish national style. These include the ballets *El Amor Brujo* (Love The Magician, first performed at Madrid in 1915) and *El Sombrero De Tres Picos* (The Three-Cornered Hat, London, 1919), the orchestral piece *Noches En Los Jardines De España* (Nights In The Gardens Of Spain, 1915) and the opera *La Vida Breve* (The Short Life, first performed at Nice in 1913).

Fauré, Gabriel (1845–1924). French classical composer, best known for his choral work *Requiem* (1887), the orchestral piece *Pavane* (1887) and the *Dolly Suite* (1897) for piano duet.

Ferrier, Kathleen (1912–1953). British contralto known for her singing in opera and oratorio. The role of Lucretia in Britten's opera *The Rape of Lucretia*, first performed at Glyndebourne in 1946, was written for her.

Field, John (1782–1837). Irish classical composer, resident in Russia from 1803. His best-known works are his 19 piano nocturnes, a form that he invented.

Fischer-Dieskau, Dietrich (1925–). German baritone renowned for his performances of lieder and operatic roles.

Flagstad, Kirsten (1895–1962). Norwegian soprano known for operatic roles, particularly in Wagner's operas.

Fleetwood Mac British rock group formed in 1967 and originally comprising Peter Green (1946–), Jeremy Spencer (1948–), John McVie (1945–) and Mick Fleetwood (1947–). Albums include *Kiln House* (1970), *Future Games* (1971) and *Rumours* (1977).

Foster, Stephen (1826–1864). American songwriter who wrote about 200 popular songs, including *Camptown Races* (1850), *The Old Folks At Home* (1851), *Jeannie With The Light Brown Hair* (1854) and *Beautiful Dreamer* (1864).

Franck, César (1822–1890). French classical composer, best known for *Symphonic Variations for Piano and Orchestra* (1885) and *Symphony in D minor* (1888).

Franklin, Aretha (1942–). American soul singer, raised on gospel music. Her albums include *I Have Never Loved A Man The Way I Love You* (1967), *Amazing Grace* (1972) and *Young, Gifted And Black* (1972).

Frescobaldi, Girolamo (1583–1643). Italian classical composer, known principally for his organ works.

Friml, Rudolf (1879–1972). Czech composer of musicals, resident in America from 1906. His best-known shows are *Rose Marie* (first performed in New York in 1924) and *The Vagabond King* (New York, 1925).

G

Gabrieli, Andrea (*c* 1510–1586) and **Gabrieli, Giovanni** (*c* 1556–1612). Italian classical composers (uncle and nephew), both organists at St Mark's, Venice, who pioneered the use of the orchestra in choral music, often with singers divided into several choirs.

Gay, John (1685–1732). English poet known for *The Beggar's Opera*, first performed in London in 1728, in which he set words to popular tunes of the time.

Gershwin, George (1898–1937). American songwriter and composer. His musical shows include *Lady Be Good* (first performed in New York in 1924), *Funny Face* (New York, 1927), *Girl Crazy* (New York, 1930) and the film *Shall We Dance?* (1937). Many of the lyrics of Gershwin's songs were written by his brother Ira Gershwin (1896–1983). Among George Gershwin's best-known other works, which make use of jazz and American folk music, are the orchestral pieces *Rhapsody In Blue* (1924) and *An American In Paris* (1928), the *Concerto in F* (1925) for piano and orchestra, and the opera *Porgy And Bess* (New York, 1935).

Gibbons, Orlando (1583–1625). English classical composer, notably of anthems and madrigals.

Gigli, Beniamino (1890–1957). Italian tenor renowned for his moving portrayals of operatic roles.

Gilbert, W. S. [William Schwenk] (1836–1911). British dramatist who wrote the words and lyrics of many operettas for which Arthur Sullivan (1842–1900) composed the music. These include *Trial By Jury* (first performed in London in 1875), *The Sorcerer* (London, 1877), *H.M.S. Pinafore* (London, 1878), *The Pirates Of Penzance* (New York, 1879), *Patience* (London, 1881), *Iolanthe* (London, 1882), *Princess Ida* (London, 1884), *The Mikado* (London, 1885), *Ruddigore* (London, 1887), *The Yeomen Of The Guard* (London, 1888) and *The Gondoliers* (London, 1889).

Gillespie, Dizzy (1917– , real name John Birks Gillespie). American jazz trumpeter who pioneered the bebop style of jazz with Charlie Parker.

Glass, Philip (1937–). American composer of minimal music and operas, including *Einstein On The Beach* (first performed at Paris in 1976) and *Akhnaten* (Stuttgart, 1984).

Glazunov, Alexander (1865–1936). Russian classical composer, best known for his ballet *The Seasons* (first performed at St Petersburg in 1900) and the *Violin Concerto in A minor* (1904).

Glinka, Mikhail (1804–1857). Russian classical composer, generally considered to be the father of Russian music. His major works include the operas *Ivan Susanin* (A Life For The Tsar, first performed at St Petersburg in 1836) and *Ruslan And Ludmilla* (St Petersburg, 1842).

Gluck, Christoph (1714–1787). German classical composer of importance in the development of opera. His operas include *Orpheus And Eurydice* (first performed at Vienna in 1762), *Alceste* or *Alcestis* (Vienna, 1767), *Iphigenia In Aulis* (Paris, 1774) and *Iphigenia In Tauris* (Paris, 1779).

Goodman, Benny (1909–). American jazz clarinettist and band leader who pioneered the swing style of jazz on forming his own band in 1934. Goodman has also played classical music, and Bartók and Copland composed music for him.

Gould, Glenn (1932–1982). Canadian classical pianist renowned for his recordings of J. S. Bach.

Gounod, Charles (1818–1893). French classical composer known mainly for his opera *Faust* (first performed at Paris in 1859), and *Ave Maria* (1859), which is a melody written to the first prelude of J. S. Bach's *Well-Tempered Clavier*.

Grainger, Percy (1882–1961). Australian composer, resident in Britain from 1901 and the United States from 1914. Known for the pieces *Shepherd's Hey* (1911), *Molly On The Shore* (1918) and *Country Gardens* (1918).

Granados, Enrique (1867–1916). Spanish classical composer of piano works in Spanish national style, notably *Goyescas* (1911), which he also arranged as an opera (first performed in New York in 1916).

Grieg, Edvard (1843–1907). Norwegian classical composer of music in Norwegian national idiom. His major works include *Piano Concerto in A minor* (1868), *Peer Gynt* (1875), and *Holberg Suite* (1884).

Guido d'Arezzo (*c* 992–*c* 1050). Italian monk who conceived the idea of the tonic-solfa system, in which notes are indicated by names such as *doh, re, mi* etc that give their relation to the tonic or home note (*doh*) of the music.

Guthrie, Woody (1912–1967). American folk singer, best known for his songs *This Land Is Your Land* and *So Long, It's Been Good To Know You* (1935).

H

Haitink, Bernard (1929–). Dutch conductor. Principal positions: Concertgebouw, Amsterdam; London Philharmonic Orchestra; Glyndebourne Opera.

Hammerstein II, Oscar (1895–1960). American librettist and lyricist who wrote the words of musical shows by Rudolf Friml (*Rose Marie*), Richard Rodgers (*Carousel, The King And I, Oklahoma, The Sound Of Music, South Pacific*), Sigmund Romberg (*The Desert Song*) and Jerome Kern (*Show Boat*).

Handel, George Frideric (1685–1759). British classical composer born in Germany (as Georg Friederich Händel), resident in Britain from 1712. Leading baroque composer, especially of opera and oratorio. His major works include the operas *Julius Caesar* (first performed in London in 1724) and *Xerxes* (London, 1738), and the oratorios *Saul* (1739), *Israel In Egypt* (1739), *Messiah* (1742) and *Judas Maccabeus* (1747). Handel's best-known orchestral works are *Water Music* (1717) and *Music For The Royal Fireworks* (1749), and he also composed many concertos, especially for the organ. Handel's most famous pieces are the *Hallelujah Chorus* from *Messiah*, and *Arrival of The Queen Of Sheba* from the oratorio *Solomon* (1749).

Harris, Roy (1898–1979). American classical composer, best known for his *Third Symphony* (1937).

Haydn, (Franz) Joseph (1732–1809). Austrian classical composer who developed classical forms such as the symphony and string quartet. Among the best-known of his 104 symphonies are the *Clock Symphony* (No 101 in D major – 1794), *Drum-Roll Symphony* (No 103 in E flat major – 1795), *Farewell Symphony* (No 45 in F sharp minor – 1772), *London Symphony* (No 104 in D major – 1795) and *Surprise Symphony* (No 94 in G major – 1791). Haydn also composed about 80 string quartets, of which the best-known is the *Emperor Quartet* (No 77 in C major – 1797) for the use of the tune that subsequently became the national anthem of Austria and Germany. Among Haydn's other major works are the oratorios *The Creation* (1798) and *The Seasons* (1801), more than 20 operas and several concertos, of which the best known is the *Trumpet Concerto in E flat major* (1796).

Haydn, (Johann) Michael (1737–1806). Austrian classical composer (brother of Joseph Haydn), best known for the *Toy Symphony* (1780), composed with Leopold Mozart.

Heifetz, Jascha (1901–). American classical violinist, born in Russia. Commissioned Walton's *Violin Concerto* (1939).

Hendrix, Jimi (1942–1970). American rock guitarist, resident in Britain from 1966. Albums include *Are You Experienced?* (1967) and *Electric Ladyland* (1968).

Henze, Hans Werner (1926–). German classical composer who has worked in several styles and whose music often has a political viewpoint. He has composed several operas, including *The Young Lord* (first performed in Berlin in 1965), *The Bassarids* (Salzburg, 1966) and *We Come To The River* (London, 1976), and the chamber works *Kammermusik* (1922–30).

Hindemith, Paul (1895–1963). German classical composer, resident in United States from 1940. His best-known works are the opera *Mathis Der Maler* (Mathis The Painter, first performed at Zurich, 1938) and a symphony (1934) based on it, the orchestral work *Symphonic Metamorphoses Of Themes By Weber* (1943).

Hines, Earl (1905–), American jazz pianist who pioneered jazz piano playing in his work with Louis Armstrong in the 1920s.

Holliday, Billie (1915–1959). American jazz singer renowned for the sensitivity and individual jazz phrasing she brought to a song. Her records include *All Of Me* (1941), *God Bless The Child* (1941) and *Strange Fruit* (1944).

Holst, Gustav (1874–1934). British classical composer, famous for the orchestral suite *The Planets* (1916). His other works include the choral piece *The Hymn Of Jesus* (1917), the overture *Egdon Heath* (1927) and the opera *The Perfect Fool* (first performed in London, 1923).

Honegger, Arthur (1892–1955). Swiss classical composer, resident in France, known for the orchestral piece *Pacific 231* (1923) and the oratorio *Le Roi David* (King David, first performed at Mézières in 1921).

Horne, Marilyn (1929–). American mezzo-soprano, known for her roles in opera.

Horowitz, Vladimir (1909–). Russian pianist, resident in America from 1928.

Humperdinck, Engelbert (1854–1921). German classical composer, best known for the opera *Hansel And Gretel* (first performed at Weimar in 1893).

I

Ives, Charles (1874–1954). American composer of highly original classical works, little known in his lifetime. They include five symphonies, the piano sonata *Concord* (1915), the orchestral works *The Unanswered Question* (1906) and *Three Places in New England* (1914), and the witty organ piece *Variations On America* (1891, later orchestrated).

J

Jackson, Michael (1958–). American pop singer who rose to fame as a boy with the family group The Jackson Five, securing an immediate hit with *I Want You Back* in 1969. Albums include *Off The Wall* (1979) and *Thriller* (1982).

Janáček, Leoš (1854–1928). Czech classical composer known mainly for his operas, which include *Jenůfa* (first performed at Brno in 1904), *Katya Kabanová* (Brno, 1921), *The Cunning Little Vixen* (Brno, 1924), *The Makropoulos Affair* (Brno, 1926) and *From The House Of The Dead* (Brno, 1930). Other works include the orchestral pieces *Taras Bulba* (1918) and *Sinfonietta* (1926), and the choral work *Glagolitic Mass* (1927).

John, Elton (1947– ; born Reg Dwight). British pop singer, renowned for his showmanship. Albums include *Tumbleweed Connection* (1971), *Goodbye Yellow Brick Road* (1973) and *Captain Fantastic And The Brown Dirt Cowboy* (1975).

Joplin, Scott (1868–1917). American ragtime composer, best known for the rags *Maple Leaf Rag* (1899) and *The Entertainer* (1902), and the ragtime opera *Treemonisha* (first performed at Atlanta in 1972).

Josquin Des Près (c 1440–1521). Flemish classical composer, one of the first to write really expressive music. His works include about 17 masses, at least 100 motets and many songs.

K

Karajan, Herbert von (1908–). Austrian conductor, principally of the Berlin Philharmonic Orchestra.

Kern, Jerome (1885–1945). American songwriter, best known for the musicals *Showboat* (first performed at New York in 1927) and *Roberta* (New York, 1933). His songs include *Old Man River* (1927), *Smoke Gets in Your Eyes* (1933) and *All The Things You Are* (1939).

Khachaturian, Aram (1903–1978). Russian composer, best known for the ballets *Spartacus* (first performed at Leningrad in 1956) and *Gayane* (Perm, 1942), which contains the famous *Sabre Dance*.

King, B. B. (1925– ; real name Riley King). American blues guitarist and singer, whose most successful hits include *Three O'Clock Blues* (1951), *Everyday I Have The Blues* (1955), *Sweet Sixteen* (1960) and *The Thrill Is Gone* (1969).

Kirkpatrick, Ralph (1911–). American harpsichordist and expert on the works of Domenico Scarlatti.

Klemperer, Otto (1885–1973). German conductor. Principal positions: Los Angeles Philharmonic Orchestra, Philharmonia and New Philharmonia Orchestras.

Kodály, Zoltán (1882–1967). Hungarian classical composer, best known for the opera *Háry János* (first performed at Budapest in 1926) and the orchestral suite *Dances of Galánta* (1933).

Kreisler, Fritz (1875–1962). Austrian violinist, acclaimed as the greatest violinist of his time.

L

Lehár, Franz (1870–1948). Hungarian composer of operettas, the best-known being *The Merry Widow* (first performed at Vienna in 1905). Other operettas include *The Count of Luxembourg* (Vienna, 1909) and *The Land of Smiles* (Berlin, 1929).

Ligeti, György (1923–). Hungarian classical composer known for his experimental pieces. Many of his works, such as *Atmospheres* (1961), make use of unusual sound effects.

Liszt, Franz (1811–1886). Hungarian classical composer known for his 13 symphonic poems, a form that he invented, and his bravura piano pieces, notably the 19 *Hungarian Rhapsodies* (1846–85), the *Piano Sonata in B minor* (1853) and three piano concertos. His other works include the *Faust Symphony* (1857), the orchestral work *Mephisto Waltz No 1* (1861) and the piano piece *Liebestraum No 3* (1850).

Lloyd-Webber, Andrew (1948–). British composer of musicals, which include *Jesus Christ Superstar* (first performed at New York in 1971), *Evita* (London, 1978) and *Cats* (London, 1981).

Lully, Jean-Baptiste (1632–1687). Italian-born classical composer, resident in France, who was important in the development of ballet and opera. His operas include *Alceste* (first performed at Paris in 1674) and *Armide* (Paris, 1686). Also known for music to Molière's play *Le Bourgeois Gentilhomme* (1670).

M

Maazel, Lorin (1930–). American conductor. Principal positions: Cleveland Orchestra, Vienna State Opera.

Machaut, Guillaume de (c 1300–1377). French classical composer, important in the development of polyphonic music. His works include *La Messe De Notre Dame* (one of the earliest masses, possibly composed in 1364), several motets and many songs.

Mahler, Gustav (1860–1911). Austrian classical composer of highly romantic works, particularly his ten symphonies, noted for their grand scale. These are No 1 in D major – 1888, No 2 in C minor (*Resurrection*) –1894, No 3 in D minor – 1896, No 4 in G major – 1900, No 5 in C sharp minor (which includes the famous *Adagietto*) – 1902, No 6 in A minor – 1904, No 7 in E minor – 1905, No 8 in E flat major (*Symphony Of A Thousand*) – 1906, No 9 in D major – 1909, No 10 in F sharp minor – unfinished (completed by Deryck Cook in 1964). Mahler's other works include the song-symphony *Das Lied Von Der Erde* (The Song Of The Earth, 1908), and the song cycles *Lieder Eines Fahrenden Gesellen* (Songs Of A Wayfarer, 1885) and *Kindertotenlieder* (Songs On The Death Of Children, 1904).

Marley, Bob (1945–1981). Jamaican singer-songwriter who, with his band The Wailers (formed in 1963), popularized reggae music. Albums include *Catch A Fire* (1972), *Natty Dread* (1975) and *Exodus* (1977).

Mendelssohn, Felix (1809–1847). German classical composer, renowned for his revival of J. S. Bach's music as well as for his own elegant and poetic compositions. These include several well-known overtures, notably *A Midsummer Night's Dream* (1826), *The Hebrides* or *Fingal's Cave* (1830), *Calm Sea And Prosperous Voyage* (1832) and *Ruy Blas* (1839), and five *Symphonies*: No 1 in C minor – 1824, No 2 in B flat major (*Hymn Of Praise*) – 1840, No 3 in A minor (*Scottish*) – 1842, No 4 in A major (*Italian*) – 1833, No 5 in D major (*Reformation*) – 1832. His other works include the oratorios *Saint Paul* (1836) and *Elijah* (1846), the *Violin Concerto in E minor* (1844), the piano pieces *Songs Without Words* (1829–1845), the *Octet* for strings (1825) and two piano concertos.

Menuhin, Yehudi (1916–). British violinist born in the United States, known for his classical playing as well as for his interest in jazz and Indian music.

Messiaen, Olivier (1908–). French classical composer of exotic music drawing on several different sources, including birdsong. His major works include *L'Ascension* (The Ascension, 1934), *Quatuor Pour La Fin Du Temps* (Quartet For The End of Time, 1941), *Turangalîla Symphony* (1948) and *Catalogue Des Oiseaux* (Catalogue Of Birds – 1958).

Milhaud, Darius (1892–1974). French classical composer, known mainly for the ballet *La Création Du Monde* (The Creation Of The World, first performed at Paris in 1923) and *Scaramouche* (1937) for two pianos.

Miller, Glen (1904–1944). American band-leader of World War II, known mainly for his theme tune *Moonlight Serenade* (1939).

Monroe, Bill (1911–). American country musician who established bluegrass music with his band, the Bluegrass Boys, in 1938.

Monteverdi, Claudio (1567–1643). Italian classical composer who composed the first major operas in Europe and developed techniques of orchestration. His three surviving operas are *Orfeo* (Orpheus, first performed at Mantua in 1607), *Il Ritorno D'Ulisse* (The Return of Ulysses, Venice, 1640) and *L'Incoronazione Di Poppea* (The Coronation of Poppaea, Venice, 1642). He also composed much vocal music, including more than 250 madrigals.

Morton, Jelly Roll (1885–1941, real name Ferdinand Morton). American jazz pianist and composer who, with his band the Red Hot Peppers, was important in the development of jazz in the 1920s.

Mozart, Wolfgang Amadeus (1756–1791). Austrian classical composer who brought the symphony, concerto and sonata to elegant perfection, and who developed opera into a highly expressive art. Among the best-known of his 41 symphonies are the *Paris Symphony* (No 31 in D major – 1778), the *Haffner Symphony* (No 35 in D major – 1782), the *Linz Symphony* (No 36 in C major – 1783), the *Prague Symphony* (No 38 in D major –

1786), the *Jupiter Symphony* (No 41 in C major – 1788), but most famous is the *Symphony No 40 in G minor* (1788). Mozart composed 27 piano concertos of which the *Piano Concerto No 21 in C major* (1785) is most popular. Among Mozart's many other concertos, the best-known include the *Clarinet Concerto in A major* (1791), the *Flute and Harp Concerto in C major* (1778) and the *Horn Concerto No 4 in E flat major* (1786). Other popular orchestral works include the serenade, *Eine Kleine Nachtmusik* (A Little Night Music, 1787). Mozart's chamber music includes 17 piano sonatas and 26 string quartets. The operas most performed are *Idomeneo* (first performed at Munich in 1781), *Die Entführung Aus Dem Serail* (The Abduction From The Seraglio, Vienna, 1782), *Le Nozze Di Figaro* (The Marriage of Figaro, Vienna, 1786), *Don Giovanni* (Prague, 1787), *Così Fan Tutte* (So Do All Women, Vienna, 1790) and *Die Zauberflöte* (The Magic Flute, Vienna, 1791). Mozart also composed much church music, including 17 masses.

Mussorgsky, Modest (1839–1881). Russian classical composer, best known for the piano work *Pictures At An Exhibition* (1874, orchestrated by Ravel in 1922), the orchestral piece *Night On The Bare Mountain* (1867) and the opera *Boris Godunov* (first performed at St Petersburg in 1874).

N

Nielsen, Carl (1865–1931). Danish classical composer, known for his six symphonies and the opera *Masquerade* (first performed at Copenhagen in 1906).

O

Offenbach, Jacques (1819–1880). French composer, born in Germany, renowned for his operettas. Of the 100 or so that he composed, the best known are *Orphée Aux Enfers* (Orpheus In The Underworld, first performed at Paris in 1858) and *La Belle Hélène* (Beautiful Helen, Paris, 1864). Offenbach also composed a serious opera *Les Contes D'Hoffmann* (The Tales of Hoffmann, Paris, 1881).

Oistrakh, David (1908–1974) and **Oistrakh, Igor** (1931–). Russian violinists, father and son.

Oldfield, Mike (1954–). British rock composer, known mainly for his album *Tubular Bells* (1973).

Orff, Carl (1895–1982). German classical composer, best known for the cantata *Carmina Burana* (1937).

P

Paganini, Nicolò (1782–1840). Italian violinist, renowned for his virtuosity, and composer. His works include *24 Caprices* (1805) for solo violin, and six violin concertos.

Palestrina, Giovanni (c 1525–1594). Italian composer of church music, including nearly 100 masses.

Parker, Charlie (1920–1955). American jazz alto-saxophonist who pioneered the bebop style of jazz along with Dizzy Gillespie (1917–). Among his great recordings are *Koko* (1945), *Night In Tunisia* (1946), *Donna Lee* (1947), *Parker's Mood* (1948) and *Now's The Time* (1953).

Pears, Peter (1910–). British tenor, known mainly for his singing of the music of Benjamin Britten (1913–1976).

Penderecki, Krzysztof (1933–). Polish classical composer who has explored new ways of playing instruments in his music. He is known mainly for his *Threnody For The*

Victims of Hiroshima (1960) and *St Luke Passion* (1965).

Peterson, Oscar (1925–). Canadian jazz pianist, known internationally for his virtuoso playing, usually with his own trio.

Pink Floyd British rock group formed in 1966 and originally comprising Syd Barrett (1946–), Roger Waters (1944–), Richard Wright (1945–) and Nick Mason (1945–). David Gilmore (1946–) replaced Syd Barrett in 1968. Albums include *Dark Side Of The Moon* (1973) and *The Wall* (1980).

Police British rock group formed in 1977 and comprising Sting (1951– ; real name Gordon Sumner), Stewart Copeland (1952–) and Andy Summers (1942–). Albums include *Ghost In The Machine* (1981) and *Synchronicity* (1983).

Porter, Cole (1891–1964). American songwriter, renowned for his catchy tunes and witty lyrics. His shows include *Anything Goes* (first performed at New York in 1934) and *Kiss Me Kate* (New York, 1948). Among his many famous songs are *Let's Do It* (1928), *Night And Day* (1932), *You're The Top* (1934) and *I've Got You Under My Skin* (1936).

Poulenc, Francis (1899–1963). French classical composer, often of elegant witty music. His works include the ballet *Les Biches* (The Does, Monte Carlo, 1924) and the operas *Les Mamelles De Tirésias* (The Breasts Of Tirésias, Paris, 1944) and *Les Dialogues Des Carmélites* (The Dialogues Of The Carmelites, Milan, 1957).

Presley, Elvis (1935–1977). American singer who was the most popular rock and roll star of the 1950s. See page 115.

Previn, André (1929–). American conductor. Principal positions: London Symphony Orchestra, Pittsburgh Symphony Orchestra.

Price, Leontyne (1927–). American soprano renowned for dramatic roles in opera.

Prokofiev, Sergei (1891–1953). Russian classical composer of many well-known works in standard forms. These include seven symphonies of which No 1, the *Classical Symphony* (1917), is most popular; several concertos; the operas *The Love Of Three Oranges* (first performed at Chicago in 1921) and *War And Peace* (Leningrad, 1946); and the ballets *Romeo And Juliet* (Brno, 1938) and *Cinderella* (Moscow, 1945). Best known of all his works is the suite *Peter And The Wolf* (1936).

Puccini, Giacomo (1858–1924). Italian opera composer. His operas include *Manon Lescaut* (first performed at Turin in 1893), *La Bohème* (Turin, 1896), *Tosca* (Rome, 1900), *Madame Butterfly* (Milan, 1904), *La Fanciulla Del West* (The Girl Of The Golden West, New York, 1910) and *Turandot* (Milan, 1926 – unfinished and completed by Franco Alfano).

Purcell, Henry (1659–1695). English classical composer, mainly known for his operas *Dido And Aeneas* (first performed in London in 1689) and *The Fairy Queen* (London, 1692), and the choral work *Ode For St Cecilia's Day* (1683).

R

Rachmaninov, Sergei (1873–1934). Russian classical composer of highly romantic music, resident in Switzerland and the United States from 1918. His works include three symphonies and four piano concertos, of which the *Piano Concerto No 2 in C minor* (1901) is best known. Other popular pieces include the *Prelude in C sharp minor* (1892) for piano, and the *Rhapsody On A Theme Of Paganini* (1934) for piano and orchestra.

Rameau, Jean-Philippe (1683–1764). French classical composer, known for his harpsichord music and also important in the development of opera and ballet.

Ravel, Maurice (1875–1937). French classical composer, renowned for his brilliant orchestral and piano music. His major orchestral works include the ballet *Daphnis And Chloe* (first performed at Paris in 1912), *La Valse* (The Waltz – 1920), *Bolero* (1928) and two *Piano Concertos* – No 1 in D major (for the left hand only – 1930), and No 2 in G major (1931). Ravel's piano music, much of which he also orchestrated, includes *Pavane Pour Une Infante Défunte* (Pavane For A Dead Infanta, 1899), *Gaspard De La Nuit* (1908) and *Ma Mère L'Oye* (Mother Goose, 1910). Ravel also composed two short operas – *L'Heure Espagnole* (The Spanish Hour, first performed at Paris in 1911) and *L'Enfant Et Les Sortilèges* (The Child And The Spells, Monte Carlo, 1925).

Reeves, Jim (1923–1964). American country singer whose songs achieved great popularity after his death.

Reich, Steve (1936–). American pioneer of minimal music, notably with *Drumming* (1971).

Reinhardt, Django (1910–1953). Belgian jazz guitarist, generally recognized as the first major European jazz musician. Known for his records with the Quintet of the Hot Club of France and the jazz violinist Stéphane Grapelli (1908–) from 1934 to 1939.

Respighi, Ottorino (1879–1936). Italian classical composer, best known for the orchestral work *The Fountains of Rome* (1916) and the ballet *La Boutique Fantasque* (The Fantastic Toyshop, first performed in London in 1919), in which he arranged several of Rossini's most popular pieces.

Riley, Terry (1935–). American pioneer of minimal music, notably with *In C* (1964) and *A Rainbow In Curved Air* (1970).

Rimsky-Korsakov, Nicolai (1844–1908). Russian classical composer, best known for the brilliant orchestral works *Scheherezade* (1888) and *Capriccio Espagnol* (1887). He also composed several operas, including *The Snow Maiden* (first performed at St Petersburg in 1882) and *Le Coq D'Or* (The Golden Cockerel, Moscow, 1909). The famous *Flight Of The Bumble Bee* comes from the opera *The Legend Of Tsar Sultan* (Moscow, 1900).

Rodgers, Richard (1902–1979). American composer of musicals, with lyrics by Lorenz Hart until 1942 and then by Oscar Hammerstein II. His shows include *On Your Toes* (first performed in New York in 1936), *Pal Joey* (New York, 1940), *Oklahoma* (New York, 1943), *Carousel* (New York, 1945), *South Pacific* (New York, 1949), *The King And I* (New York, 1951) and *The Sound of Music* (New York, 1959).

Rodrigo, Joaquín (1901–). Blind Spanish classical composer, known principally for *Concierto De Aranjuez* (1939) and *Fantasia Para Un Gentilhombre* (Fantasia For A Gentleman, 1954), both for guitar and orchestra.

Rolling Stones British rhythm and blues group, formed in 1962 and originally comprising Mick Jagger (1944–), Keith Richard (1944–), Brian Jones (1944–1969), Bill Wyman (1941–) and Charlie Watts (1942–). Albums include *Beggar's Banquet* (1968) and *Let It Bleed* (1969).

Romberg, Sigmund (1887–1951). Hungarian composer of operettas, resident in the United States from 1909. His most popular operettas are *The Student Prince* (first performed in New York in 1924) and *The Desert Song* (New York, 1926).

Ross, Diana (1944–). American popular singer who rose to fame with her group the Supremes in 1964 before becoming a solo singer and actress in 1969. Her singing roles in films include *Lady Sings The Blues* (1973) and *The Wiz* (1978).

Rossini, Gioacchino (1792–1868). Italian classical composer, known mainly for his operas. The best-known of these include *L'Italiana In Algeri* (The Italian Girl In Algiers, first performed at Venice in 1813), *Il Barbiere Di Siviglia* (The Barber of Seville, Rome, 1816), *La Cenerentola* (Cinderella, Rome, 1817), *The Thieving Magpie* (Milan, 1817), *Count Ory* (Paris, 1828), and *Guillaume Tell* (William Tell, Paris, 1839). Rossini also composed some church music, notably *Stabat Mater* (1841), and his music is used for the ballet *La Boutique Fantasque*. See Respighi, Ottorino.

Rostropovich, Mstislav (1927–). Russian cellist, resident in the West from 1974, for whom Britten composed several works. Also known as a conductor.

S

Saint-Saëns, (Charles) Camille (1835–1921). French classical composer, now known principally for the orchestral entertainment *Carnival Of The Animals* (1886), but which he did not allow to be publicly performed in his lifetime. Saint-Saëns composed much orchestral music, the *Danse Macabre* (1874) being popular, and wrote 13 operas, of which the best known is *Samson And Delilah* (first performed at Weimar in 1877).

Satie, Erik (1866–1925). French classical composer, known principally for the piano pieces *Trois Gymnopédies* (1888) and *Trois Gnossiennes* (1890) and the ballet *Parade* (first performed at Paris in 1917).

Sax, Adolphe (1814–1894). Inventor of the saxhorn family of brass instruments (patented in 1845), and the saxophone family of woodwind instruments (patented in 1846).

Scarlatti, Alessandro (1660–1725) and **Scarlatti, Domenico** (1685–1757). Italian classical composers, father and son. The elder Scarlatti was important in the development of opera and the cantata, composing about 100 operas and 600 cantatas, while the younger Scarlatti was equally prolific in keyboard music, composing more than 550 single-movement harpsichord sonatas.

Schoenberg, Arnold (1874–1951). Austrian composer, resident in the United States from 1933. His early works, highly romantic in style, include *Verklärte Nacht* (Transfigured Night, 1899) for strings and the choral work *Gurrelieder* (1900–1911). From about 1908, Schoenberg began to compose atonal (keyless) works, notably *Erwartung* (1909) and *Pierrot Lunaire* (1912). This development culminated in the twelve-note or serial method of composition, which Schoenberg employed from 1923 onwards. His major twelve-note works include *Variations For Orchestra* (1928) and the unfinished opera *Moses And Aaron* (first performed at Zurich in 1957).

Schubert, Franz (1797–1828). Austrian classical composer, renowned for the poetic and lyrical qualities he brought to classical forms and songs. He composed nine *Symphonies* – No 1 in D major (1813), No 2 in B flat major (1815), No 3 in D major (1815), No 4 in C minor (*The Tragic Symphony*, 1816), No 5 in B flat major (1816), No 6 in C major (1818), No 7 in E major (sketched out only in 1821), No 8 in B minor (*The Unfinished Symphony*, 1822) and No 9 in C major (*The Great Symphony*, 1828). Schubert also wrote 15 string quartets of which *Quartet No 14 in D minor* (*Death And The Maiden*, 1824) is the best-known; other well-known chamber works include the *Piano Quintet in A major* (The Trout Quintet, 1819). Among Schubert's piano works are several popular piano sonatas, impromptus, moments musicaux (musical moments) and piano duets, the latter including the famous *Marches Militaires* (1818). Schubert also composed more than 600 songs, including the song cycles *Die Schöne Müllerin* (The Fair Maid Of The Mill, 1823) and *Die Winterreise* (The Winter Journey, 1827).

Schumann, Robert (1810–1856). German classical composer of romantic music. His works include four *Symphonies* – No 1 in B flat major (*The Spring Symphony*, 1841), No 2 in C major (1846), No 3 in E flat major (*The Rhenish Symphony*, 1850) and No 4 in D minor (1851) – and several concertos, of which the *Piano Concerto in A minor* (1845) is best known. Schumann also composed much piano music, notably *Papillons* (Butterflies, 1831), *Carnaval* (Carnival, 1835), *Kinderscenen* (Scenes Of Childhood, 1838) and *Kreisleriana* (1838), and some 250 songs, including the song cycle *Dichterliebe* (Poet's Love, 1840) and *Frauenliebe Und Leben* (Woman's Love And Life, 1840).

Schwarzkopf, Elisabeth (1915–). German soprano, known for operatic roles and recitals.

Scriabin, Alexander (1872–1915). Russian classical composer, known for his mystical orchestral works *The Poem of Ecstasy* (1908) and *Prometheus* (1910).

Segovia, Andrés (1893–). Spanish guitarist primarily responsible for the revival of the guitar as a classical instrument.

Shankar, Ravi (1920–). Indian sitar player noted for his promotion of Indian music in the West. He has also composed music for films and ballets.

Shostakovich, Dmitri (1906–1975). Russian classical composer known for his 15 symphonies and 15 string quartets, of which the best known are the *Symphony No 5 in D minor* (1937), and *Symphony No 7 in C major* (The Leningrad Symphony, 1941) and the *Quartet No 8 in C minor* (1960). The latter two works depict events in World War II, while the fifth symphony was written to atone for his second opera, *Lady Macbeth of Mtsensk* (first performed in Leningrad in 1934), which fell foul of the Soviet authorities.

Sibelius, Jean (1865–1957). Finnish classical composer of music with national associations, especially the orchestral works *Karelia Suite* (1893), *The Swan of Tuonela* (1893) and *Finlandia* (1899). Sibelius also wrote seven symphonies and the orchestral piece *Valse Triste* (1904).

Sinatra, Frank (1915–). American popular singer who rose to fame as a big-band singer in the 1940s and then became a film actor. Renowned for the rhythmic drive of his singing.

Smetana, Bedřich (1824–1884). Czech classical composer, known mainly for the set of six symphonic poems *Má Vlast* (My Country, 1894), of which the most popular is *Vltava* (1880), and the opera *The Bartered Bride* (first performed at Prague in 1866).

Smith, Bessie (1894–1937). American blues singer who influenced many later jazz and popular singers. Famous records include *St Louis Blues* (1925), *Careless Love* (1925), *Reckless Blues* (1926) and *Young Woman's Blues* (1926).

Solti, Georg (1912–). British conductor, born in Hungary and resident in several other countries from 1939. Principal positions: Covent Garden Opera, Chicago Symphony Orchestra, London Philharmonic Orchestra.

Sondheim, Stephen (1930–). American songwriter, known for the shows *Company* (first performed in New York in 1970) and *A Little Night Music* (New York, 1973). He also wrote the lyrics of *West Side Story*. See Bernstein, Leonard.

Sousa, John Philip (1854–1932). American bandleader and composer of many famous marches, including *The Washington Post* (1889), *Liberty Bell* (1893) and *Stars And Stripes Forever* (1897).

Springsteen, Bruce (1949–). American rock singer. Albums include *Greetings From Asbury Park* (1973), *Born To Run* (1975) and *Born In The USA* (1984).

Stockhausen, Karlheinz (1928–). German experimental composer who has explored in depth new ways of creating music and making sounds. He first advocated total serialization, notably in *Zeitmasse* (Tempos, 1956) for wind quintet and *Gruppen* (Groups, 1957) for three orchestras. Stockhausen was also a pioneer of electronic music, and his most important electronic works include *Gesang Der Jünglinge* (Song Of The Youths, 1956), *Kontakte* (Contact, 1960) and *Hymnen* (Anthems, 1967), as well as pieces in which instruments are treated with electronic devices, notably *Mikrophonie I* (for tam-tam, 1964) and *Mantra* (for two pianos, 1970). A further important work is the contemplative *Stimmung* (Mood, 1968) for six singers. In 1977, Stockhausen began his vast opera cycle *Licht* (Light), which will comprise seven operas named after the days of the week. By 1983, two parts (Thursday and Saturday) had been completed.

Stokowski, Leopold (1882–1977). American conductor, born in Britain. Principal positions: Philadelphia Orchestra (1912–1938), New York Philharmonic Orchestra (1946–1950), Houston Symphony Orchestra (1955–1960).

Stradivarius Latin name of famous Italian family of violin makers, notably Antonio Stradivari (1644–1737).

Strauss, Johann (the elder, 1804–1849). Austrian classical composer, known mainly for the *Radetzky March* (1848). Father of Johann Strauss the younger.

Strauss, Johann (the younger, 1825–1899). Austrian classical composer, known for his dances and operettas. Among his most famous dances are the waltzes *The Blue Danube* (1867) and *Tales From The Vienna Woods* (1868). His best-known operettas include *Die Fledermaus* (The Bat, first performed at Vienna in 1874) and *The Gipsy Baron* (Vienna, 1885). The famous operetta *Wiener Blut* (Vienna Blood, Vienna, 1899) was compiled from music previously composed by Strauss.

Strauss, Richard (1864–1949). German classical composer, mainly of symphonic poems and operas in highly romantic idiom. His symphonic poems include *Don Juan* (1889), *Tod Und Verklärung* (Death And Transfiguration, 1889), *Till Eulenspiegel* (1895), *Also Sprach Zarathustra* (Thus Spake Zarathustra, 1896), *Don Quixote* (1897) and *Ein Heldenleben* (A Hero's Life, 1898). Strauss' major operas include *Salome* (first performed at Dresden in 1905), *Elektra* (Dresden, 1909), *Der Rosenkavalier* (Dresden, 1911), *Ariadne Auf Naxos* (Ariadne On Naxos, Stuttgart, 1912), *Die Frau Ohne Schatten* (The Woman Without A Shadow, Vienna, 1919) and *Arabella* (Dresden, 1933).

Stravinsky, Igor (1882–1971). Russian-born composer, resident in Switzerland from 1914, France from 1920 and the United States from 1939. Stravinsky's music, renowned for its vigour, falls into three periods. The first, marked by its originality, includes four ballets – *L'Oiseau De Feu* (The Firebird, first performed at Paris in 1910), *Petrushka* (Paris, 1911), *Le Sacre Du Printemps* (The Rite of Spring, Paris, 1913) and *Les Noces* (The Wedding, Paris, 1923) – and the stage work *L'Histoire Du Soldat* (The Soldier's Tale, Lausanne, 1918). Stravinsky then composed in a neoclassic idiom using styles of the past. These works include the ballets *Pulcinella* (Paris, 1920), which is based on the music of Giovanni Pergolesi (1710–1736), and *Apollo* (Washington, 1928); the oratorio *Oedipus Rex* (1927); the choral work *Symphony Of Psalms* (1930); *Dumbarton Oaks* (1938) for small orchestra and Stravinsky's only opera *The Rake's Progress* (Venice, 1951). In his last period, Stravinsky adopted the twelve-note or serial method of composition pioneered by Schoenberg. These works include the ballet *Agon* (New York, 1957) and the choral works *Threni* (1958) and *Requiem Canticles* (1966).

Sullivan, Arthur See Gilbert, W. S.

Suppé, Franz von (1819–1895). German classical composer known mainly for his overtures. These include *Morning, Noon And Night In Vienna* (1844), *Poet And Peasant* (1846), *Beautiful Galathea* (1865) and *Light Cavalry* (1866).

Sutherland, Joan (1926–). Australian soprano, resident in Switzerland from 1960, known for her operatic roles.

T

Tatum, Art (1910–1956). Blind American jazz pianist, capable of great virtuosity in solo improvisations. Records include *Tiger Rag* (1933), *St Louis Blues* (1940) and *Willow Weep For Me* (1949).

Tchaikovsky, Peter Ilyich (1840–1893). Russian classical composer of very melodic music in romantic style. His major orchestral works include six *Symphonies* – No 1 in G minor (*Winter Dreams*, 1866), No 2 in C minor (*Little Russian*, 1872), No 3 in D major (*Polish*, 1875), No 4 in F minor (1878), *Manfred Symphony* (not numbered, 1885), No 5 in E minor (1888) and No 6 in B minor (*Pathétique*, 1893); the *Romeo And Juliet Fantasy Overture* (1869), *1812 Overture* (1880) and *Hamlet Overture* (1888); three piano concertos, the *Piano Concerto No 1 in B flat minor* (1875) being the best known; and the *Violin Concerto in D major* (1878).

Tchaikovsky is also renowned for his ballets, notably *Swan Lake* (first performed at Moscow in 1877), *The Sleeping Beauty* (St Petersburg, 1890) and *The Nutcracker* (St Petersburg, 1892), and the operas *Eugene Onegin* (Moscow, 1879) and *The Queen Of Spades* (St Petersburg, 1890).

Te Kanawa, Kiri (1944–). New Zealand soprano renowned for her operatic roles.

Telemann, Georg (1681–1767). German classical composer, possibly the most proflic of all composers. His works, in many forms, include 40 operas, more than 100 cantatas and some 600 orchestral suites and overtures.

Tippett, Michael (1905–). British composer, notably of four operas – *The Midsummer Marriage* (first performed in London in 1955), *King Priam* (Coventry, 1962), *The Knot Garden* (London, 1970) and *The Ice Break* (London, 1977). His other major works include the *Concerto For Double String Orchestra* (1939), the oratorio *A Child Of Our Time* (1941), and four symphonies.

Toscanini, Arturo (1867–1957). Italian conductor. Principal positions: La Scala, Milan; NBC Symphony Orchestra.

V

Varèse, Edgard (1883–1965). French-born experimental composer, resident in America from 1915, who explored dissonant and unusual instrumental sounds and was a pioneer of electronic music. His major works include *Ionisation* (1931) for percussion, *Density 21.5* (1936) for platinum flute, and the electronic works *Déserts* (1954) and *Poème Électronique* (1958).

Vaughan Williams, Ralph (1872–1958). British classical composer of lyrical music influenced by folk song. In addition to nine symphonies, his major works include the *Fantasia On A Theme of Thomas Tallis* (1910)

for strings, the song cycle *On Wenlock Edge* (1909), the choral work *Serenade To Music* (1938), the opera *Hugh The Drover* (first performed in London in 1924) and the ballet *Job* (London, 1931).

Verdi, Giuseppe (1813–1901). Italian opera composer. His operas include *Nabucco* (first performed at Milan in 1842), *Macbeth* (Florence, 1847), *Rigoletto* (Venice, 1851), *Il Trovatore* (The Troubadour, Rome, 1853), *La Traviata* (The Woman Gone Astray, Venice, 1853), *Un Ballo In Maschra* (A Masked Ball, Rome, 1859), *La Forza Del Destino* (The Force Of Destiny, St Petersburg, 1862), *Don Carlos* (Paris, 1867), *Aida* (Cairo, 1871), *Otello* (Othello, Milan, 1887) and *Falstaff* (Milan, 1893).

Vickers, Jon (1926–). Canadian tenor, known for his dramatic and heroic roles in opera.

Villa-Lobos, Heitor (1887–1959). Brazilian classical composer, best known for his nine-part work *Bachianas Brasileiras* (1930–45) which is intended to express the spirit of J. S. Bach in Brazilian style. The most popular parts are No 2, *The Little Train*, and No 5 for soprano and eight cellos.

Vivaldi, Antonio (1678–1741). Italian classical composer, known for more than 400 concertos (principally in concerto grosso form). His best-known work is *The Four Seasons* (1725), a set of four violin concertos.

W

Wagner, Richard (1813–1883). German opera composer. His operas are *Rienzi* (first performed at Dresden in 1842), *Der Fliegende Holländer* (The Flying Dutchman, Dresden, 1843), *Tannhäuser* (Dresden, 1845), *Lohengrin* (Weimar, 1850), *Tristan Und Isolde* (Tristan And Isolde, Munich, 1865), *Die Meistersinger Von Nürnberg* (The Mastersingers of Nuremberg, Munich, 1868), **Das Rheingold* (The Rhine Gold, Munich, 1869),

Die Walküre (The Valkyrie, Munich, 1870), *Siegfried* (Bayreuth, 1876), *Götterdämmerung* (The Twilight Of The Gods, Bayreuth, 1876) and *Parsifal* (Bayreuth, 1882). The four operas marked * form the opera cycle *Der Ring Des Nibelungen* (The Ring Of The Nibelung, usually called The Ring).

Walton, William (1902–1983). British classical composer, known mainly for *Façade* (1922), originally a set of poems for reciter and six instruments but later orchestrated and used as ballet music. Walton's other major works include the overture *Portsmouth Point* (1925), two symphonies (1935, 1960), concertos for violin (1939) and viola (1929), the oratorio *Belshazzar's Feast* (1931) and the opera *Troilus And Cressida* (first performed in London in 1954).

Waters, Muddy (1915– ; real name McKinley Morganfield). American rhythm and blues singer and guitarist who influenced many popular singers and groups. Hits include *Rollin' Stone* (1950), *I've Got My Mojo Working* (1954) and *Hoochie Coochie Man* (1954).

Weber, Carl Maria von (1786–1826). German classical composer, known mainly for the piano piece *Invitation To The Dance* (1819), later orchestrated and used for the ballet *Le Spectre De La Rose* (first performed at Monte Carlo in 1911). Weber also composed the operas *Der Freischütz* (The Marksman With The Magic Bullets, Berlin, 1821) and *Oberon* (London, 1826).

Webern, Anton (1883–1945). Austrian classical composer who developed Schoenberg's twelve-note method of composition. His works include *Five Pieces For Orchestra* (1913) and *Symphony* (1928).

Weill, Kurt (1900–1950). German classical composer, resident in the United States from 1935, known mainly for stage works of which Bertolt Brecht (1898–1956) wrote the words. These are *Die Dreigroschenoper* (The Threepenny Opera, first performed in Berlin, 1928), which includes the famous song *Mack The Knife*, *Happy End* (Berlin, 1929), *The Rise And Fall Of The City Of Mahagonny* (Leipzig, 1930) and *Die Sieben Todsünden* (The Seven Deadly Sins, Paris, 1933).

Who, The British rock group, formed in 1964 and comprising Roger Daltry (1943–), Pete Townshend (1945–), John Entwistle (1946–) and Keith Moon (1947–1978). Albums include *Tommy* (1969) and *Quadrophenia* (1973).

Williams, John (1942–). Australian guitarist resident in Britain from 1952. Known for his virtuoso classical playing and work with the rock group Sky.

Wolf, Hugo (1860–1903). Austrian classical composer, principally of songs. His song cycles include *Mörike Lieder* (Mörike Songs, 1888), settings of 53 poems by Eduard Mörike (1804–1875).

Wonder, Stevie (1950–). Blind American pop singer and musician who has worked successfully in several different styles. See page 120.

Z

Zappa, Frank (1940–). American rock composer and guitarist who, mainly with his group The Mothers Of Invention, has created music of great technical expertise, often satirical in intention. His albums include *Absolutely Free* (1966) and *Hot Rats* (1969).

Index

Figures in *italic* denote photograph or illustration

Photographic acknowledgements

Archiv für Kunst und Geschichte, Berlin 131 bottom; Archiv Produktion 78 bottom left; Arts Council of Great Britain/Contemporary Music Network/Jaques Witt 37 top; Erich Auerbach 12, 25 top right, 25 bottom, 26, 67, 145 top and bottom; Clive Barda title page, 23 top, 28, 40 bottom right, 66, 82, 84, 144 bottom; BBC Copyright 158 top; BBC Hulton Picture Library 73 top, 74 bottom, 81; BBC Hulton Picture Library/Bettmann Archive 50 bottom, 107, 108 bottom, 110–111, 113 bottom right, 141 top; Bulloz 97 top; The British Library 152; Bruce Coleman/Pekka Helo 79; Donald Cooper 106 left; Cucumber Studio/Peter Shelton 121 bottom; Decca Record Company 157, 168 top; Deutsche Grammophon Production/S. Lauterwasser 71 top; Douglas Dickens 20, 51, 55 top, 55 bottom; Zoë Dominic 132 top; Format/Valerie Wilmer 15 top, 21 left, 60–61, 109 top, 111 right, 112, 118 bottom; Giraudon 53 left, 69 bottom (Louvre, Paris), 130 left, 132 centre (Bibliothèque Nationale, Paris), 136 bottom, 137, 143 right; Griffith Institute, Ashmolean Museum, Oxford 123 top left; Robert Harding 57, 63 top left & bottom right; H.G.P.L. 22 bottom right, 33, 39 bottom, 43, 52 top, 52 bottom (UNESCO), 60, 65 (Courtesy of the Country Music Foundation Library & Media Center), 70, 74 top (Museum of Fine Arts, Boston), 80 (Mozart Museum, Salzburg), 83, 89 (D'Oyly Carte Opera Trust), 102 bottom, 108 top, 119 top (Courtesy of the Country Music Foundation Library & Media Center), 117 bottom, 120 top (CBS Records), 123 bottom (University of Philadelphia Museum), 124, 126–127, 128 right (Bibliothèque Nationale, Paris), 129 right, 131 top, 132 bottom left (Ashmolean Museum, Oxford) 133, 135 top (Internationale Stiftung Mozarteum, Salzburg), 136 top (Beethovenhaus, Bonn), 140–141 (Abbey Aldrich Rockefeller Folk Art Collection), 143 left, 143 centre, 150, 158 bottom (RCA Records), 168 bottom; Michael Holford 78 bottom right; Marion and Tony Morrison/South American Pictures 63 bottom left; Illustrated London News Picture Library 48; Kobal Collection 75, 91, 104, 106 right; Alex von Koettlitz preface, 88 top, 93, 138 top and bottom; Laurie Lewis 56 top, 86–87, 88 bottom; London Features International 10 top (Mike Putland), 23 bottom (Mike Putland), 78 top (Paul Cox), 113 bottom left (Andy Freeburg/Retna), 110 top, 109 bottom, 114 bottom (SKR), 115 bottom (Frontline Pictures), 116–7 top, 117 right (Ebet Roberts Photography), 120 bottom (Simon Fowler/Frontline Pictures), 121 top; Mansell Collection 68, 69 bottom right, 69 top, 97 bottom, 103, 129 left;

Mary Evans Picture Library 72 centre, 73 bottom, 138 centre left; MAS, Barcelona 130 top right and centre, 130 bottom right and centre (Monasterio del Escorial, Madrid); F. Arborio Mella 128 left, 138 centre right; Mike Davis Studio 72 bottom, 90 bottom, (Jesse Davis), 94 top, 95, 96 top, 96 bottom (Jesse Davis), 98, 99 (Jesse Davis), 100 (Jesse Davis), 135 bottom (Jesse Davis), 142–3; Reproduced by courtesy of the Trustees, The National Gallery, London 27; Carlos Olms Private Collection, London 16; Panasonic UK/Technics 46; The Performing Rights Society 167 top (Professional Photo Services); Philips 165; Philips Records 164; Phonogram International 13 (Werner Neumeister); Polydor 47; Polygram Classics 10–11; David Redfern 10 bottom, 18, 18–19, 21 right, 25 top left, 29 top right, 30 bottom left (Richard E. Aaron), 31, 35 top left, 37 bottom (Collin Fuller), 39 top (Tony Russell), 102 top, 111 top left (Beryl Bryden), 113 top (William Gottlieb), 114 top (Jacob Ger), 118 top, 119 bottom, 154, 162–163; Rex Features 38 bottom, 94 bottom (Globe Photos Inc), 167 bottom (Clive Dixon); The Royal College of Music 72 top; SCALA 86 top; Marion Scott 151; Brian Shuel 17; Pennie Smith 45; Spectrum 71 bottom; Steinway & Sons 147 (Michael Glazebrook); Syndication International 115 top; Third Eye Productions 50 bottom; Colin Thomas Photography 54 top; Alan Titmuss 49 top; Paul Tomlinson 161; Jean Vertut 122, 123 top right; The Victoria & Albert Museum, London 25 right, 156; The Visual Connection 167 centre (Chris Foster); Wales Tourist Board Photo Library 85; Wide World Photos 40 bottom left; Yamaha 146 (Rex Caves Photography); ZEFA 14, 15 bottom, 22 bottom left, 34 (H. G. Trenkwalder), 38 top (Gunter Heil), 49 bottom (by kind permission of Syco Systems), 58, 59 (J. Bitsch), 62 (Kurt Gobel), 63 top right (Günter Heil), 64 top, 64 bottom (W. Berssenbrugge), 86 bottom, 90 top, 135 centre (Damm).

Artists

Ray Burrows; Vince Driver; Emma Hughes; Tony Morris (Linda Rogers Associates); Oxford Illustrators; Sylvia Tate; Brian Watson (Linden Artists).